All In One Collection

Off-Grid
Solar Power Systems

Beginners

A Technical Guide on How To Design, Install, and Maintain Grid-tied and Off-Grid Systems For Your Home, Tiny House, RV, Cabin, Boat, or Yurt.

Advanced

Best Components for Various Sized Systems

Planner

Staying organized is the key to moving forward building a Solar Array

Written by: Den Collier

Table of Contents
Beginners

Advanced

Introduction

"We are like tenant farmers chopping down the fence around our house for fuel when we should be using Nature's inexhaustible sources of energy -- sun, wind, and tide... I'd put my money on the sun and solar energy. What a source of power! I hope we don't have to wait until oil and coal run out before we tackle that."

- Thomas Alva Edison,

American Inventor and Businessman

Lving off-grid or being self-sustainable is a trend that is becoming more and more popular among Americans who seek a more independent way of life. There are many stories of people becoming digital nomads who rent an RV to travel across the country while living and working remotely. Others like to go camping on their fully equipped solar-powered RV or simply enjoy living off-grid on a boat and sailing across the West Coast, the East Coast or even sailing across other latitudes.

There are also people who just decide to go off-grid with the objective of eliminating their electricity bill and increasing their reliability against power outages, which in some areas, like California, have been increasing in the past few years due to grid stability issues and wildfires.

Many others are also concerned about the impact that fossil fuels are having on our planet and choose to live a more sustainable and Eco-friendly lifestyle by offsetting their energy consumption from contaminating sources and making the switch to a clean renewable energy source.

Maybe you can relate to some of these stories, or maybe to several of them as I do myself. But, whether you are a green energy enthusiast, someone who likes to live outdoors and travel constantly, whether you simply dislike high electricity bills, or simply have an interest in building your own solar power project, this book was made for you.

Now, I know that you must be excited as much as I am to get started, but first, if you want to make the switch to living off-grid, one of the first questions you may ask yourself is:

Why solar energy?

Fossil Fuels – Hard to Leave Them Behind

Fossil fuels have been the conventional source of energy over the last 150 years. Since the industrial revolution began, the consumption of fossil fuel sources like natural gas, crude oil, and coal has been rising dramatically since the 1900s. These sources of energy are not only required to generate electricity to power our homes but also play an important role in the

transportation sector. Since the introduction of the automobile in 1908 by Henry Ford, there has been an exponential increase in the consumption of these energy sources because they were seen as the only solution at that time to boost the expansion of transportation across the world.

The high amounts of energy density that fossil fuels have, made them the most logical choice for the development of the transportation and electricity sector. As a valuable comparison, while natural gas has an energy density of 53.1MJ/kg, a lithium-ion battery has only 0.504MJ/kg.

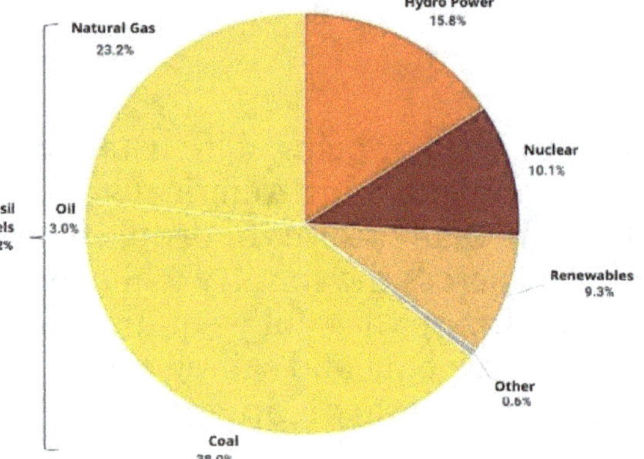

This big difference, plus the convenience of costs and easy transportation, paved the way for fossil fuels to become the dominant source of energy in the world up to date.

However, as years went by we realized that this convenience for our progress was starting to have an impact on our planet. Despite this, the Earth has had many cycles of ice ages and warmer periods.

In the last century, the temperature of the planet has risen unexpectedly fast and the conclusion that scientists have reached is that human activity is driving this more recent rapid increase.

In fact, according to data from the National Aeronautics and Space Administration (NASA), the temperature of the Earth has increased up to 1°C in the last century.

Recent studies from the Intergovernmental Panel on Climate Change (IPCC) and the US Global Change Research Program have indicated that an increase of 1.5°C above pre-industrial levels will probably occur in the next 20 years. From this point forward, the effects of climate change will start to increase and be felt all across the world. However, if no drastic measures are taken to reduce fossil fuel consumption, the increase is likely to reach 2°C, a point from which, the effects of climate change will be irreversible with worse consequences such as long drought seasons, as well as increased intensity and frequency of natural phenomena such as ice storms, hurricanes, tornado's, floods, or wildfires. All of this will have a tremendous impact on our food and energy supplies, as well as on human health.

Predicting this devastating outcome of events, nations from all across the world united into an initiative commonly known as the Kyoto Protocol that commits state parties to reduce greenhouse gas emissions, and therefore reduce fossil fuel consumption. This agreement was signed in 1997

Solar Energy: Cornerstone for Sustainable Living

Now, while we want to protect our planet, we also want to continue enjoying our current lifestyle. We want to continue growing with technology development and make use of all the amenities that the industrial and digital revolution have given to us. Therefore, the key is to make a change for a more sustainable energy mix that allows us to generate electricity in a clean way.

This is where renewable energy sources stepped in. Hydropower, biomass, geothermal, tidal, and wind energy, all of them valuable alternatives to fossil fuels, however, most of them are highly site-dependent or are suitable only for large scale development projects, making them hard to implement in our daily lives on a single basis.

On the other hand, solar energy has the flexibility to work in any region across the world and is suitable for both large industrial development as well as for residential or small type applications.

Before the industrial revolution, the sun gave us everything we needed to sustain our living, providing heat and light for us, as well as for plants and animals, which we need to survive. Today, the sun gives us one more thing, electricity. Thanks to the introduction of solar panels, now we can generate electricity to sustain our living in this digital era, making it a cornerstone of sustainable living anywhere in the world.

This is why I opt for solar power as a valuable ally to make your off-grid life, sustainable, easy, and clean.

However, for someone who is not familiar with solar power, I know that the setup and design process to install your own PV system can be challenging and even scary because after all, we are working with electricity. This is why I am writing this book, to make this setup process easy to follow, as well as to offer you valuable resources to get the best possible outcome.

Here you will learn everything you need to know about solar energy and learn the step-by-step process to build and connect your own photovoltaic (PV) project at home. After reading this book you will be able to know in detail:

- Benefits of solar energy
- How solar power works
- Basic electrical concepts
- The most important components of an off-grid solar system
- Perform practical calculations to assess your energy requirements
- Types of PV Systems
- Size and select the best components
- Build your entire off-grid PV system for your RV, boat, home, cabin or yurt.
- Perform appropriate maintenance to the solar system
- Happily, live off-grid with solar power!

With all of this clear in mind let us get that PV project started!

Part - I
ALL ABOUT SOLAR POWER
Chapter 1
Solar Energy 101

Expect the unexpected is the motto of the survivor and the well-prepared. In practice, you can power your small shack, tiny home, and cabin with standard gas generators, but they will only get you so far. These generators demand a constant flow of fuel, release greenhouse gas emissions, have short lifespans, and produce loud noises while operating, disrupting your comfortable way of life. Installing off-grid solar systems is the way to go for the survivalist and the environmentalist that wants to get in touch with nature while enjoying the technological comforts and benefits of society.

Now, before jumping to the technical design details, you must first learn the basics behind solar energy. In this chapter, we will go through the principles of solar energy, how it works, its applications, and get an answer to your most recurring questions about this technology.

Solar Energy: What is It and How Does It Work?

The sun is the largest celestial body within the solar system. This massive star is constantly working as a fusion reactor, producing 3.86 x 1023 kW of power, but only 1.74 x 1014 kW of those reaches the Earth,

which is the equivalent of more than 7,700 times the capacity of The Three Gorges Dam, the power plant with the largest capacity in the world. With such a massive source of clean energy, it is reasonable that the scientific community on Earth has put on a considerable effort to harness its power.

The Basics of Solar Radiation

Solar radiation refers to the electromagnetic waves constantly being emitted by the sun, which are comprised under the solar spectrum. The solar spectrum perceived in space includes electromagnetic waves with wavelengths going from 100 nm to 3,000 nm, but thanks to the atmosphere of the earth, only a small percentage of these waves are perceived on earth.

The solar spectrum perceived on earth includes wavelengths of 280 – 3,000 nm, comprising ultraviolet radiation and visible light under the short waves category, and infrared radiation under the long-wavelength category.

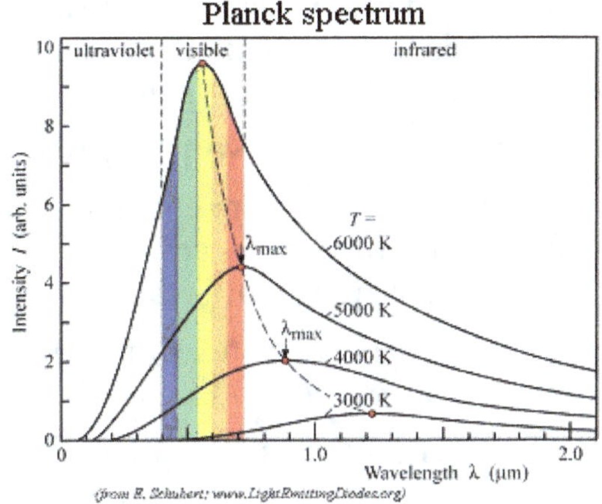

Ultraviolet radiation features wavelengths of 10 nm to 400 nm, while visible light which is the most important for humans to see, has a wavelength range of 380 to 700 nm, which includes all the colors of the rainbow. Finally, infrared radiation has wavelengths of 700 nm to 2,500 nm.

Energy From the Sun

The energy from the sun perceived on Earth is measured in kilowatt-hours per square meter per day (kWh/m2/day), this number also receives the name of Peak Sun Hours (PSH), which is the equivalent to the number of hours that a solar system will produce power at its nominal power output.

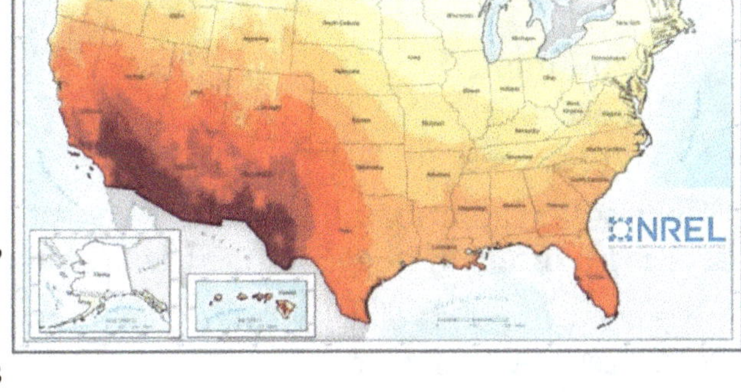

States in the U.S. perceive around 4 to 5.75 kWh/m2/day, varying on the state. Considering the solar resource in your state is of great importance to estimate the power output of your solar system.

NREL

Basic Principles

While now you know that solar radiation perceived per state varies between 4 to less than 6 kWh/m2/day, it is important to know what causes these variations. The daily solar radiation can vary depending on the following factors:

- Geographic location
- Time of day
- Season
- Local landscape
- Local weather

All these factors may improve or worsen the solar radiation perceived by a PV system at any given state. Factoring the regular weather, landscape, the seasons, and other factors in the list will help you understand how solar radiation is impacted at your property, which may affect the power output of your off-grid DIY solar system

Diffuse and Direct Solar Radiation

Another aspect to consider when talking about solar radiation is diffuse and direct solar radiation. Direct solar radiation indicates the amount of sunlight that is directly perceived by your solar panels.

On the other hand, diffuse solar radiation is a result of the radiation scattered, absorbed, and reflect by bodies located in the air or the landscape.

The bodies that can affect the radiation and be the cause of diffuse solar radiation are the following:

- Air molecules
- Water vapor
- Clouds
- Dust
- Pollutants
- Forest fires
- Volcanoes

Diffuse solar radiation allows for a PV system to produce power, even when there is no direct sunlight impacting the modules.

The output of your solar PV system will result from the combination of these two sources of radiation.

How Is Electricity Produced From Sunlight?

Solar power can be as simple as connecting photovoltaic (PV) modules to a solar system or solar generator and powering your appliances. However, there is a complex and interesting process running behind that allows the conversion of photons (small particles with electromagnetic energy found in the visible light) into electricity that can be used by your appliances and electronics. Solar energy can be converted into electricity, thanks to a phenomenon called the photovoltaic effect. PV modules feature p-doped (positively charged) and n-doped (negatively charged) semiconductor materials in the absorber layer, which is the layer in charge of absorbing sunlight and converting it to electricity. Modules also include

layers that help conduct electricity through the closed circuit to power the load. The photovoltaic effect starts when a photon impacts the solar cell, exciting an electron (negatively charged particle).

As the electron gets excited and moves out of its position, this creates an electron hole (known just as a hole) on an atomic level, creating what is known as an electron-hole (e-h) pair.

When the e-h pair is created, the electron moves from the valence band (the part of the semiconductor material with more electrons) to the conduction band (the band with fewer electrons). As electrons are freed from the valence band onto the conduction band, they are conducted out of the cell through the electrodes or busbars, which are metal conductors soldered to the cells.

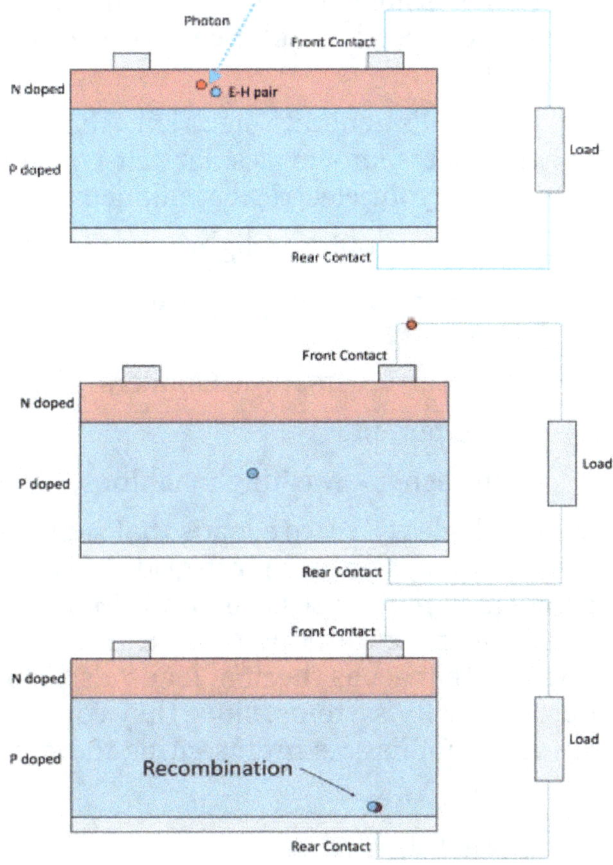

Electrons are finally transported through the closed circuit of the load, flowing in the form of electricity.

After electrons powered the load, they go back to the solar panel through the conductors in the closed circuit, pairing with a hole, ending that particular e-h pair in a process known as the recombination process. Only the visible range of the solar spectrum is used for this process.

What Is Solar Energy Used For?

After understanding how energy from the sun can be harvested by a solar system, you should also understand its applications. Solar energy is extremely versatile and can be used for several purposes as can be seen below.

Electricity Generation

One of the most important applications of solar energy is electricity generation, possible only thanks to the photovoltaic effect. As we have seen in the previous section, solar cells convert energy from incoming sunlight into electricity.

Solar cells generate electricity that can be stored or consumed locally, achieving what is known as solar self-consumption. Solar energy can be used to power your electrical appliances including:

- Indoor and outdoor lighting systems.
- Regular electronics like computers, TVs, gaming consoles, and others.
- Fridges, freezers, or ice makers.
- Water pumps.
- Dishwashers, washing machines, and others.

Electric Vehicles (EVs) are loads that represent a high consumption, therefore requiring a larger off-grid PV system to fully charge a vehicle, impractical in most cases. Air conditioning systems also demand high demands of energy although they can still be powered by solar energy. Appliances that act as thermal loads also represent a high consumption and require larger PV systems, since they convert electricity directly into heat. Some of the appliances representing thermal loads are the following:

- Electric stoves
- Cloth dryers.
- Home heating systems.
- Water heating systems.

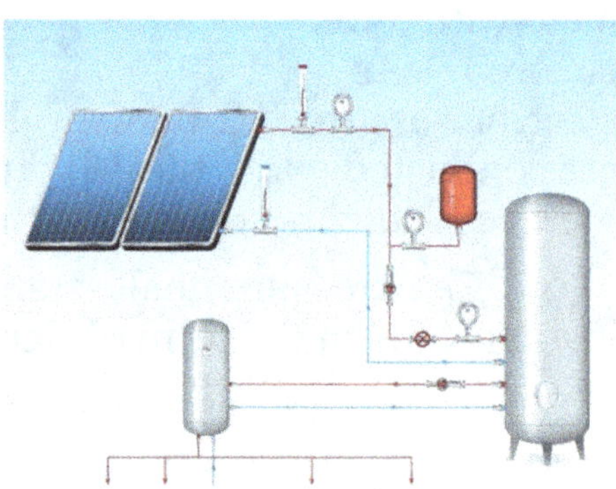

One of the benefits of solar energy is that it is extremely flexible. Thanks to the different applications for solar energy, some of these aforementioned loads, can be replaced by using other solar energy applications, like the thermal energy applications explained in the following section.

Thermal Energy

Converting solar radiation into thermal energy or heat is another common application for solar energy. This principle allows for the installation of solar water heaters and space heaters, increasing the temperature of the air or water acting as a carrier fluid, to 150 or 200 °F.

Thermal energy applications can efficiently convert 20 to 80% of the solar energy into heat by using flat-plate collectors.

Here, the infrared component of the solar spectrum is used to generate heat. Flat-plate collectors are devices featuring a blackened metal plate and a frontal insulator made out of glass layers. These devices allow the entrance of visible light, heating the carrier fluid inside, and capturing the heat within the plates. To take better advantage of solar radiation, flat-plate collectors are designed with large surface areas up to 430 square feet, even in the sunniest parts of the world.

Other Applications

Even though heat and electricity generation are the most common applications for solar energy, this resource can be used for many other applications. Some countries have installed desalination plants that produce clean drinking water by processing saltwater through solar power.

Other applications involve the use of silicon-based artificial leaves that split water into hydrogen and oxygen, to produce hydrogen, featuring a process similar to the photosynthesis seen in plants.

The Solar Market Today

Solar energy is so versatile that it has become the most attractive renewable energy source, growing in the U.S. at an average rate of 33.3% per year. This energy nowadays is used in residential, commercial, and utility-scale applications.

The U.S. currently has an installed solar capacity of over 121 Gigawatts (GWs), which is the same capacity required to power 23 million homes.

Solar Energy Pros and Cons

Solar energy presents incredible advantages as a result of its flexibility, return on investment, and several other points in favor. This is also why solar installations made up the largest share of newly installed capacities in 2020 and previous years. Let us take a look at the pros and cons of this technology, especially when going fully off-grid.

Advantages

- Solar energy is **environmentally friendly,** meaning that it does not release any greenhouse emissions that damage the environment.

- **Does not produce sonic contamination** or noise.

- Solar energy is a **renewable energy** source that does not consume natural resources in the process.

- Solar energy allows partial or total **energy independence.**

- Requires **low maintenance.**
- **Financial incentives** are available at the Federal and sometimes at the state level.
- Is **flexible and adaptable** to every customer's needs
- Is a **matured technology.**

Disadvantages

- Requires **high upfront investment.**
- **Performance varies on location** and across the seasons.
- Requires **battery backup system** to power loads at night
- May **require a large space** for installation.

Is Solar Right for You?

Going entirely off-grid with solar energy is one of the best choices you can make for the environment and maximize your energy independence, but it is important that you truly understand what this means. Regular size PV systems are suitable to cover most of the loads at home, including regular electronics, fridges, and other appliances.

It is important to notice, however, that when going off-grid with solar energy, energy efficiency will always have to be the backbone of your power consumption habits.

Solar is not always the best choice to power thermal loads like dryers or electric stoves for long periods, since these loads represent a high-power consumption that will take up most of your generation capacity.

You can enjoy some of these loads like a clothing dryer, but you might have to create habits of reducing power consumption in other areas of the home while the dryer is running. The same goes for cooking with an electric stove instead of a gas burner.

Aside from learning new energy consumption habits focused on energy usage optimization, location and available space are quite important.

PV systems require a medium to large rooftop area or an opened ground area to install ground-mounted solar panels.

The location also has to be considered regarding the available solar resource taking into account average radiation and shading objects. You can check out the Solar Resource Map & QR code page 11 to analyze the PSH at your property. If you live in a home that has a nice solar resource and the property is located in an open area with practically no shade for the location of the solar system, this might be a suitable option for you and your family.

If, however, you live on an RV or a boat, since you may your location constantly, this can be quite variable but every time you park your RV at a campsite, you will need to watch out for nearby obstacles or trees that could impact your solar panels.

Solar Power

Solar energy is often confused with solar power, but these are individual concepts. Solar power is the instantaneous generation capacity of a PV system, considering the ability of the system to convert solar energy radiation into electric power, which is measured in Watts (W) or kilowatts (kW). This provides a reference for the rate at which solar energy is being converted into electricity.

Solar Power vs. Solar Energy

While solar power is considered at any particular instant, solar energy is a concept related to time. This means that solar energy is the accumulation of solar power produced during a certain period like an hour or a day.

Solar energy is measured in Watt-hour (Wh) or kilowatt-hour (kWh).

A useful analogy to understand the difference between solar power and solar energy is using a water pipe. A water pipe will have a certain flow of water depending on its gauge, the instantaneous amount of water passing through a pipe at any given time is the same as solar power.

On the other hand, the liters of water that are being drawn from a water tank in an hour would be the analog to solar energy.

When tying these two concepts in electrical terms, solar energy can be understood as the accumulated power output of a solar system during an entire hour. Considering this, a solar system producing a constant power output of 1,000W for an hour will produce 1,000Wh in solar energy.

The Future of Solar Energy

Solar energy installations are rapidly growing across the world. More and more nations are making the switch to solar energy to increase their renewable energy mix. Electricity grids in South Australia for instance, are largely running on solar power throughout the day, while the government is working on initiatives to incentivize the introduction of energy storage devices coupled with solar systems. The same happens in California. Capacities are expanding and countries are competing with each other in this sector as can be seen here.

Solar Power Capacity and Cost

This graph shows references for historical growth data in the last 10 years up to 2020, but in the first quarter of 2022, the world solar industry finally achieved the milestone of installing 1 TW (1,000 GWs) in solar capacity.

China is still currently leading the way as the country with the largest wind and solar capacities, generating 17.3% of its energy with renewable technologies. Other important countries and groups of countries with considerably large solar capacities are India, Japan, the United States, and the European Union.

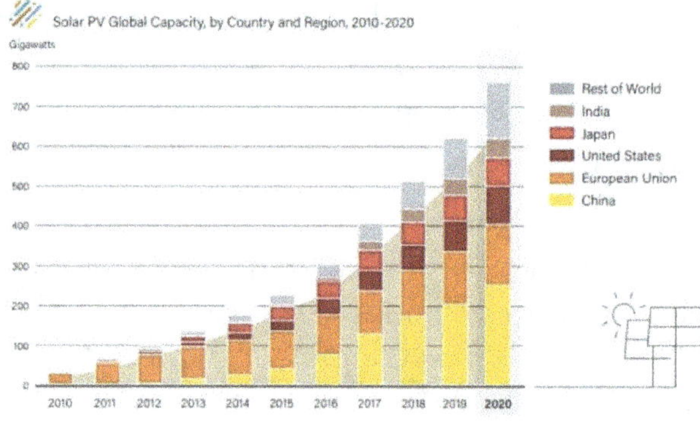

The interest of the world in solar energy is not entirely surprising. This technology is constantly improving its efficiency and reducing its costs, producing lower Return of Investment (ROI) periods. From 2016 to 2021, the hardware cost for a solar system was reduced by 45%, which made installing PV systems more financially attractive with faster ROIs. Costs for residential and commercial applications are now cheaper than ever and more and more projects are expected to continue. The solar industry also holds thousands of jobs in the US, reaching up to 230,000 workers as of 2020.

Challenges and Anticipated Solutions

The solar industry is constantly innovating and researching better and more practical solutions for the future. This section of the chapter addresses some of the most common challenges found for certain problems for solar power and the anticipated solutions that the solar industry has found for them.

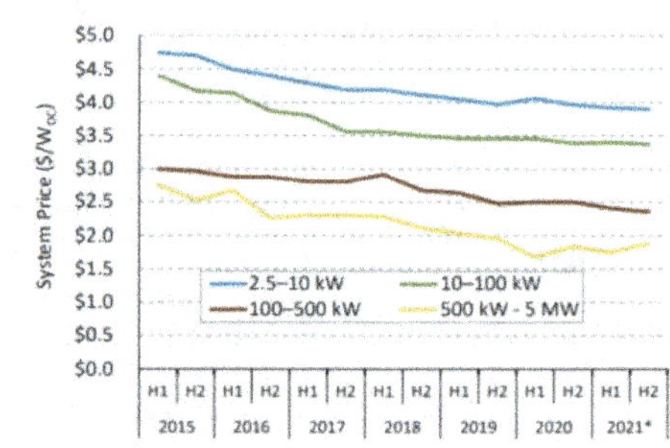

Photovoltaics at night

Solar systems produce an impressive power output during the day, especially when solar radiation levels reach a high point during clear sky summers. The problem with photovoltaics is that these systems cannot produce power at night, which is why most utilities resort to fossil-fuel-derived power to meet the demands of consumers. The main solution for this problem is battery storage, whether it is on the side of the utility or the customer.

Battery systems represent a resilient solution to store solar energy generated during the day, powering the load at night. Innovative and advanced power distribution grids are implementing smart grid solutions, relying on home battery storage systems, electric vehicles (EVs), and utility scale storage systems to supply power during the night when there is no photovoltaic generation.

Another interesting solution that completely avoids the nighttime problem is the generation of solar power directly from space, which is currently being studied at Caltech.

This is an ambitious project relying on photovoltaic technology, ultra-light deployable spacecraft structures, and laser beaming wireless power transfer, to generate solar power directly in space and transfer it wirelessly to Earth.

Space optimization for utility-scale power plants

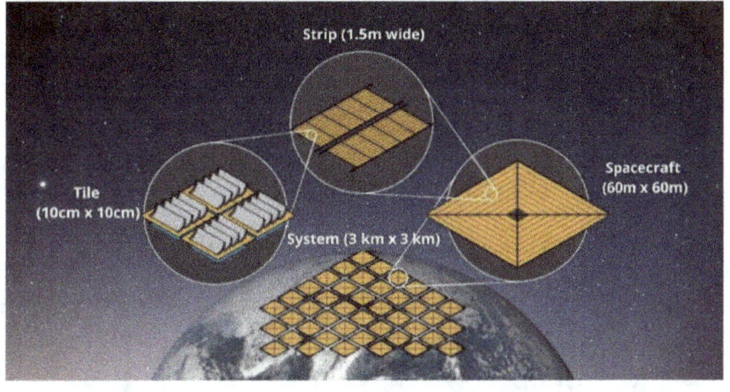

A concerning problem for photovoltaic technology is the required space for utility-scale power plants. These solar installations require large areas of ground space, causing a concerning problem for farming and wildlife habitats.

One of the most innovative solutions pursues the installation of power plants on the roofs of warehouses, capped landfills, or even contaminated mines. This space optimization alternative represents a viable solution for the space requirement of utility-scale power plants.

Solar Fuels

Solar energy can be harnessed for thermal and power applications, but this renewable energy has its limits.

One major setback for solar energy is the inability to replace regular fossil fuels like gas or oil, in applications like the powering of vehicles, boats, aircraft, construction tools, and a diverse range of applications.

While it is true that solar energy cannot directly produce fuel, it is one of the required components to grow plankton and algae, which are components used in the production of alternative fuel. The scientific community is currently investigating different options to

produce alternative fuels, looking to reduce fuel consumption and make a positive impact on the environment.

Frequently Asked Questions About Solar Power

• What are the states across the U.S. that receive more solar radiation?

The Solar Resource Map on page 12 illustrates that the southwestern region of the U.S. perceives the highest radiation, between 5.00 to 5.75 PSH or more. This mainly features the states of California, Arizona, New Mexico, Texas, Nevada, Utah, Colorado, and Oklahoma. Other states like Florida, Georgia, Alabama, Louisiana, and Mississippi also receive a good amount of solar radiation.

• What type of solar radiation reaches the Earth?

Solar radiation is divided between short waves and long waves. Short waves perceived on Earth include a fraction of the UV radiation, (around 10% of the UV radiation with wavelengths of 280 - 315 nm) and visible light (wavelengths of 400–780 nm) Infrared radiation generated by the sun (wavelengths of 780 - 3,000 nm) is entirely perceived on Earth, making up for most of the heat perceived from the sun.

• What is a renewable energy source?

Renewable energy sources are a particular type of energy that is inexhaustible, featuring an entirely natural process.

This includes:

- **wind energy**
- **hydro power** ....from flowing water
- **biomass** ....from plants
- **geothermal energy...**from stored heat inside the Earth
- **solar energy**

Since these sources of energy are found in nature, they do not generate any negative impact on the Earth's atmosphere.

The road so far...

In this chapter, we dealt with the basic concepts of solar energy, the perceived radiation on Earth, and its most important applications for heat and electricity generation. Let's see in the following chapter what photovoltaic technology has to offer...

Chapter 2

The Power of the Sun, in the Palm of Your Hands

Photovoltaic (PV) power is one of the major solar energy applications, granting people the ability to harness energy from the sun and convert it into electricity. Humans have used solar energy for hundreds of years mainly for heating purposes, but with the rapid development and improvement of photovoltaics in the last few decades, this application has become very important for the present and future of humanity. In the previous chapter, you learned the basics of solar energy. With this ground base knowledge, we can now go deeper into further solar photovoltaic concepts. Now, in this chapter, you will learn more about photovoltaic technology including:

- A bit of history
- How does PV work
- Different technology variations
- Design aspects and their impact on the performance of PV modules.

A Short History of Solar Panels

The first recorded use of solar energy in a practical way dates back to the 7th Century B.C. when humans used a magnifying glass to ignite a fire. Romans and Greeks also used solar energy during the 3rd Century B.C. to light torches.

Installation by Charles Fritts, New York, 1884

It was not until the discovery of the photovoltaic effect in 1839 by Edmond Becquerel that humanity had its first hint that this energy could be used not only to generate fire and heat but also to generate electric power.

Portrait of Edmond Becquerel

In 1883, 44 years after Becquerel paved the way for photovoltaics, Charles Fritts created the first solar cells by coating selenium over a thin layer of gold, creating a solar panel with a 1 – 2% efficiency. Even though humans understood in practice the photovoltaic effect, this was not studied until 1887 by Heinrich Hertz and Lenard in 1902, but none of them could truly explain the effect. It was not until 1905 that Albert Einstein published a paper that delivered a complete explanation of what would be known as the photoelectric effect. This discovery awarded him the Nobel Prize in physics in 1921. In 1941, 58 years after the invention of the first solar panel, Russel Ohl patented the first silicon solar cell, which gave way to the creation of the first silicon solar panel in 1954 by Bell Laboratories, being the precursor for the most popular solar panel technology used in present days.

How Do Solar Panels Work?

As we mentioned in the previous chapter, the sun works like a giant natural nuclear reactor, releasing small amounts of energy in the form of photons. Photons reach the Earth by traveling through 93 million miles in around 8 minutes and 20 seconds. In total, the solar resource capacity perceived on Earth is around 173,000 terawatts (TW), which is 10,000 times more power than the necessary to power the entire planet. Now, when a photon hits a solar panel, it generates solar power under the photovoltaic effect, but how exactly are solar panels wired in order to work like this? Solar panels are made by soldering solar cells together in series, parallel, or series-parallel connections, which allows them to increase the power output of the solar module. At the same time, solar panels, are connected in series, parallel, or series-parallel configurations, to create a solar array that can cover the power demands of an average household.

When solar panels are hit by photons, they generate solar power and do so in the form of direct current (DC) through a closed circuit.

Electrons in DC flow in a single direction, from negative to positive terminals within the circuit (in this case the output cables of the solar panels). After passing through the load, electrons go back to the solar panel through the negative terminal of the closed circuit.

How Does the Weather Affect Solar Power?

Heat

Since solar panels are placed outdoors and require photons to reach the absorber layer within the cell, they can be deeply affected by the weather.

While sunny days with clear skies are the best to produce higher power outputs for a single module, the excess heat can also generate an undesired effect in which the solar power output is reduced. The ideal scenario is having high solar radiation as well as low or average ambient temperature values since modules have better performance at lower temperatures.

Clouds

Expecting cloudy days to be entirely bad is a common mistake among solar homeowners, but this is not precisely the case. Just like when you go out on a cloudy day and you can still get sunburned, solar panels can perceive photons from solar radiation that penetrate through clouds, producing solar power from diffused radiation. While it is true that power output for a solar system during cloudy days is not the same as during a sunny day with clear skies, cloudy days still can make for decent solar power generation.

Soiling: Snow and Dust

Another weather-related problem affecting the output of a solar system is snow and dust. Both of these affect solar panels in two ways:

- Snow and dust particles falling from the sky might catch photons supposed to impact solar panels, slightly reducing the power production at the module. This might cause trouble, but it is not the major concern for solar panels.

- Particles of snow and dust accumulating at the surface of your solar panel can drastically reduce the production of the module.

This last aspect is why it is important to perform regular maintenance with sufficient water to the module, as well as remove snow or dust particles from the surface of your panel (especially after a snow or dust storm). Performing regular maintenance to your panels will keep the system operating in top shape.

Do Some States Get More Solar Energy than Others?

Turning back a few pages and checking the Solar Resource Map page 12 will show you that U.S. states like California, Arizona, Utah, Oklahoma, Texas, Florida, and similar southern states, receive more radiation than

others, causing them to have more solar energy available. However, this is not a reason for you to get discouraged about generating solar power in another state.

Some states have very high radiation values across the year, but as previously mentioned, states in the north can also generate a good amount of solar power. Considering that solar efficiency is higher at lower temperatures, states in colder locations like Connecticut, New York, New Jersey, and similar ones, are still excellent locations to install solar systems that will grant large savings to your future.

What are Solar Panels Made of?

Solar panels use crystalline silicon solar cells to produce solar power and feature a large protecting design around these cells. The most important materials used to manufacture solar panels are the following:

- Crystalline silicon (for the solar cells).
- Ethylene-vinyl acetate copolymer foam, better known as EVA.
- Tempered glass.
- Metal for the back sheet.
- Aluminum for the frame.
- Silver or copper for the connections between cells
- Junction box

The solar panel is manufactured using the structure seen on the next page. Solar cells are soldered to create the desired circuit for the module and then are sandwiched between EVA layers (a polymer resin placed to protect solar cells, soften shocks and vibrations). To provide an additional layer of support and robustness, a metal back sheet is placed on the rear side and tempered glass with an aluminum frame on the front side of the module.

Finally, diodes designed to protect the circuit of the solar panels are placed within the junction box alongside the cables that go out from the module. Different types of solar panels and different design technologies might feature slight variations in the materials.

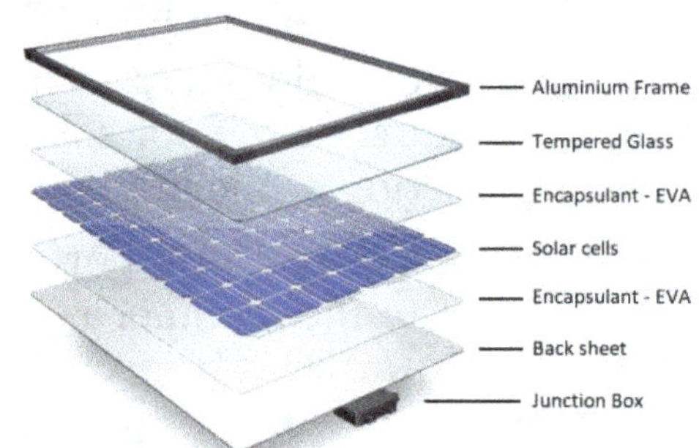

Additional Important Solar Panel Parts

The typical solar panel installed in your future off-grid solar system, will not be only manufactured by soldering solar cells together, PV modules

also require additional components to operate correctly. These components are:

- **Bypass diodes**: Partially shaded solar panels on your rooftop, will stop generating and act as resistors, consuming power and producing heat, causing a fire hazard. To avoid this, bypass diodes are installed in reversed bias to isolated strings of solar cells in the panel, known as sub-strings. This diode keeps the cells from consuming power and acting as a resistor.

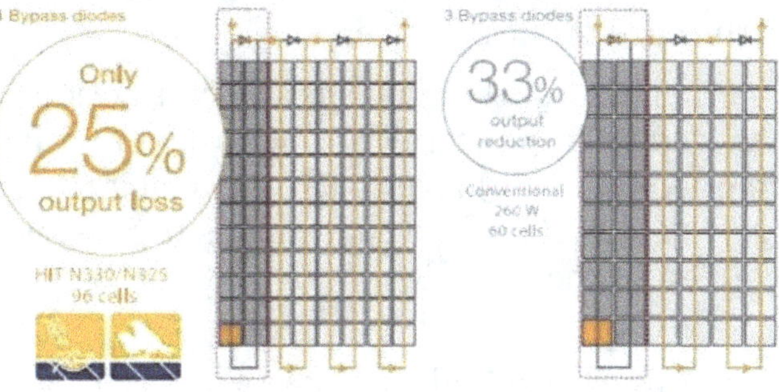

As a cell is partially shaded, the whole substring will stop generating, which might cause the output of the panel to be reduced to 1/3 or 1/4 of its capacity, depending on how many diodes are installed.

- **Cables**: Solar cells soldered together do not have enough reach to be connected to the rest of the system or the load.

To solve this, solar panels include cables that extend the positive and negative terminals of the module, allowing you to connect the panel to the array or the load itself.

- **Connectors:** Connectors are designed to plug and attach the positive and negative terminal of a module to the load or the rest of the system. There are many types of solar connectors like the MC3, Solarloks, Tyco, Amphenol, and T-Joints, but the most popular one is the MC4 connector, which is the safest and more robust in the solar industry.

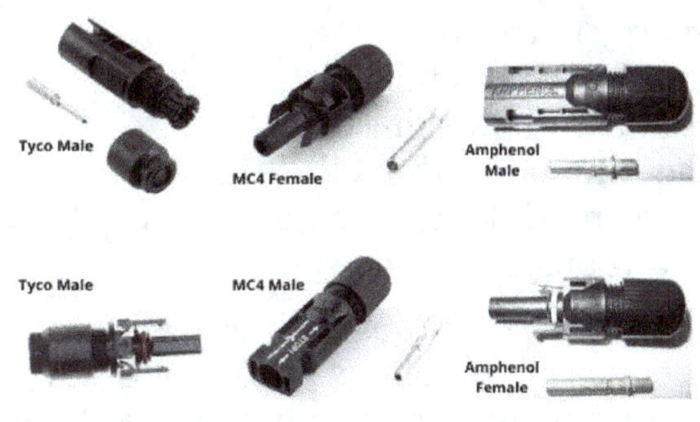

Photovoltaic (PV) Cells – The Underlying Unit of a Solar Panel

Solar Cell Structure and Operation

The ability of a solar cell to generate power from solar energy is a result of the structure used to create each cell.

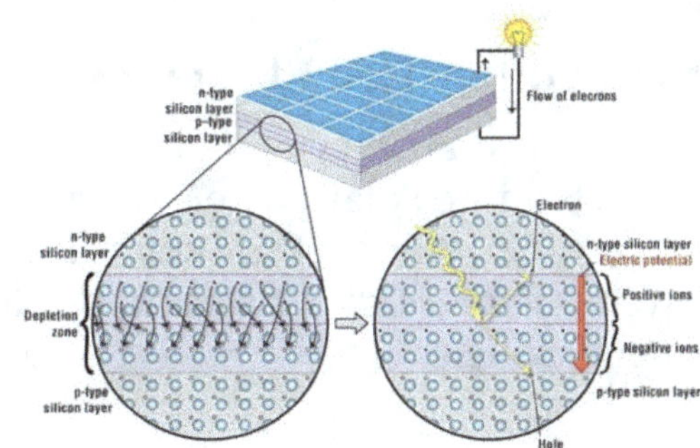

This technology has been constantly improving since 1883 when the first solar cell was created.

As the light reaches the solar cell, it goes through a protective glass that is designed to keep the inner materials of the solar cell intact. An anti-reflective coating is placed below the glass, allowing the photons to pass the coat while trapping them inside.

As the photon goes into the module, it finds the absorber layer, which is the core of the solar cell.

The absorber layer is a P-N junction constructed with a positively charged (P-Type) semiconductor layer with extra holes and a negatively charged (N-Type) layer with extra electrons. These two layers together, create an electric field that makes it possible for the photovoltaic effect to happen in the cell.

When the electrons get excited inside the absorber layer as a result of the photovoltaic effect, they are transported out of the cell through the busbars, which eventually send the energy to the load. Busbars are metal conductors working as the contacts of the cell and set in place to close the circuit for the system . Some modules also feature a back sheet polymer to increase the durability and robustness of the cell.

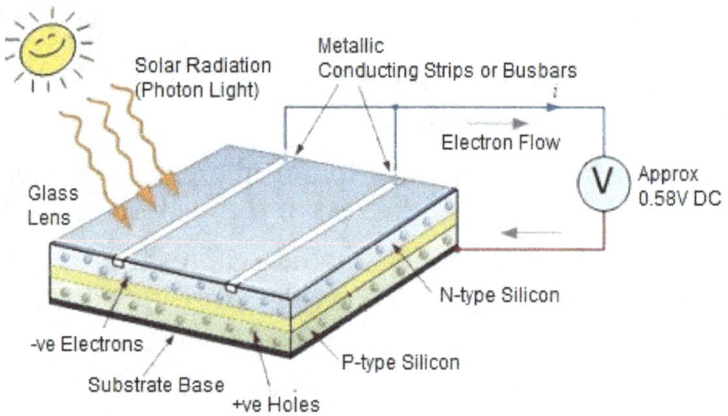

Disregarding the surface area of a solar cell, any single solar cell will produce a low voltage output of 0.5V, which is why solar panels have to feature several solar cells soldered together in order to increase the voltage. To create solar panels with 17 − 35 V outputs, solar cells have to be soldered together, going from 36 cells for 17V solar panels up to 72 cells for 35V solar panels.

Photovoltaic Cell Efficiency

The efficiency of a photovoltaic cell is the ratio of solar energy converted into solar power. Increasing the efficiency of solar panels is one of the research pillars of the solar industry that is constantly searching for ways to increase the power output for a single solar cell and reduce the cost of solar panels.

The most efficient solar panels manufactured by superior brand names like Sunpower, LG Solar, REC Solar, Panasonic, Jinko Solar, and others, feature efficiencies ranging from 20.43% to 22.80%. The most efficient solar cells ever created, featuring the most advanced technology, have achieved a conversion efficiency of 39.2% for Standard Test Conditions (STC) and 47.1% for a concentration of 143 suns.

To test the efficiency of a single solar cell or PV module, the solar industry came up with a standardized test that became the norm for solar cells and solar panels. This test measures the conversion efficiency of a cell at the power equivalent of one sun or 1,000 W/m2 at a temperature of 25°C. These testing conditions are called STC or Standard Test Conditions and they can be used to effectively compare the performance of multiple solar panels. The drawback to this method is its done under artificially induced conditions.

The best test is NOCT (normal operating cell temp) which gives more realistic watt output values per tested panel.

Different Types of Photovoltaic Cells

In the constant mission of the solar industry to increase the efficiency of solar panels and reduce the cost of USD per watt ($/W) for solar systems, researchers have tested different materials and come out with different types of photovoltaic cells. Some of the most popular ones are the aforementioned crystalline silicon and thin-film solar cells, but there are also other interesting technologies available.

Crystalline Silicon Cells

Crystalline silicon solar cells are the most popular type of solar technology used in the solar industry. These are divided between *monocrystalline* and *polycrystalline* silicon:

Monocrystalline

Monocrystalline silicon (Mono c-Si) solar cells are manufactured using a single wafer or slice of crystalline silicon with a thickness of 156 to 200 nm, created by using a method known as the Czochraslki process. A single wafer of material reduces the chances of impurities, resulting in a better performance for the cell.

This matured technology has a large market share of 36.0% and has achieved its highest recorded efficiency at 25.4% for a single solar cell. This type of solar panel is the most used in new installations across the US.

Polycrystalline

Polycrystalline silicon (Poly c-Si) is a material manufactured by melting together a large number of monocrystalline silicon pieces. Wafers made with this material have a thickness of 160 to 240 μm, and a higher

level of impurity, resulting in a lowered performance compared to Mono c-Si. Solar cells with Poly c-Si have achieved high conversion efficiencies of 24.4% and a market share of 54.9%. This type of solar panel is widely used thanks to its accessible pricing.

Thin-Film Cells

Another important variation of photovoltaics that you should know about is thin-film solar cells. These are solar cells manufactured using a wide variety of materials for the absorber layer, featuring a wafer with a thickness of 1 μm or around 0.5% the thickness of crystalline silicon wafers.

With a thinner absorber layer, thin-film photovoltaics are more versatile for a wide variety of applications.

CIGS and GaAs

Copper Indium Gallium Selenide (CIGS) and Gallium Arsenide (GaAs) solar cells are two of the most attractive thin-film photovoltaic technologies. They feature excellent performance, and high conversion efficiency, and are very popular for space applications.

CIGS solar cells are created by embedding Gallium into a Copper Indium Selenide (CIS) matrix, featuring a solar cell that has achieved a high recorded efficiency of 23.4%. On the other hand, GaAs solar cells have a highly complex manufacturing process, producing solar cells with a high conversion efficiency of 29.1%.

While CIGS solar cells are widely used for commercial and industrial applications, they are also used in space applications.

GaAs solar cells, on the other hand, are more efficient but are highly expensive, which is why they are mainly reserved for space applications that require a high conversion efficiency in limited installation space.

CdTe and a-Si

Cadmium Telluride (CdTe) and Amorphous Silicon (a-Si) are two important thin-film solar cells, highly popular for their variety of applications. While CdTe solar cells are mainly used for commercial and industrial applications, a-Si solar cells are implemented in low consumption electronics like calculators in past decades and battery rechargers in current days, however, another important application is the creation of building Integrated Photovoltaics (BIPV) windows which replace regular windows and generate power. The highest recorded efficiency for a CdTe solar cell is set at 22.1% while for a-Si solar cells, is barely 14.0%.

Other Types of Solar Cells

Other important types of solar cells are Perovskite and Organic cells. They are usually categorized as thin-film photovoltaics since they feature wafers with similar thickness, but this is a fairly common mistake.

Organic Cells

Organic solar cells are an important photovoltaic technology that is currently under study due to its potential to produce large volumes of cost-effective solar cells. Organic Cells feature organic polymers with small organic molecules in the material for the absorber layer. These cells are highly adaptable, lightweight, and entirely customizable. The highest recorded efficiency for an organic solar cell is set at 18.07%. **Perovskites**

Perovskite solar cells might easily be the future of the solar industry. These cells are produced from a family of crystals called perovskites, with the most popular one being Methylammonium lead triiodide (CH_3NH_3).

Perovskite is a promising solar technology since it has the potential to produce a high conversion efficiency with a record set at 29.15%, and it features a much lower manufacturing cost than crystalline silicon.

These solar cells are still under thorough research since they have to overcome certain limitations like extending their lifetime, improving mass-producing manufacturing processes, and others, for them to be viable.

Comparing The Different Types of Photovoltaic Cells

Comparing technical specifications and characteristics of photovoltaic cells is a great method to understand how they differ from each other. In the following table, we compare all of these types.

Solar Panel Design Technology

Solar panels can feature a wide variety of design technologies. They yield different benefits and advantages by increasing light absorption, reducing power losses, or providing other benefits while they can use the same type of solar cell. In this section of the chapter, you will understand how all of these technologies work and their advantages.

Comparing different types of Photovoltaic cells

Applications	Costs/Watt	Temp. Coefficient	Lifespan	Highest Efficiency	
Residential & Industrial	$0.16 /W - $0.46/W	-0.39% / C	25 - 30 Years	25.40 %	Monocrystalline Silicon (mono c-Si)
Residential & Industrial	$0.24 /W	-0.387% / C		24.40 %	Polycrystalline Silicone (poly c-Si)
Commercial & Industrial	$0.40 /W	-0.172% / C	30 Years	22.10 %	Cadimum Telluride (CdTe)
Commercial & Industrial Space Applications	$0.60 /W	-0.36% / C	25 Years	23.40 %	Copper Indium Gallium Selenide (CIGS)
Mostly building-integrated photovoltaics	$0.69 /W	-0.234% / C	10 Years	14.00 %	Amorphous Silicone (a-Si)
Mostly space applications	$50 /W	0.09% / C	15 Years in space (5 more years than c-Si)	29.10 %	Gallium Arsenide (GaAs)
Residential, commercial, Industrial, BIPV, & Space applications	$0.16/W	-0.13% / C	30 months (2.5 years)	29.15 %	Perovskites
Wearable electronics, biomedical devices, smart windows, greenhouses	$1.00/W - $2.83/W	-0.13% / C	1300h (54 days or 1.8 months)	18.07 %	Organic

IBC

Interdigitated Back Contact (IBC) restructures the solar cell to place the frontal busbar at the back. The increased frontal surface receiving light and other structural differences increases the efficiency for Mono c-Si solar cells from 25.4% to 26.7%and reduces the thermal losses.

PERC

Passivated Emitter and Rear Contact (PERC) is a solar cell design that implements dielectric surface passivation and dielectrically displaced rear metal reflector. These two increase the efficiency of the module by around 0.86%, by increasing the light absorption and reducing power losses that are caused by a common phenomenon called electron surface recombination.

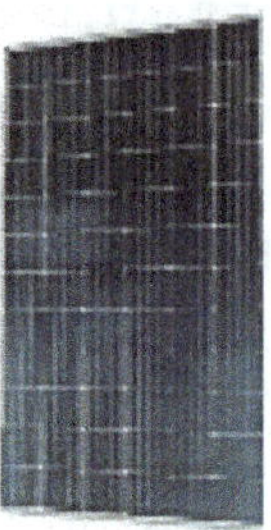

The surface recombination process happens when a hole and an electron recombine at the surface of the module before the electron flows as electricity through the load. This can be caused by impurities in the material, manufacturing defects, or several other reasons. By adding the passivation layer, surface recombination is reduced, which increases the efficiency of the module.

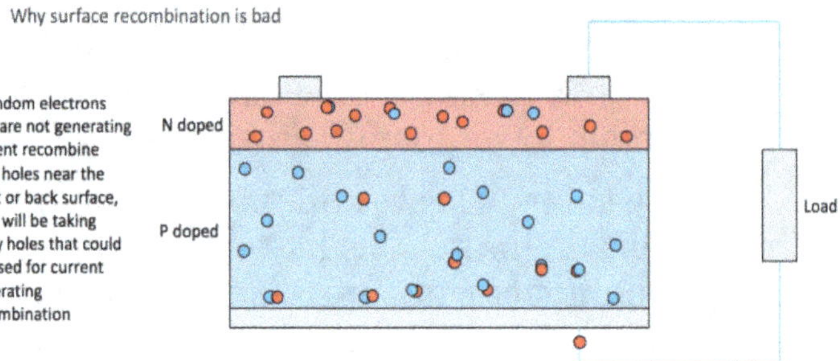

Half-Cell

The half-cell design uses traditional wafers with half the surface area. This fits two solar cell arrays in one single module. The subtle modification reduces power losses produced under Joule's Law by up to 1/4 or 75%. The resulting PV module has an increased power output of 2% to 4%, featuring fewer power losses and a reduced temperature for hot spots and regular operation.

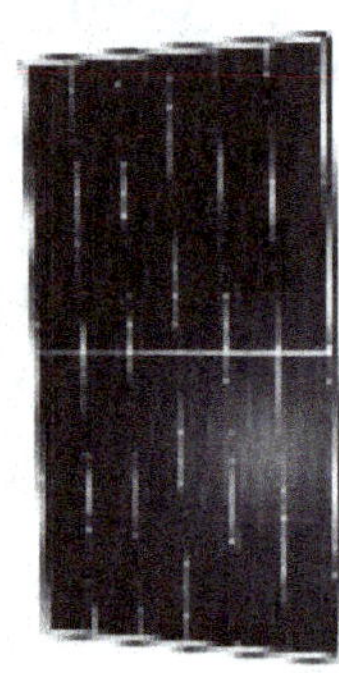

Bifacial

Bifacial design technology restructures solar cells to give them the ability to absorb light from the front and rear sides of the cell. Since Bifacial technology can generate power by absorbing light from both sides, it can take full advantage of the albedo resource which is comprised of diffused solar radiation being reflected from the ground up. thin wafers in the absorber layer, granting flexibility to the module. This design technology does not particularly increase efficiency or reduce power losses, but it does increase available applications. Flexible solar panels can bend to a certain

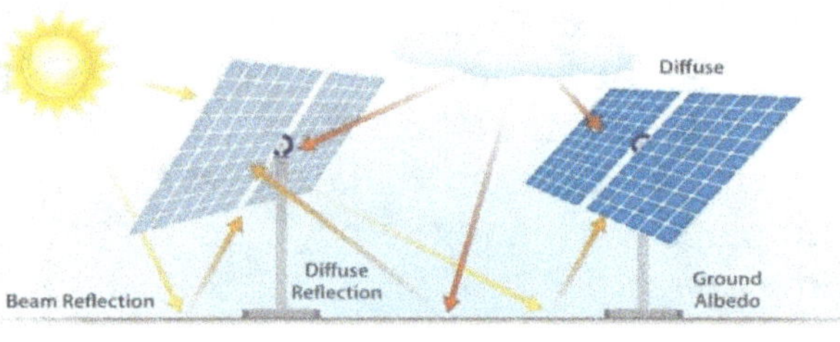

degree and perfectly adapt to the shape of curved surfaces, roofs of RVs, decks of boats, and many others.

All Black Solar Panels

All black solar panels exchange white back sheets and silver metal frames of traditional modules, for all-black back sheets and frames. They also include IBC technology to remove metal busbars from the front side of the cell. While this technology does not provide additional efficiency or performance advantages, it is the superior aesthetic design for solar panels.

Frequently Asked Questions (F.A.Q.)

- Can Solar Panel Design Technologies Be Combined for a Single PV Module?

One of the best advantages of photovoltaics is how flexible and adaptable this technology is.

Most of the design technologies for solar panels can be combined in a single PV module, accumulating advantages for each technology. For instance, you can have Bifacial PERC, Bifacial IBC, and even combine other technologies to create PV modules with excellent performances.

- How Much Weight Can the Tempered Glass of a Solar Panel Withstand?

Tempered glass for solar panels is tested specially to withstand hail and severe storms. Some modules manufactured by large companies can withstand up to 2,400 pascals of wind loads and up to 5,400 pascals of snow loads. What you should never do, even though they can withstand it, is walk on top of your PV modules, since this can entirely void the warranty.

- What Is the Shockley-Queisser Limit?

The Shockley-Queisser limit is defined as the theoretical maximum conversion efficiency of a solar cell. This is calculated for a single p-n junction semiconductor, considering how much power can be extracted from a photon. The limit is set at 33.7%, which is the theoretical maximum conversion efficiency for a solar panel. PV modules featuring multi-junction for the absorber layer, can in theory surpass that limit.

The Road So Far

We have learned about basic aspects of solar photovoltaic cells and energy, as well as the different types of solar panels that you can find on the market But, how can you use this knowledge to set up your off-grid power generation project? Let's find out more about this in the following chapters, starting with the basics of off-grid systems and understanding their difference with grid-tied solar systems.

Chapter 3

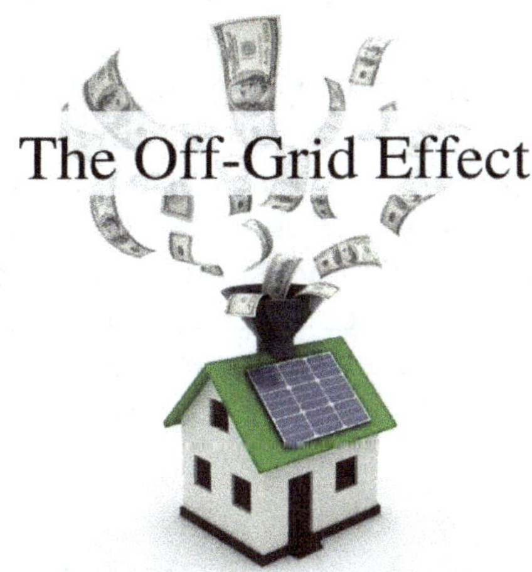

The Off-Grid Effect

One of the biggest questions in everyone's mind is why they go for solar if they are using electricity from other means like wind, water, and coal. The answer to this question is that solar contains tons of advantages besides electricity. This chapter will show some important reasons why homeowners go towards solar.

Provide financial saving

If you are employed or have a business, you always search for financial savings ideas.

The first one is that solar power energy will reduce electricity bills. Everyone around the world is worried about rising electricity bills. But through using solar power energy, a person can easily generate free energy from the system for more than 25 years.

The second one is that while energy costs are increasing it will not affect a person using solar energy. Every year, the cost of energy will be increased in every part of the world. If a person has invested in solar energy, then his cost will be locked. Saving a lot of money as the electricity cost increases with time.

The third advantage is that solar energy will also increase the value of the property. Solar power will decrease the energy bills and increase the cost of the property in Real Estate value.

The fourth one is that solar energy is a good return on investment. Through a solar energy system, a person can get more than a 20% return. As the solar life span is increasing so its return on investment will also increase.

Environmental benefits from solar

The next important advantage gained from solar energy is environmental benefits. From the environmental protection agency, the production of electricity is contributing 27% of carbon emissions in America. Fossil-fuel power plants are contributing to carbon emissions along with increasing air pollution levels. With the help of solar energy, the goal is to protect the environment. In that, there will be no carbon footprints in the solar energy system. It is also possible for a person to offset the need for carbon-emitting generation by connecting them with the grid. By using solar energy in residential areas, it will become possible to eliminate about 3 to 4 tons of carbon emission per year, this is equal to growing 100 trees annually.

Other benefits of solar energy

There are also other benefits of solar rather than environmental and financial savings. It means moving towards solar energy will help to increase local jobs. When local jobs are increased then it will also be contributing to the local economy. Therefore, if a person is investing in solar energy then it is better for the economy of a country.

Many solar parts are interchangeable

Solar power system parts include solar panels, inverters, charge controller and batteries. All of these parts are combined to run any solar power system which makes it possible to increase its capacity saving money and time by attaching the best parts.

Solar systems don't require direct solar energy

It is also possible for solar panels to produce energy during cloudy weather or dim conditions.

But it will only decrease the level of energy, but this power is enough to charge up the battery during the rainy season and at night.

Better energy produced from cheaper solar panels

With the passage of time, solar panel technology is also improving and moving from poly-crystalline to mono-crystalline. But the older technology is cheaper compared with new models of solar panels and also better. Like, poly-crystalline solar panels are providing lower costs per watt of power. Although they don't overheat at higher temperatures and also produce higher power. These panels are not bigger than their alternatives.

Benefits of off-grid solar power systems

As the rate of electricity bills increases, many people around the globe are shifting toward renewable power resources. The fact is that these resources are providing advantages to the environment and allow a person to spend less money on electricity.

In grid-tied systems, a person who has installed solar panels on their roof can easily supply energy to the grid. But an off-grid system, a person is only providing solar energy to their home. It is related to the idea of standalone. But there are a lot of benefits if a person is moving towards an off-grid system by using solar panels.

One of the major disadvantages of investing in a grid-tied system is that the homeowner may struggle with power outages, and he will also depend on other professionals. The cost of such a system is also high.

But if a person is using an off-grid solar system then he can avoid power outages, less professional cost, reduce electricity costs, and an easy installation. This is the reason why it is attractive for people if they wanted to save money and the environment at the same time.

Avoiding power outages

If a person is shifting off-grid then he will never face any kind of unpredictable power outages. Mainly because you are not connected with the power source of the city that is facing power interruptions due to sleet storms, freezing rain, and load shedding.

Power outages at home may create a lot of problems and make living conditions uncomfortable. The power outage may interrupt for hours, stress out families, and also stops your daily routine. It is extremely difficult to live without power and energy at home. Waiting for power to be restored is frustrating.

For reliable energy at home, an off-grid solar system is the best choice. This system is connected with batteries. The batteries are charged with solar panels and provide power energy at home during bad weather conditions like rain, winds, heatwaves, and cold snaps. The required equipment of any off-grid system is standalone.

Easy installation

Off-grid systems are quite easy to install. The required equipment connected with off-grid solar systems is not depending on the grid. Therefore, the installation process is straightforward and does not rely on complex infrastructure. In the grid-tied systems, only professionals can provide services and connect them with the electric grid. But the off-grid system can be installed by the homeowner if he had a little bit of information regarding its tools and connection. The complete process for installing an off-grid system is not complex so there is no need to hire a professional installer.

Off-grid solar power system, alternative source for rural areas.

Many individuals who live in rural areas face various problems regarding electricity. The rate of power outages in rural areas is comparatively higher than in cities. Rural areas also face complete blackouts. Whenever they need to provide water to their fields they require tube wells, which are powered by electricity. But due to the blackout, they can't water their crops. If an off-grid system is installed, this would greatly improve their success in farming and growing food for their families.

Off-grid systems keep the environment clean

Solar energy is taken from the sun and is considered a renewable energy resource.

This energy resource is greener and healthier for the environment as opposed to fossil fuel energy. If a person is using an off-grid or on-grid system, both of them are good for the environment.

Grid-tied is common among solar system owners as they can rely on the power grid along with the rest of the city while an off the grid solar system means users are independent at providing power to their home.

Compared to a grid-tied system, this type of solar power relies on batteries to store the electricity harnessed by the solar panels.

EASY ALTERNATIVE FOR RURAL AREAS

Electricity is one of the most significant problems of residents of rural and remote areas as these areas are prone to blackouts.

Since rural and remote areas have fewer infrastructures, connecting to the main electrical grid can be a challenge and incredibly costly but off-grid solar energy systems offset this significant role.

People who live in areas away from the main grid can save money through off-grid systems. These systems make it so users don't have to pay extra to connect to anything.

It gives people the freedom to live anywhere while being able to produce and control power.

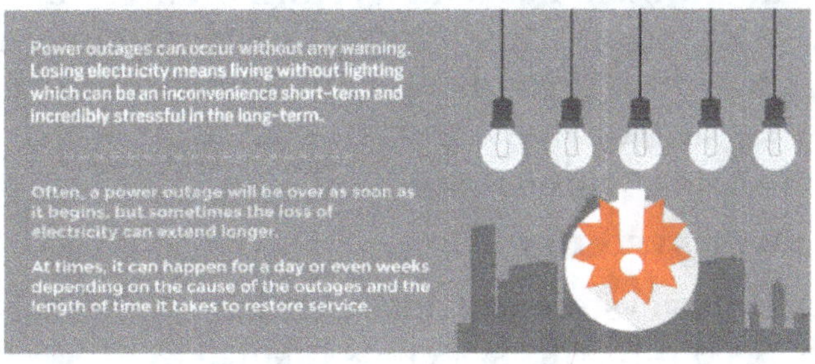

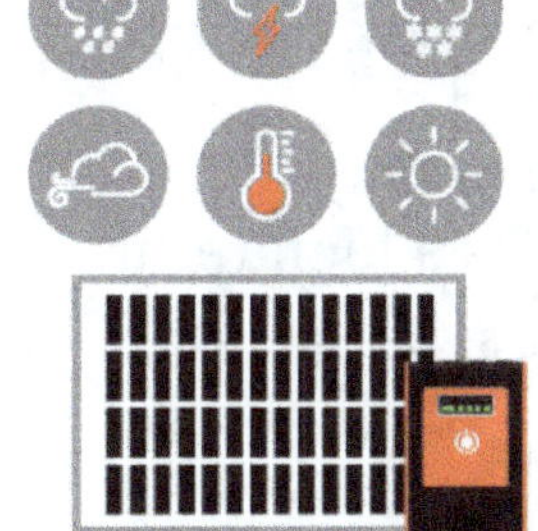

Types of solar systems

There are three important types of solar power systems. These include on-grid solar power systems, off-grid solar power systems, and hybrid solar power systems. This section will take a look at the vital benefits, features, components, and applicability of these types of solar power systems.

On-grid solar power systems

In its features, this particular system contains a large utility-scale model. It is possible to draw night power from the grid and it also provides supply to the grid.

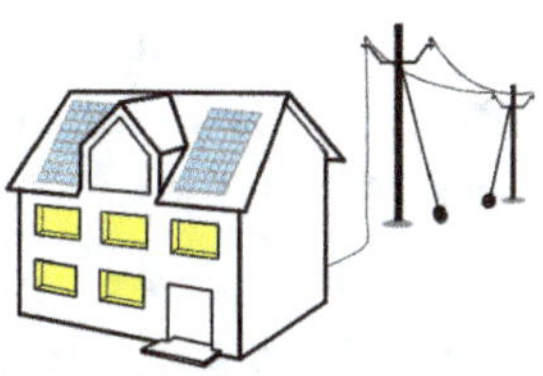
On Grid Systems

In its components, there are solar panels, a grid-tie inverter, a green meter, and a grid. In its benefits, there will be low electricity bills. It provides a faster return on investment and also better savings. This system is only applicable in urban areas with high-quality grid connectivity.

Off-grid solar power systems

In its features, this system is completely independent. The off-grid system life span is quite long. Also, this system is hassle-free.

Off-Grid Systems

In its components, there are solar panels, inverters, and a battery system. In its benefits, there will be no electricity bills after installing this system. The particular system has a high return on investment. It is an independent system of the grid. The off-grid solar system is applicable to any place around the world. It can be used in homes or offices. It can be applied in microgrids, urban areas, and rural areas. It is also applicable in the agricultural and construction sectors.

Hybrid solar power systems

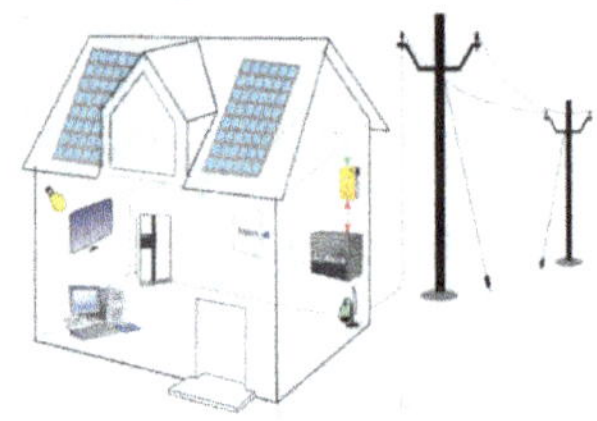

In its feature, this system provides surplus supply to the grid. Secondly, this system is taking night power from the battery. Therefore, there will be no blackouts. In its components, there are solar panels, battery systems, hybrid inverters, and a green meter used for net metering. In its benefits, there will be low electricity bills and provides a high return on investment.

Hybrid Systems

The hybrid system is applicable in homes or offices, rural areas, micro-grids, and also agricultural sectors.

The difference between On-grid and off-grid solar energy

On-grid and off-grid solar energy are very different from each other. This section will discuss the differences in these systems in detail.

Difference 1: Your access to electricity

Electricity access from an off-grid system

If a person has access to electricity from an off-grid system then it means their home is not connected to the grid.

The fact is that in an off-grid system, there are solar panels, which are making power energy and provide energy to the home and batteries. This person is relying on the sun's energy.

However, in this system, a person may face a complete blackout when there is no sun for a week and the batteries ran out. When a power system is completely off-grid then it means a person gets electricity when the sun is shining, or when the charge from the sun is stored in batteries and they can get electricity at night or in harsh weather.

If you have no batteries, then there will be no electricity at night and also less electricity during cloudy days. Extra electricity will not be available, a person can only use energy that is produced by the panels.

Electricity assesses from an On-grid solar system

If a person is going to install an On-grid solar system then there will be no blackouts. Another point is that if solar panels are not generating

enough electricity to power heavy machines at home, then a person can take energy from the grid.

Difference 2: Excess production of solar energy

Excess produced in Off-grid solar systems

The energy from solar is depending on the size of the system. If the size of the system is huge that covers all your appliances like air conditioners, iron, oven, and water pump at the same time then you have 10kva system. Therefore, at peak hours of the day, it will generate more than 9kva solar power energy. If your load is only 4kva, then excess energy will be stored in the battery. Further, if the batteries are charged then excess energy generated from solar is useless in an off-grid system. Many off-grid solar system owners have increased the number of batteries to cover the demand at night and also in cloudy weather. It means that excess electricity is useless in an off-grid solar power system if there are not enough batteries for the load.

Excess production in On-grid solar power system

If an excess amount of electricity is produced in an On-grid system, then it would be beneficial for it. Many people who wanted to cover 100% of their energy usage benefit from using an on-grid solar power system.

In the peak hours of the day, solar energy will generate excess energy. This excess energy will charge up the batteries.

When the batteries are charged then it will transfer power to the grid and the grid will compensate for your electricity bills through using net metering.

With this net metering, a person can give units to the grid, and then the grid will compensate for electricity bills. Whenever a person is providing energy to the grid then it will give advantages in the form of extra credits or compensation in future electricity bills.

Difference 3: What will happen when the grid goes down?

The Grid goes down in an off-grid system.

In the off-grid system, the solar energy is working as a standalone and makes power that is stored in batteries and used in homes. During power outages, there will be no problem with the off-grid system having no connection of the home to the grid and generating its own energy.

During bad weather or storms, the power outage duration will be high because of the lack of sun. During this period, the off-grid system will rely on its own sources from the batteries during outages or complete blackouts.

The Grid goes down in the on-grid system

When the home is connected to the grid and the solar system then a person can easily take electricity from the grid at any time. But there are some rules to it. In a grid-tied solar system, whenever the grid is down then you will have zero electricity if there is no battery system connected at home.

It means that the underwriters' laboratories require that the solar power system should be shut down when the grid is down. It is only for the safety of the workers when they are repairing the power lines.

It is one of the huge disadvantages of a grid-tied system compared with an off-grid system. If a person is using an On-grid system, then he must attach batteries. These batteries will provide power when the grid is not connected to it.

Difference 4: Billed for electricity

The Electricity bill for using an Off-grid solar power system.

It means that if a solar power system is not connected to the grid system then there will be no electricity bills. But with no electricity bills, the Off-grid solar power systems are highly expensive because it requires extra solar panels and batteries to complete the demand of the home at any time.

Electricity bills for an On-grid solar power system.

If a person is using an on-grid solar power system, then there are still some minimal charges present in the electricity bill even when the solar system is providing 100% energy.

In the electricity bill, there are charges for delivery and a service fee. This cost is regarding the connection of homes or businesses with the grid. It contains a flat rate, and it will not impact the use of electricity. The next point in the electricity is regarding demand charges. These types of charges are linked with commercial properties. Therefore, a person has to pay these charges when electricity is consumed during peak hours. The main reason behind it is that a large amount of energy will be used at one time will put pressure on the grid.

The electricity rates will be higher at that time. But it is possible to decrease these demand charges. During peak hours, the whole home system must be cut off from the grid and shifted on batteries. Through this, batteries will manage that time and when it is over, the system will be connected to the grid again.

Hybrid solar energy systems.

It is a system, that is connected to the grid and also contains a battery bank that is storing unused electricity.

The fact is that hybrid solar systems are more expensive because it requires extra batteries and panels. If there is no extra battery, then the system will take energy from the grid. But it is able to use energy when the grid is down. It will also decrease the demand charges for businesses.

How solar works in on-grid, off-grid and hybrid systems.

All working solar power systems operate on one basic principle. Converting solar energy into DC power. which is also called the photovoltaic effect. After this, the particular DC power will be stored in the batteries and also transferred to the inverter.

Then the inverter will convert the DC power into AC which is used as electricity in homes or offices. It is dependent on the size of the system, and also a connection with the grid for extra credits or storing power energy in batteries.

Types of solar power systems

There are three types of solar power systems are given below

On-grid solar power system: This system is also known as grid-tie or grid-feed solar system.

Off-grid solar power system: This system is also called as a stand-alone power system.

Hybrid solar power system: This system is a grid-connected solar system that contains batteries.

Main components of a solar system

This section will show information regarding the main components of a solar system

Solar panels

As the rate of technology is increasing, solar panels are also improving.

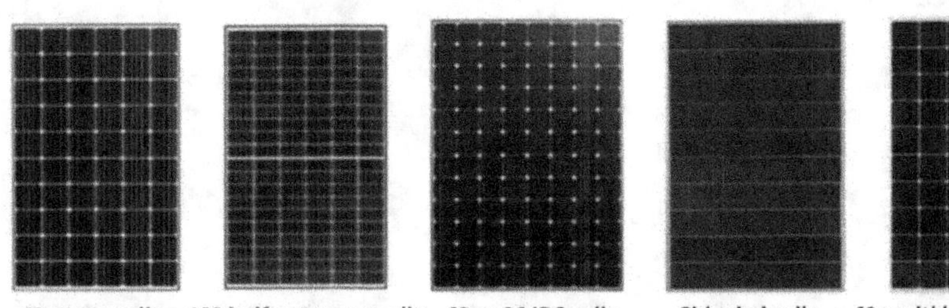

Modern solar panels are made from photovoltaic cells. These cells generate direct electricity from sunlight. All of these PV cells are linked together in the solar cells and connected with each other through cables. Only sunlight is producing electricity. These solar panels are also called solar modules. These panels are connected together in the form of a string creating a solar array. The required amount of solar energy generated by the panels depends on its orientation, the tilt angle of the solar panels, and any losses due to shading from dirt and ambient temperature. The efficiency of the panels

also factors into this. There are a lot of solar panel manufacturers on the market. Therefore, it is important to know which is better.

Solar inverters

Popular Solar Panel Sizes

When solar panels are generating DC electricity, it can be stored in batteries only, otherwise, it is useless. Therefore, it is important to convert the DC electricity into AC so it can be used in homes and businesses. The

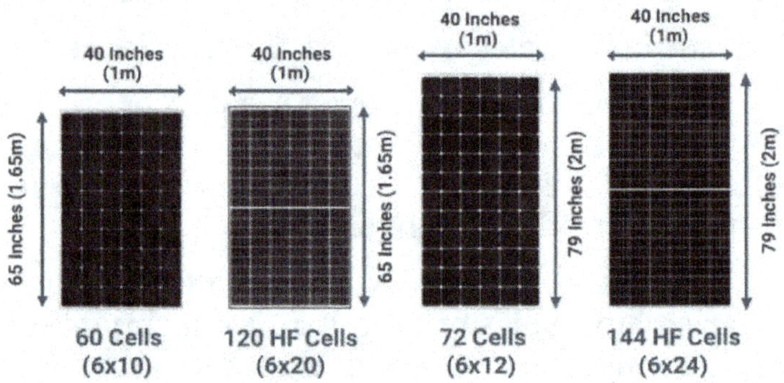

conversion of DC into AC is done by the solar inverter. In the string inverter system, the number of panels that's connected creates DC electricity. After this, the particular DC electricity will be converted into AC.

But in the micro-inverter system, every panel contains its own micro-inverter that is attached to the rear side of the panel.

In that case, the panels are still producing DC electricity but its converted into AC through inverters.

In some advanced string inverter systems, there are some small power optimizers present. These optimizers are attached to the back side of each panel system. These power optimizers are monitoring and control each panel properly. It also ensures that every panel is operating at maximum efficiency level under various conditions.

Batteries

The required batteries used for a solar power system are of two types, lead-acid and lithium ion.

There are other types of batteries like sodium-ion and redox flow batteries, But in a modern energy storage system, rechargeable lithium-ion batteries are the best. These batteries are available in various shapes and sizes. You can configure these batteries in various ways.

The capacity of the battery is measured in Amp-hours for lead-acid batteries and kilowatt-hours for lithium-ion batteries. But it is not possible

to use 100% of the battery capacity. The lithium battery is supplying about 90% of the available capacity per day. On the other hand, the lead-acid batteries are only supplying 30 to 40% capacity per day It is also possible to discharge a lead-acid battery, but it is only done in emergency situations.

The off-grid solar power system is connected with off-grid inverters. The battery system for an off-grid system must be large. This particular system must have enough power to sustain the system for more than 2 days. On the other hand, the hybrid solar system is using low-cost battery inverters and does not require a huge battery system.

Electricity switchboards

In any solar power system, the AC electricity is generated from the panels, then it is sent to the switchboards. From switchboards, it will connect with various appliances in the home. This process is called as net metering. The excess amount of electricity generated by the solar system will be sent to the electricity grid by using an energy meter. In some countries they use Gross metering in which the solar energy is exported to the electricity grid.

Hybrid systems export excess solar electricity to the grid and also store in the batteries. Hybrid inverters are connected to the backup switchboard.

These switchboards will allow important loads that will be powered on through panels during blackouts or grid outages.

Working with an on-grid system

Grid-tied solar systems are used by many businesses and homes. These particular systems are not using any batteries, solar or micro inverters. The required solar panels are connected with the electricity grids. If an excess amount of power is generated by the solar panels, then it will export to the grid.

During grid incidents, if the solar system is still feeding electricity in the damaged grid, then it will create problems during the repairs. The hybrid solar system has the ability to isolate itself from the grid during a blackout also called islanding. Batteries easily supply power during a blackout.

The meter: In an On-grid system, there is a meter that is measuring the rate of excess electricity from solar panels. It will calculate how much power is exported or imported from the grid.

The metering system: In various states and countries, the metering is different. According to this, the meter is only involved in measuring the rate of electricity exported to the grid. In some states, the meters measure solar electricity produced by the system. The electricity of the home will run by the meter before reaching the switchboard. In some states, the meter is measuring both export and import electricity to the grid. The customer is charged on a monthly or yearly basis.

The electricity grid: The solar system at home will send power to the grid. Then this energy can be used by other consumers on the grid. When the solar system is not working then a person is using more electricity than they are producing. It is dependent on the solar system for how much electricity the system is exporting to the grid.

Working with an Off-grid system

The required off-grid system is not connected with the electricity grid. Due to this fact, it requires a battery storage system. The off-grid system must be designed in such a way that it can provide energy throughout the year in various weather conditions.

This system must have enough battery storage that can meet the demand of the home during the winter or summer season. Due to the high cost of solar panels and also the batteries, the off grid solar power system is expensive compared with other systems. But after new technologies, the cost of the batteries is decreasing so there will be a growing market for off-grid solar systems.

The battery bank: It is the main part of the Off-grid solar power system. In the day times, solar energy is creating an excessive amount of electricity. This excess energy is stored in the battery bank. On the other hand, when the battery bank is fully charged then it will not take any electricity from solar. If the solar array is not working on cloudy days or when it rains then power will be supplied from this bank.

Backup generator: Sometimes, there will be no storage in the battery if there is no solar for 3 or more days. Completing the energy demand, a backup generator must be installed at home. This generator will complete demand in harsh days and also charge up the batteries.

Working with hybrid systems

The hybrid systems are connected with the grid and also charge the batteries in various configurations. As the battery cost is decreasing with time, the hybrid system contains various batteries that are connected to the

solar power system. During peak hours, this system is generating excess energy and it is stored in the batteries and also providing power to the grid system. Therefore, at night, the system is cut off from the grid and imported electricity from it.

But batteries are supported at night to minimize the electricity bills. The hybrid systems are also charging the battery during cheap off-peak hours and complete the electricity demand of the home.

The battery bank: This system contains a battery bank. In this bank, the solar power will be stored in it and then used at night or during power outages. Furthermore, when the battery bank is fully charged then it will not receive any power from the solar system. The required energy from the battery can be discharged when energy is consumed at home.

The hybrid system can be shifted towards the battery during peak hours so maximum advantage can be taken.

The electricity grid and the meter: It depends on the required hybrid solar system. If the number of solar panels is high, then it will become possible for the system to charge the battery in less time. Then the excess electricity will be provided to the grids through meters. If the batteries are not charged properly, then the hybrid system will take power from the grid.

Is Off-grid solar legal?

It is an important question for the consumers that are going to shift towards it. The government and power companies have figured out how to lock you into a power bill.

According to this, the legal opinions are agreeing that solar generation is legal in the US. It is also included as a constitutionally protected right. But state and local governments have the right to restrict. Therefore, some of them are charging their customers who generate their own energy through solar.

The electric code connected with off grid solar systems

The government had applied the NEC to all electrical installations rather than moving vehicles and tiny homes.

These restrictions are because low voltage DC systems are less dangerous. They are simple to install as a temporary off-grid power system and it is also invisible to the regulations. The government is unable to find one running USB cables and extension cords.

Minimum usage charge applied for Grid-connected solar

Power companies are fighting back. States are promoting higher usage charges when they install grid-connected solar systems. It means that

the consumer has to pay for high power usage even if he is producing power from solar. But there is no legal basis to give bills to off-grid customers.

The main secret of Legal Off-Grid solar

- Connect with a low voltage DC system as much as possible.

• Apply for temporary installation at home and it will not constitute a permanent installation.

- Do not ever connect your home or any part with the grid.

- One of the best ways to do this is that just make sure that the home is portable.

Laws related to Off-grid solar systems

There are some important laws related to off-grid solar systems that are given below.

The national electric code

The required NEC contains important significance regarding solar panels. Moreover, all 50 states are adopting this code. If someone is going with a professional solar installer then, he must follow all regulations present in the code. Further, if someone is not a professional installer then he must have a good reference and follow up on all regulations.

HOAs and Covenants

Many rural plots of land are sold through bylaws or covenants. Whenever a person buys land, he has to sign an agreement. It means that the owner has to protect the property from devaluing. Due to this, some considerations in the law will also limit the number of solar panels and also the overall size of the solar installation.

Municipal Nuisance laws

It is important for every city that had passed an ordinance that is limiting the residents what they are going to do with their land. There is no such information present regarding the city code that is prohibiting solar panel installation. They can get in by using a back door like city beautification ordinances.

Part – II

Chapter 4

EXPLORING ELECTRICITY

Definitions and Types

What is electricity and how does it work?

Electricity is considered as a secondary energy source that is created at an atomic level because of the attraction of electrons and protons. It is generated when electrons are moved around, and energy is moved down the conductive wires traveling into our businesses and homes.

Electricity is worked by getting various conducting elements together and create a flow of an electron-stealing pattern. This flow of electrons is also called current. The conductors must be insulated so that electrons will move in one direction only.

In today's world, electricity is considered as the main thing that is powering various appliances, examples are computers, cell phones, air conditioners and electric heaters and the lights in and around our home. It is not easy to escape from the world of electricity. But what is electricity? It is the most difficult question.

Due to this, there is only an abstract representation of it that is present in our surroundings.

The fact is that electricity is considered as a natural phenomenon, and it occurs throughout nature. It is briefly defined as the flow of electric charge. This upcoming section will show how these electric charges flow in a conductor.

Going atomic

To understand the fundamentals of electricity, it is important to start with atoms.

Every element of the earth is made up from atoms and it is a basic building block. These atoms are combined with each other to make molecules. The size of the atom is about 0.1nm. In a copper penny there are 2.3044×10^{22} atoms. Explaining more detail, it is important to take a look at the required building blocks of them like protons, electrons and neutrons.

Building blocks of an Atom

The complete atom is made from the combination of three particles: neutrons, protons and electrons. In every atom there is a nucleus in which neutrons and protons are present. In the orbits surrounding the nucleus are electrons.

There is at least one proton present in an atom. The number of protons of an atom defines its chemical properties.

The total number of protons is considered its atomic number. On the other hand, the purpose of neutrons is quite important. The neutrons are keeping the protons in the nucleus and also defining its isotopes.

Electrons are the critical part for electricity. In a complete balanced state, the number of electrons and protons are equal. It means in copper if the nucleus contains 29 protons, then it will be surrounded by an equal number of electrons. The electrons of an atom are not bound forever with an atom. The outer orbit of electrons is known as valence electrons. Whenever an outside force is applied then valence electrons will escape the required orbit of the atom and become free. These free electrons are involved in moving the charge from one place to another

Flowing charges

As the electricity is made from the flowing of electricity and charge. This charge is considered the property of matter. There are two types of charge, positive and negative. Through charge carriers, the charge is moved from one place to another.

The electrons are carrying the negative charge and protons carry a positive charge. But neutrons are neutral. The charge of electrons and protons is important because they are exerting an electrostatic force on each other.

Electrostatic force

The electrostatic force is such a force that it can operate between varying charges. Equal charges repel each other but opposite charges attract.

The amount of force acting on the charge depends on their distance. Due to the electrostatic force, electrons will be pushed and attracted to protons. This particular force is part of the glue that holds atoms together.

Making charges flow

Electrons present in the atoms are considered the charge carrier. Electrons contain a negative charge. If an electron is free from an atom, then electricity will be created. The fact is that electrons

present in the valence electrons are less likely to be attracted to the nucleus. Therefore, it can be freed easily when applying less force on them.

The one valence electron present in copper is a free electron. This electron is attracted by the positively charged atom. Due to this, the electron is ejected and moved toward the next electron and fills up free space. This chain effect of the electrons is making an electric current.

Conductivity

There are some elements that are releasing their electrons better than others. For obtaining good results in electron flow, just attach a valence electron lightly to the atom. The conductivity of an element is dependent on the bond of the free electron. Elements that contain less conductivity are insulators. Elements with higher conductivity are conductors like copper, iron, silver, brass, and gold.

Static or current electricity

There are two types of electricity: current and static. But in electronics, the current electricity is common rather than static electricity.

Static electricity

Static electricity is present opposite charges on the object are separated by an insulator. Static electricity exists only when the group of opposite charges can easily find a path between each other. When the charges are finding the means of equalizing then static a discharge phenomenon will occur.

The attraction of charges will be so high that they can easily go through the insulators. But the discharging of static current would be harmful, and it is depending on the required medium. The main example of static discharge is lightning.

Current electricity

It is an important type of electricity that is making electronic gizmos possible. This type of electricity is applied only when there is a constant flow of charges. This type of electricity is opposite to static electricity in which the charges are gathered and remain at rest.

Types of electric current

The facts are showing that there are two types of electric current. The first is AC and the second is DC current.

Direct current (DC)

The direction of this type of current is the same. The required electric current will be generated from solar, battery, and wind power that are DC. When the direction of the current is the same, then the value of the frequency is zero. Therefore, in this current, the one end is positive and the second one is negative.

Alternating current

The direction of the alternating current will keep on changing.

The required value of AC current will be moved in one direction, and it is increased from zero to maximum and falls down from zero to minimum and again repeats the same cycle again. Due to this, its graph is looking like a wave, and it is known as a sine wave. The frequency of AC current is about 50 Hz. Moreover, one side of the AC current is a phase and the other is neutral.

Electric fields

Now the next point is how electrons are moved through matter to make electricity. A source is required that will induce the flow of electrons and this comes from the electric field.

What is a field

A field is considered a tool used for modeling physical interaction involving no observable contract. It is not possible to see a field, but its effect is quite real. Although everyone is familiar with one kind of field, and it is Earth's gravitational field. Due to this field, everything is attracted to Earth. At various points of the field, its strength varies

Electric fields

By using electric fields, it's possible to understand the flow of electricity. It is defined as the main pushing or pulling force in the required space between charges. From Earth's gravitational force, there is only one 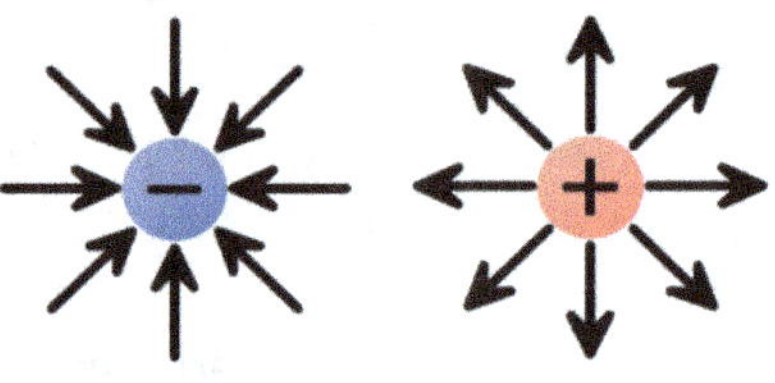 difference and that is the Earth's field is attracting other objects but the electric field is pushing charges away. The required direction of the electric field is defined through the positive test charge direction.

The main purpose of an electric field is to provide a pushing force that is used to induce a current.

The Direction of positive and negative charge Electric potential (energy)

Whenever electricity is used to power various things, it means the energy is transformed. Electronic circuits have the ability to store energy and also transfer it from one form to another. Stored energy is also known as electric potential energy.

Potential energy

To understand potential energy. Energy is the ability of a body to perform work. It means that when one object is moved towards another then energy is consumed. There are various forms of energy like mechanical, electrical, and chemical. Potential energy is related to stored energy when the object is at rest. It is also possible to control potential energy but when the object is in motion, it is converted into kinetic energy.

Electric potential energy

The mass in a gravitational field contains gravitational potential energy and a charge in an electric field has electric potential energy. The potential energy of a charge is showing how much energy is stored in it. When it is moved by an electrostatic force then this charge exerts kinetic energy.

Electric potential

The potential energy accounts for the electric potential. The electric potential shows how much energy is stored in electric fields. Which models the behavior of the electric field. Also, the electric potential is not the same as electric potential energy. In the electric field, an electric potential is the amount of electric potential energy stored and divided by a total number of charges at a certain point. The electric potential has a unit that is joules per coulomb.

Electricity in action

• To make electricity, you need to review the required ingredients used to make it.

• The flow of charge is called electricity and these charges are carried through free-flowing electrons.

• The negatively charged electrons are present in the last orbit and loosely held to an atom of conductive material.

• A properly closed circuit is providing a path so that electrons can flow continuously.

• On the other hand, the charges are moved by an electric field. This source will push the electron from low to high potential energy.

A short circuit

Batteries are considered the primary energy source that is converting chemical energy into electrical. Two important terminals of the battery are connected to the whole circuit. The

one terminal is connected with the positive part of the circuit and the second one is with the negative. There is an electric potential difference present between these terminals.

Illuminating a light bulb

A circuit will be made by attaching a battery to the bulb. The positive terminal and negative terminal of the battery are connected to the bulb. Therefore, when a light bulb is connected with the batteries through wires then a functional circuit is created. In this circuit, the electric field is affecting the whole circuit at every instant. When the switch is closed then electrons are moved toward the electric field. But when the switch is opened, then the transfer of electrons will be stopped.

Basic units and glossary of terms

Terms	Definitions
Alternating current	The current that can easily reverse its direction at regular intervals
Amps	It is the measuring unit of current that is flowed through a conductor
Battery	It is a single group of connected electric cells that are producing a direct current
Blackout	When there is a total loss of electric power from the grid
Capacitance	It is the ability of a component to store electric charge
Charge	The main component to produce electricity through surplus, and shortage of electrons
Current	The flow of electricity through a conduction
Conductor	The material that has the ability to transfer electrons and electric current through it.
Direct current	The electric current that is flowing in one direction
Electricity	The flow of electrons in a conductor
Generator	The machine that is converting mechanical energy into electrical
fuse	An electrical safety device that is consisted of a wire or a strip of fusible metal. This material will melt whenever the current value is increased

Insulator	A material that is not allowing any current through it
load	Such electrical devices that are using electric power
Meter	The instrument that is measuring the amount of electrical energy used by the consumer
Motor	A device that is converting electrical energy into mechanical
Power factor	The ratio of apparent power over reactive power
Solar energy	Such type of electrical energy that is produced from the sun
Spike	A small duration of increased voltage that will last only one-half of a cycle
Transformer	An electrical device that has the ability to increase or decrease voltage and current
Wind turbine	A machine that is converting wind energy into electrical

**With these out of the way,
let's see what an electrical circuit looks like...**

Chapter 5
Circuitry 101

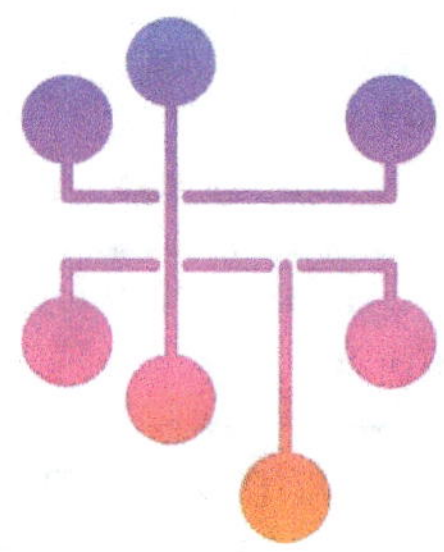

What is a circuit?

A circuit is a closed connection between the electric potential energy and a load.

Overview In this chapter, there is comprehensive information regarding the basics of a circuit in detail. If someone wanted to gain information regarding electronics then they must have a vital concept of a circuit.

Circuit basics

Voltage and how it works

The battery contains a certain number of volts in it and it is depending upon the number of cells. It is also the measurement of electrical potential produced by the battery and the grid connected with the home outlet.

When using volts, there needs to be electrical potential and it will come from electricity. It is also like a blown-up balloon. When this balloon is pinched then air present in it will do something after its release.

The electricity is only passing through the material that has the ability to conduct electricity like copper. When one wire is connected to the battery and the load, then after closing the switch the volts will move from higher to lower potential. It is like, the circuit is making a conductive path between higher voltage and lower voltage and electricity will flow along that path. If a useful thing is placed in its path like LED then the flowing electricity will move through it and light up the LED.

The simplest circuit

The simplest circuit is made by connecting the positive side of the voltage source which is a battery with the LED and the

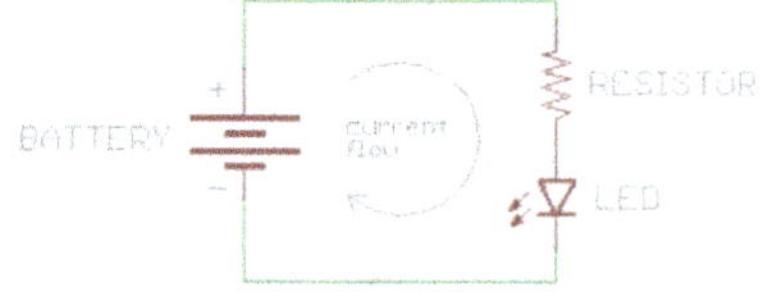

negative side is attached to the negative terminal of the battery. A resistor is placed between the battery and the LED to minimize the volts. After closing

the switch, the current and volts will flow through the circuit and light up the LED. The arrow is showing the direction of the current.

Short and open circuits

What is a load?

Before understanding this concept, let's take a look at the load concept. The main reason for making electricity is to make something useful for humans by attaching new things in an electric circuit. Therefore, when various things are put in an electric circuit then the current will flow to make noise, light up and run programs.

Whenever something is attached in the circuit and by applying current, the output is called load. At home, various appliances that a person is using are considered as load. Whenever a load is applied then it will lower the power supply. If the load value is lower than current, then it will damage the load and the power supply.

Short circuit

In simple words, if someone connect one end of the battery terminal with the other than it is called a short circuit. But never try it because it is dangerous.

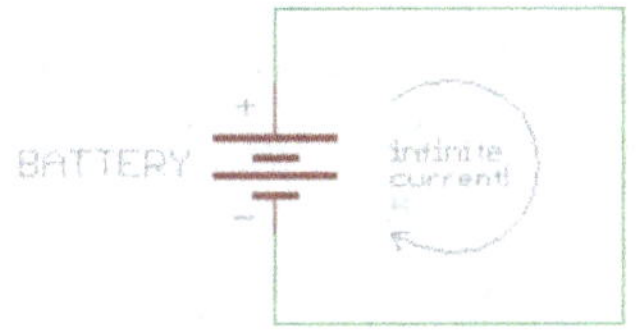

As the electrical current is flowing from higher voltage to lower and if a load is placed in the circuit then it will perform something different. Moreover, the power supply has the ability to limit the amount of current, but it is possible to increase the current depending on the load.

When there is no load present then there will be infinite current passing through the circuit.

Open circuit

The open circuit is opposite the closed circuit. In this circuit the loop is not fully connected, and it is not a complete circuit.

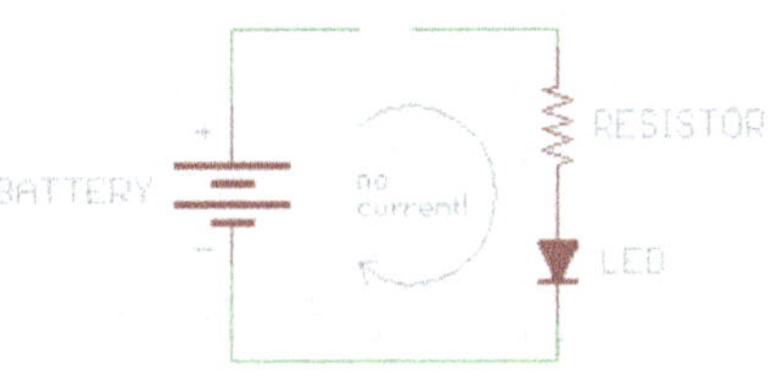

Like a closed circuit, there will be no damage gained from this circuit. But the voltage source will also not light up the LED. There are some advantages of an open circuit while calculating the voltage and current drained through a load. For this, the load is removed, and voltages are measured across it. Repeat measuring the voltages by attaching a load with it. It will show how much voltages are dropped. In the open circuit, the circuit will not work properly. The reason may be a loose connection or a broken wire. To find out from where the circuit is open you can use a multimeter.

Circuit terminology

To understand circuits, it is important to analyze a circuit. The most important components in a circuit include a capacitor, inductor, and resistor with voltage and current sources. Therefore, it is important to take a look at a glossary of terms related to circuits.

Types of circuits

There are two important types of circuits that include series and parallel circuits. Both of these circuits will be discussed in detail.

Series and parallel circuits

This section will show the vital differences between series and parallel circuits in detail.

Series circuit Nodes and current flow

For understanding a series circuit, Take the concept of a node. A node is only a fancy representation of an electrical junction that is present between two or more components.

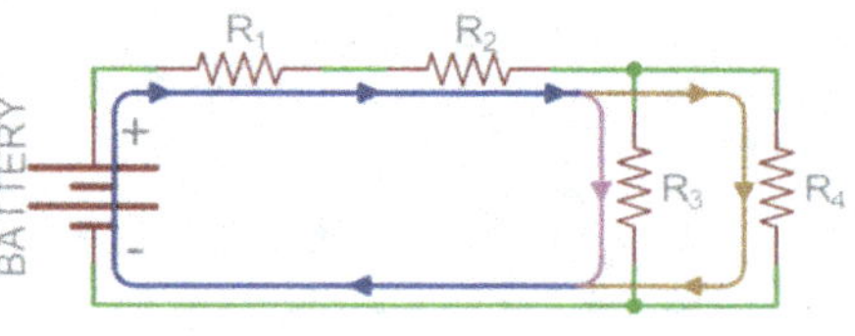

On the other hand, when a circuit is modeled on a schematic, then these nodes are showing the number of wires present between these components.

The main point is regarding the difference between parallel and series circuits. The current is flowing from a high voltage to a low voltage. In a circuit, the current will pass through every point toward a lower voltage that is called ground.

Series circuit defined

Whenever two components are in series then they will share a common node, and also the same current will pass through them.

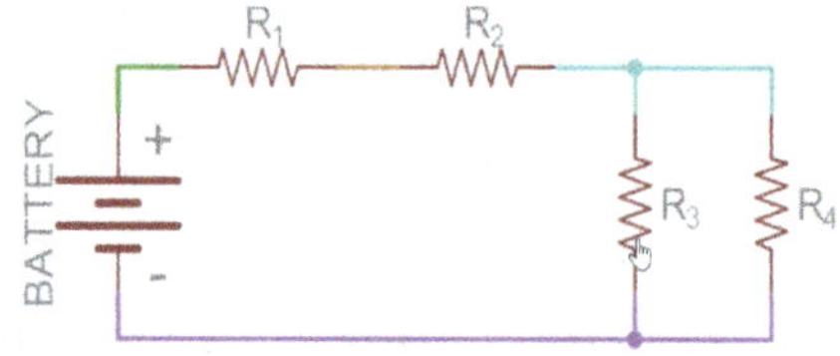

In this circuit, the current will flow in one direction only. It is started from the positive terminal and then passes through resistors and will end at the negative terminal.

Parallel circuits defined

If components are sharing two common nodes with each other, then they are in parallel. If a circuit is made from parallel components, then it is a parallel circuit. In a

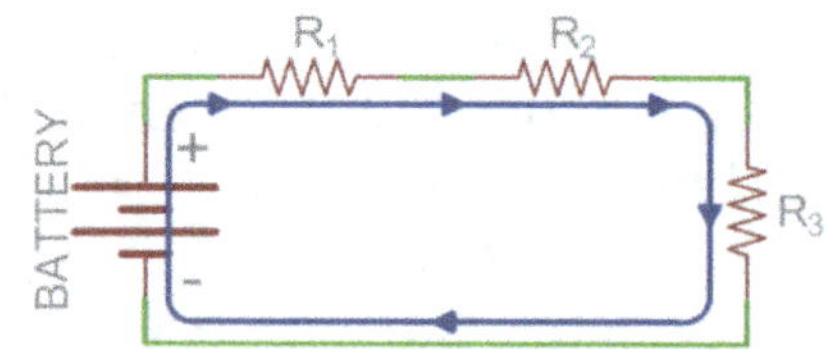

parallel circuit, the current will not be the same and it is divided. In the parallel circuit, the voltages will be the same, but the current is not the same.

From this, the node that is connected to one resistor to the battery is also connecting other resistors. The other end of the resistors is tied together to make a common node. In this circuit, the current will take three different paths so it will be different.

Series and parallel circuits working together

What happens when series and parallel circuits are working together.

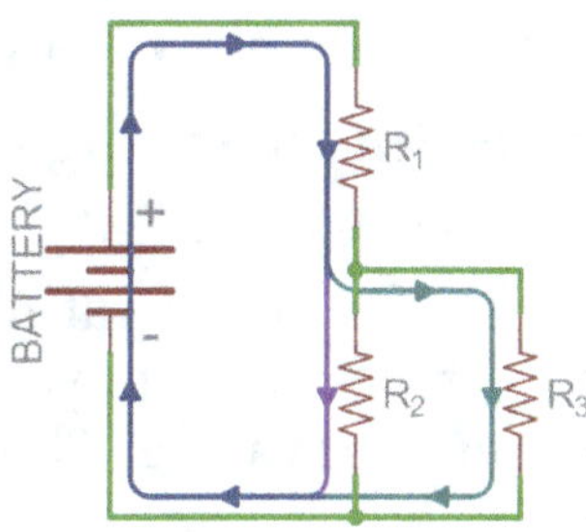

The circuit is made parallel by attaching two resistors in parallel. According to this circuit, the R2 and R3 resistors are in parallel.

Calculating equivalent resistances in series circuits

It is possible to calculate the equivalent resistance in series circuits. If 3 resistors are connected in a series that contains a value of 1ohm each. Due to this, its equivalent resistance will be found by adding these resistors.

$$Req = R1 + R2 + R3 \,, \; Req = 1 + 1 + 1 \,, \; Req = 3 \text{ ohms}$$

It will become 3 ohms. If the voltage supply contains 3 volts, then it means 1A current is flowing through the circuit.

Calculating equivalent resistance in parallel circuits

But calculating equivalent resistance in parallel is something difficult. It means that if two resistors are connected in parallel with a value of 2 each. Then its equivalent resistance will be calculated through this.

$$Req = 1 \div R1 + 1 \div R2 \,, \; Req = 1/2 + 1/2 = 1$$

Therefore, its equivalent resistance will be one ohm.

Moreover, if two resistors are in parallel, then its equivalent resistance can be calculated through this.

$$Req = R1 \times R2 \,/\, R1 + R2$$

But this method is only successful for two parallel resistors only.

Rule of thumb for series and parallel resistors

In some situations, there is a need for some creative resistor combinations. Like if a person is trying to set up a specific reference voltage,

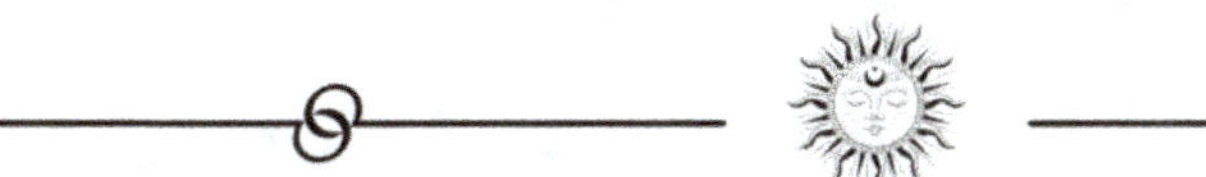

then there is a need for a specific ratio of resistors that contains standard values. It will become possible to get a high degree of precision in resistor values. It is possible to build your own resistor values.

Tip 1: Equal resistors in parallel

If N-like-value resistors are attached in parallel then it will give R/N ohms. Like, if you need a 2.5k ohms resistor. But it is not possible to get it because you only have 10k ohms resistors. Then, with 4 10k ohms, resistors can be combined in parallel will calculate like: Req = 10 ÷ 4 = 2.5k Ω

Tip 2: Tolerance

Every resistor contains its own tolerance value. Like, if there is a need of 3.2k ohm resistor, then a person will put 3.10k ohms resistors in parallel. It will provide 3.3k ohms.

This will provide a 4% tolerance from the required value. But the required circuit must be less than 4% tolerance. Due to this, a stash of 10k ohm will be measured to check the lowest value because it contains tolerance too. Moreover, if the stash of all 10k ohm resistors contains 1% tolerance then it will provide 3.3k ohms.

Tip 3: Power ratings in series/parallel

These types of series and parallel combinations of resistors are only working for power ratings. Like, if you need a 100-ohm resistor with a 2-watt rating. But there are a lot of 1k ohm resistors that are available with a quarter watt rating. Therefore, its power rating will be Power rating = 10x 0.25W

On the other hand, it is important to be extremely careful while combining dissimilar values of resistors in parallel when equivalent resistance and power rating are concerned.

Tip 4: Different resistors in parallel

When two or more different values resistors are combined in parallel then their equivalent value is less than the smallest value resistor. This may cause difficulty for a user to combine different resistor's values together and get a required value. If 10 ohm and 5-ohm resistors are connected in parallel then its equivalent value will be less than 5 Req = 1 ÷ 10 + 1 ÷ 5 = 3.33 ohms

Tip 5: Power dissipation in parallel

When dissimilar resistor values are connected in parallel, then power will be dissipated in parallel combination.

The fact is that the current through these parallel resistors is not the same. When 1k and 10k ohm resistors are connected in parallel, you will find that a 1k ohm resistor is drawing 10 times more current than 10k ohm.

Series and parallel capacitors

The combining of capacitors in series or parallel is the same as resistors but in the opposite.

Furthermore, a capacitor consists of two plates that contain a close space between them. The main purpose of a capacitor is to hold the electron in it. If the capacitance value is high then it can hold more electrons.

In series, the equivalent capacitance value will be like this:

$$Ceq = 1 \div C1 + 1 \div C2 + 1 \div C3 + 1 \div C4 + \dots 1/Cn$$

In parallel, the equivalent capacitance will be like this:

$$Ceq - C1 + C2 + C3 + C4 + \dots Cn$$

Series and parallel inductors

The series and parallel combination of inductors is the same as the resistors. But the most difficult part is that when inductors are placed close together, they contain interacting magnetic fields. Therefore, it is important to use a single component rather than 2 and more.

Series combination of inductors

$$Leq = L1 + L2 + L3 + \dots Ln$$

Parallel combination of inductors

$$Leq = 1 \div L1 + 1 \div L2 + 1 \div L3 + 1 \div L4 \dots 1 \div Ln$$

Chapter 6
Electrical Workings

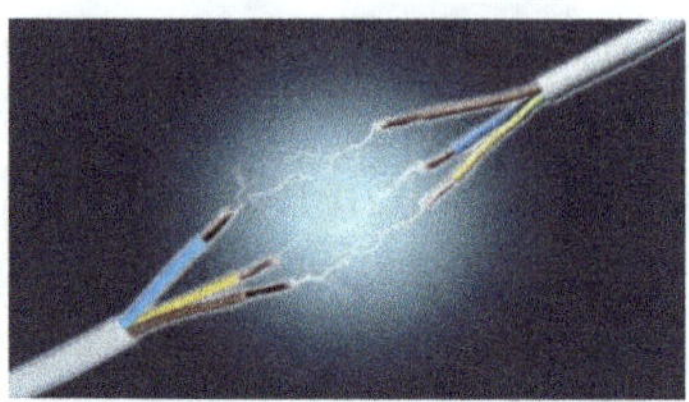

Energy vs Power

Energy

Energy is the main ability to perform work. Like, if someone is lifting a box and putting it in another place. Therefore, lifting a box requires energy. Moreover, a battery also contains certain an amount of energy in it so it can provide a given amount of fuel. The unit of energy is Joule. It means a certain number of joules are required to pick up a box. Energy is directly proportional to time.

Power

Power is related to the transmission of energy from one place to another. It is the required amount of energy that is divided by time. The unit of energy is watt, and it is given by joules per second. You need a certain amount of power to run a battery. The required energy stored in the battery can be calculated after the required amount of power is drained from it.

$P = E / t$

When the power and time are multiplied by each other then it will provide the value of energy. This is the reason why a kilowatt is a unit of power, and a kilowatt-hour is a unit of energy. Power is inversely proportional to time.

Voltage, current, resistance, and Ohm's law

This section will show some vital information regarding voltage, resistance, current, and ohm's law.

Electricity basics

All of these factors are considered the fundamental basis of electricity. Moreover, they are also considered the 3 basic building blocks to manipulate and use electricity.

At the start, it is difficult to understand these concepts because they are not visible to the naked eye. But for measuring them, you need some

tools like a spectrum analyzer, multi-meter, and oscilloscopes. With these tools, you can see the change in a system.

Electrical charge

The term electricity is related to the movement of electrons. These electrons are creating a charge that will move from one place to another to perform related work like light up various appliances. All of these appliances are operated by using the same power source.

There are three main principles of electricity that include voltage, current, and resistance.

Voltage

The voltage can be defined as the potential energy present between two points on a circuit. One point contains more charge compared with the other. The main difference between these two charges is called voltage. Voltage is measured in volts.

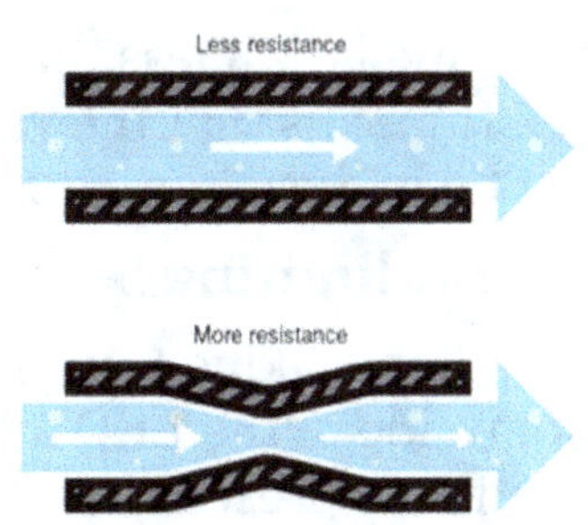

This can be explained through the example of water. Like, water is considered as a charge, the pressure provided for water to flow is the voltage and the required flow is current.

Current

The flow of a charge is called current. From the above example, the flow of water through the hose from the tank is considered current. If the pressure is high then the current will be high. Therefore, with electricity, the required amount of charge flows through the circuit in unit time. The unit of current is measured as Amperes.

If the width of the hose is thin, then less water will flow from it. This width is related to its resistance. The required phenomenon is the same for the flow of charges in electricity.

Resistance

Resistance is the required force that is stopping the flow of current. If the resistance value is high then a low current will pass through the circuit. The unit of resistance is the ohm.

From the example of a water tank, if the width of the tank is narrower, then less water will flow through it. It means its resistance is high.

Ohm's law

In simple words, the product of current and Resistance is Ohm law. Moreover, voltage and current are directly proportional to each other by keeping the resistance constant. It is given by this: V = I x R

An Ohm's law experiment

According to this experiment, a 9-volt battery will be used to power an LED which is extremely fragile. If the value of the current is fractionally high then it will burn out. It is important to give LED current, according to its current rating. The material required for this experiment includes a multi-meter, A 560-ohm resistor, a 9-volt battery, and an LED.

LED is considered a non-ohmic device.

The reason behind it is that the equation through the current flowing LED is not satisfying V=IR. The LED is introducing a new term that is voltage drop into the circuit. But in this experiment, you need to protect the LED from over-current. The current rating of LED is about 20 milliamperes or 0.020 amps. You need to find what resistor is suitable to draw 20 milliamps current through the LED.

$$V = I \times R , R = V \div I , R = 9 \div 0.020 , R = 450$$

So, if R = 500 is selected then this will happen.

$$I = V \div R , I = 9 \div 500 , I = 0.018$$

This value is still less than the current rating of LED. It will not damage the LED. It means that the value of the resistor selected to light up the LED must be higher than 450 ohms. The LED will be saved from over current.

Current limiting before or after the LED

For making things complicated, just place a current limiting resistor on one side of the LED and its working will be the same. Now imagine a river that is present in a continuous loop.

Therefore, when a dam is placed in it, the flowing of water will be stopped. Also, imagine when the water wheel is present in the river it will slow the rate of water flowing. It is not important where the location of the water wheel is but it will slow down the whole river. It means that the current limiting resistor can be placed on any side of the LED

Electrical power

With great power

Why it is important to take care of power? Power is the measure of energy transfer at a specific time. When energy is used then it will cost. The fact is that batteries are not free along with the electricity provided at home. So power is measured by how fast the money is draining from the wallet.

There are various kinds of energy that include, radiation, heat, sound, wind, nuclear, etc. Moreover, if the value of power is high then it means more energy. But it is extremely important to have a proper idea of the power used in your electronics.

What is electric power?

Electric power is defined as the amount of energy transferred in unit time.

You need to understand what energy is and how it is transferred. Energy has the ability to perform various tasks and there are different forms of energy, like chemical, mechanical, electromagnetic, electrical, and many others. Energy cannot be created or destroyed but only transformed from one form to another. Like, spinning motors are converting electrical energy into mechanical. Also, when a 9V alkaline battery is turned on then its chemical energy is converted into electrical.

Each part of a circuit is involved in producing or consuming electric energy. A consumer is involved in transforming the electrical energy into another form. Therefore, when the LED is turned on then electric energy will be transformed into electromagnetic. And the light bulb is also consuming power.

Wattage

The unit of energy is joules and power is measured when energy is transferred in unit time.

Therefore, the unit of power is joules per second, and it is called Watt.

$$\text{Watt} = W = \text{Joule} \div \text{Secon} = J \div S$$

Calculating power

Electric power can be calculated by the rate at which energy is transferred. But electric power is the product of voltage and current. Therefore, the volts are defined as joules per coulomb, and ampere is defined as the rate of coulomb over time. Shown like this this.

Power = Volts x amperes

Power = Joules $\div$ coulomb x coulomb $\div$ second = joules $\div$ second = watt

$P = V \times 1$

Power can be calculated through 2 more formulas.

$P = V2 \div R$, $P = I2 R$

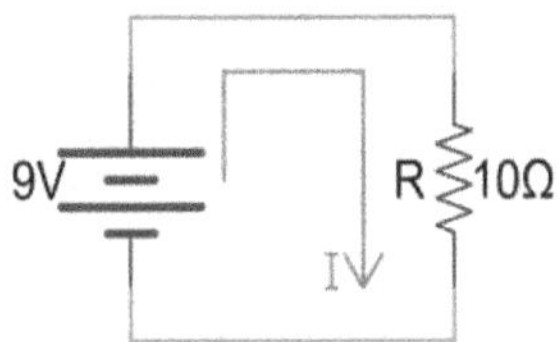

Therefore, from the above circuit, power can be calculated by:

$P = V2 \div R$, $P = 92 \div 10$, $P = 8.1$ watts

Power ratings

All electronic components are involved in transferring energy from one type to another. Here are some energies that are transferable. These energies include LED, motor spinning, and battery charging. Some energies are also undesirable and also avoidable. Such unwanted energy transfers are present in power losses. These power losses are in the form of heat. If the power loss is high then the component is heated too much and becomes undesirable. Therefore, many components are rated with maximum power that they can easily dissipate and also, can operate under this value.

Power rating of resistors

Resistors are considered the notorious culprits of power loss. The reason behind this is that when voltages are dropped across a resistor then an induced current will flow across it. It means that if the voltage value is high then the current and the power are high.

This means when 8 watts are dropped across a 0.5-watt resistor then it will burn.

Part – III

Chapter 7

OFF-GRID SOLAR SYSTEM OVERVIEW
The Major Components

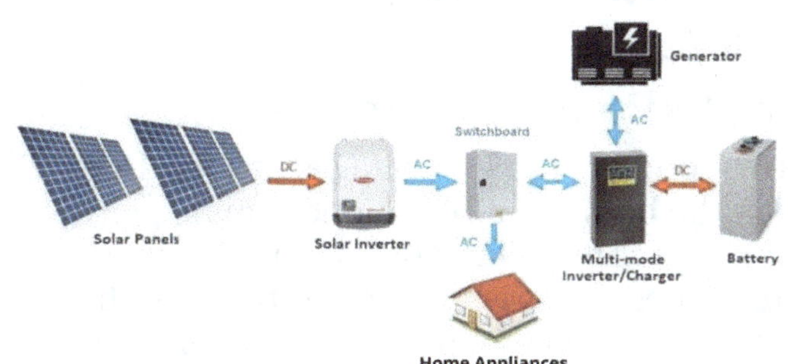

What is an off-grid solar system?

Off-grid solar systems are not connected to the grid and the sun is its only source of energy to meet the power needed. With the passage of time, off-grid solar systems can be improved. These systems are providing advantages to the environment while decreasing financial expenses.

Building an off-grid solar system

The off-grid solar system is made through solar panels which are connected in series to make a complete array of solar panels. Solar energy is then transferred to the solar charge controller, and then stored in the battery, and transferred to the inverter for use of this energy. All of these are important components of an off-grid solar system.

Solar panels

To capture sunlight from the sun solar which is mounted on rooftops and RVs consist of a lot of small photovoltaic cells. All of these photovoltaic cells are made up of semiconductor materials that are converting sunlight into electricity. There are various types of solar panels.

Semi-flexible and thin-film solar panels are lightweight and also a perfect option to use for RVs, boats, or cars. Monocrystalline and multi-crystalline are options to consider for solar panels in the system. Both of these panels are perfect for home use as well as for businesses.

The monocrystalline solar panels are more expansive compared with polycrystalline. But they are more efficient in warm weather.

Solar charge controller

The next important component is the solar charge controller that is used for the off-grid solar system. The charge controller manages the power from the panels and stores it in the batteries. This charge controller is ensuring that the batteries are not overcharged during the day and also the energy does not flow backward from the batteries to the panels at night. For the solar system, MPPT charge controllers are best, but they are more expensive than Pulse width modulation.

Off-grid power inverter

The next component is the off-grid power inverter.

The inverter converts the DC voltages of solar into AC and supplies it to all appliances in the home. This component manages the flow of AC and DC power. It is important to buy the proper size inverter according to the size of your system. These inverters are sized through their power capacity. If the solar system is 5kv then the inverter size must match the system.

The battery bank

For an off-grid solar system, the battery bank is considered the most important part. In the battery bank, a number of batteries are connected in series. Without a battery bank, the off-grid system is useless. At peak times, solar power is taken from the panels and stored in the batteries that are going to be used at night. The battery bank must have the ability to store a backup for about 3 to 4 days without sunlight. Therefore, it is important to make a battery bank that has the ability to support rainy or heavy storm days. There are two important types of batteries that can be used which include Lead-acid batteries and lithium-ion batteries.

Lead-acid batteries

The deep-cycle lead-acid batteries are commonly used in various appliances like RVs, cars, solar applications, and marine. But these batteries contain low energy density, short lifespan, moderate efficiency, and high maintenance.

Pros

- These batteries contain a low upfront cost.

- The typical price of lead-acid batteries is about 100 to 200 dollars.

Cons

The lead-acid batteries are heavy in weight. The lifespan of these batteries is low and requires a lot of maintenance. If these batteries are drained more than 50% then it will affect their life span.

Lithium Batteries

In the off-grid solar power system, deep-cycle lithium batteries are extremely useful for the battery bank.

These batteries use lithium salt to store energy.

Pros

There are a lot of advantages of lithium-ion batteries. The charging time of such batteries is fast. It is possible to use more than 80% of the rated capacity of such batteries. The weight of such batteries is lower compared with lead-acid batteries, and these batteries require no maintenance. Lithium-ion batteries contain their own internal BMS for their protection.

Cons

The upfront cost of lithium-ion batteries is expensive.

The cost of an off-grid solar system

The cost of an off-grid solar system depends on the size of the system. It is up to the user how much power he wants.

There are various categories of off-grid solar systems that are from 100 W to 20000W with a battery bank. Mostly, on houses, a 10000W system is reliable with a battery bank. The next cost is regarding the battery bank. If a lithium battery is selected then the overall cost of the off-grid solar system will be high. It is important to choose a package that can easily light up all appliances in the home.

If someone wanted to make a completely off-grid system, he is looking at a perfect investment plan. For this system, you will need 10000 W of solar panels with a 1200 Ah battery bank. The cost of the system could be more than $25000.

Other off-grid solar system equipment that's needed

Other off-grid solar systems equipment includes wires, circuit breakers, a battery monitor, and connectors. All of these components are rated to the size of the system. If these components are underrated then it is extremely dangerous for the whole system.

Disconnect and self-sustain by going off-grid

A person who has installed an off-grid system is disconnected from the grid. Therefore, you are making your own source of power which is quite beneficial because there will be no electricity bills in the future.

Basic components of a solar power system

Solar panel

Solar panels play a vital part in the quality of the production of energy and converting the solar energy into electricity and stored in the bank of batteries. There are various types of

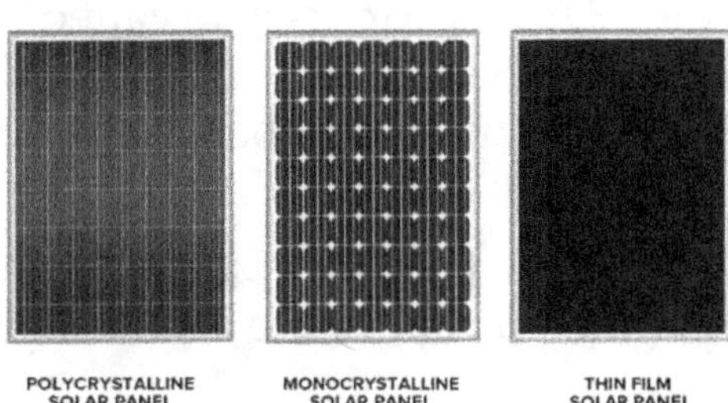

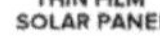

solar panels, polycrystalline solar panels, monocrystalline solar panels, and thin-film solar panels.

• Polycrystalline solar panels are made up of multi-crystalline layers and require more space. These panels are inexpensive and less efficient.

• Monocrystalline solar panels are made from a single silicon crystal and their efficiency is high and they are expensive.

• Thin-film solar panels are made from thin layers, and they are considered flexible panels. These panels require more space, and their efficiency is low and has a short lifespan

As technology increases, new technology for solar panels has been invented.

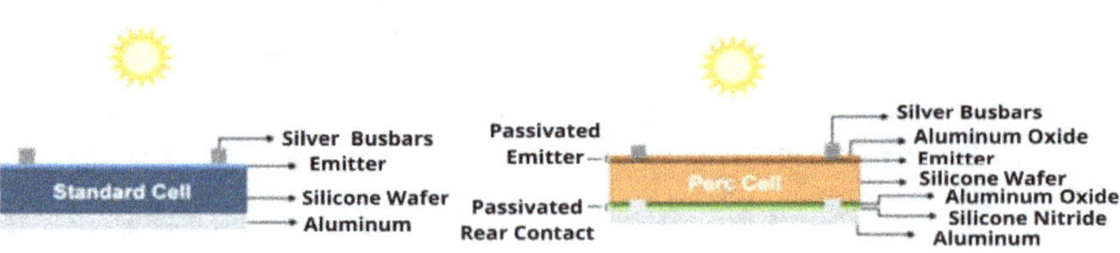

They are Passivated Emitter and Rear Cell (PERC). This particular technology is used in both polycrystalline and monocrystalline solar cells. But the main difference is that they contain an additional dielectric passivation layer on the rear side of it that absorbs all scattered solar waves.

Array junction box

The array junction box is a component that is used between the solar panels and inverter. There are some vital functions of the array junction box.

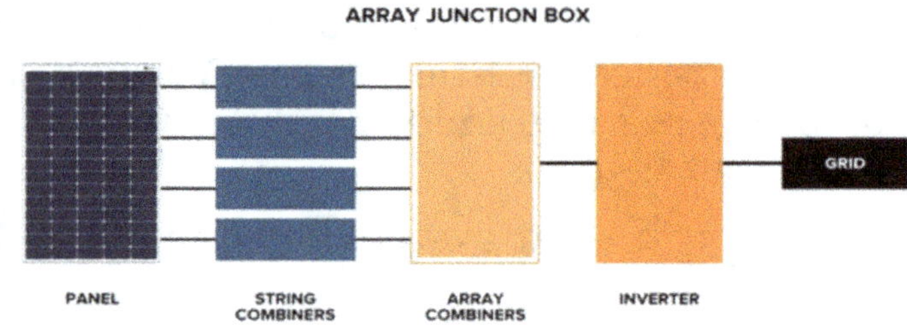

• This junction box is electrically connecting the output of various solar string wires in parallel form.
• The junction box consists of a blocking diode that is present on each string protecting the panel from reverse current.
• It is also providing protection to the system against over voltage and over current.

Inverter

The inverter is also called the heart of the solar power system. Because the inverter is connected with the solar system, the grid, and the home. The main purpose of the inverter is to convert DC from the solar panels into AC supply. Almost all appliances at home work on AC supply.

The inverter is playing an important role and synchronizing the generated power to the appliances with the help of small transformers.

There are two main types of inverters that include:

Off-grid inverters: these inverters are working independently and contain no contact with the grid.

On-grid inverters: these inverters are connected to the power grid and are the most important type of inverters used for residential areas.

Grid inverters are also classified into four sections

String inverters: these inverters are in high demand because of their durability and feasible cost. Multiple strings are connected to build a single-string inverter. One drawback, when one string is damaged then it will affect all the inverters.

Micro inverter: This type of inverter is used where space is the factor over cost. Also, where uneven shading is present in small areas. Small inverters are placed on every panel. So, when one panel is damaged then it will not affect others.

Central inverter: This inverter is similar to the string and also contains a high-capacity range. Only one inverter is used complete the demand of entire system and they are used for large utility scale applications.

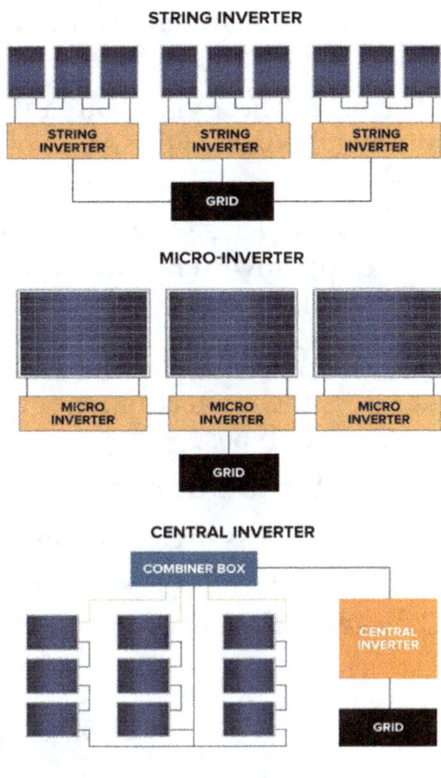

Hybrid inverter: It is a combination of off-grid and on-grid systems. These inverters are offering a lot of flexibility regarding power delivering. This inverter has the ability to choose between battery backup, solar power and also grid connectivity.

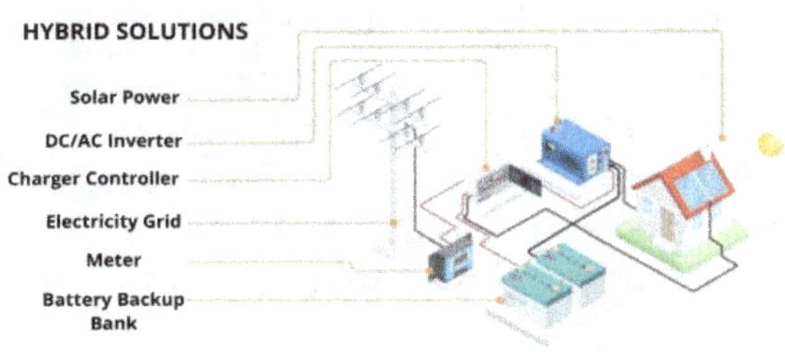

Mounting system: To support the solar system with a mounting system. There are two types of mounting fixed and track.

Fixed mounting: These mounts are stationary and also inexpensive. The mounts are unable to change position in the direction of sunlight.

Track mounting: These mounts have the ability to change their position according to sunlight.

As the direction of the sun is changing then these track mounts follow the solar radiation path and produce maximum results. These mountings are efficient and highly expensive. But for rooftop, fixed mounts are best.

Cabling system

Cables in solar power systems are considered blood vessels. These cables are responsible for transferring the current and also for the electric current from the panels towards loads. It is important to connect cables according to the system. If the cables are less efficient then power losses will happen. There are two types of cables used for solar power systems.

• **AC cable:** These cables are taken from the inverter and connected to the main switchboard of the AC appliances. These cables are only delivering AC power.

• **DC cables:** These cables are connected to the panels with each other and also with the inverter. These cables are transferring DC power generated from the solar panels.

Distribution box

It is the main component used for an electricity supply system and there are two types.

DC distribution box

This box is used to connect the output power from the solar panel to the input of the inverter. It contains DC surge protection devices.

AC distribution box

This box is distributing the electrical power from the solar inverter to the required load of the home or grid. It contains extra protective equipment like circuit breakers and surge protectors.

Meters

Meters are involved in tracking the amount of energy generated by the solar panels, utilized by the home appliance, and also how many units are sold to grids. There are three types of meter, PV meter, load meter, and net meter

• **PV meter:** this meter is connected in series with the inverter. This meter is showing how much electrical power is generated by the panels

• **Load meter:** this meter is connected with the load and measures the amount of energy consumed by the loads

• **Net meter:** this meter is connected between the distribution panel and the grid. This meter is bidirectional and also shows the information on how many units are sold to the grid and how many are utilized from the grid.

Protection device

As with lights various fault conditions are direct and indirect. The main components of the solar system can be damaged. Therefore, protection devices are used to protect these components. These protection devices include fuses, surge protectors, a grounding method, and circuit breakers.

Energy storage battery

The battery storage system is considered the most important part for the Off-grid solar power system. Without batteries, this system is useless. The extra solar energy is stored in these batteries and provide power at night or on rainy days. Rechargeable batteries are used.

Charge controllers

The main aim of charge controllers is to find the proper amount of charge taken and supplied to the battery. Charge controllers protect the battery against overcharging and reverse current. There are three types of charge controllers.

- Pulse width modulated

- Simple 1 or 2 stage controls

- Maximum power point tracking

Load center

The load center is used for both AC and DC and it consists of circuit breakers, fuses, and other switches.

Important safety precautions for installing solar power system.

During building solar array, a person is dealing with high DC voltages. Therefore, it is important to follow these guidelines.

- Use thick wire according to calculations

- Use a charge controller so it can protect the battery bank.

- Use protection devices at the DC and AC system of the solar power system to protect it against any damage.

- Attach all connections after complete knowledge, otherwise hire a professional.

The essentials

The essential components of off-grid solar power system include solar panels, battery bank, inverter, and extra components.

Generating power with solar panels

When power is generated from solar panels then it is stored in the batteries and also provided to the inverter.

Storing power with a battery bank

The battery bank is involved in storing the power taken from solar panels.

Making connections

From solar panels to inverter, DC connection wire is used to make connections. From the inverter to the load, AC connection wires are used.

Powering your devices

The solar panels are generating electricity and it is in the form of 12 Volts DC. These DC volts are enough to power up other appliances present in the home.

Building a solar power system

The solar power system is made by using solar panels, battery banks, cables, inverters, and AC appliances. When all of these components are connected with each other, then you have a solar system.

Chapter 8
A detailed guide on major components

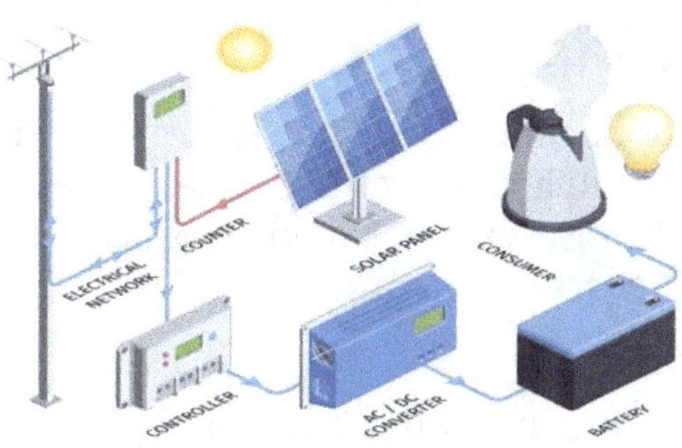

8-A: solar and mounting solutions

Solar panel efficiency

The efficiency of solar panels is the required measure of the amount of sunlight converted into electricity. If the efficiency of solar panels is 20%, then it means the panels are only making electricity from 20% of the sunlight.

The efficiency of solar panels is extremely important. If its efficiency is low, then it is not possible for them to generate enough power. Residential and commercial solar projects are use 60-cell and 72-cell panels. With the advancement of technology, solar panels' efficiency is increasing. Manufacturers are getting better at producing high-wattage panels. The output of panels is increased from 1 to 5- watt per year because of these efficiency improvements.

If high efficiency panels are used, then they will generate more watts from sunlight and the number of panels will be decreased. For small areas, high efficiency solar panels are recommended. Save money by buying high efficiency panels.

From research, the ideal efficiency rating of solar panels falls between 15 to 23%. There are also ways through which the efficiency of the solar panels can be increased.

Shading

If there is shade on the panels then it will prevent them from absorbing sunlight and it will also reduce production. Try to build a solar array in a location where shading is low and or panels are able to receive complete sunlight. It can be avoided by using micro inverters or placing panels in non-shaded areas.

Panel facing

If you want to absorb the maximum amount of sunlight, then place the panels towards the equator. They are exposed to direct sunlight for the whole day. The tilt angle of the panels is important. The panels must be tilted at an angle that is equal to the latitude.

Degradation rate over time

With the passage of time, solar may degrade and it will lose about 0.5 to 1% efficiency. But the advanced technological panels will degrade at a slower rate increasing their lifespan. The degradation rate of the panels can be found in the manufacturer's warranty.

Cleaning

Dust and dirt will accumulate on the panels. The efficiency will be decreased. It is important to have a cleaning schedule at least once a month. The efficiency will be maintained. Always use soft brushes to clean them.

Expanding further Difference between 60-cell and 72-cell solar panels

The main difference is that 72-cell solar panels are a foot taller than 60-cell. They are expensive and used to for large-scale applications. But both of them have the same cell technology.

Some dismissing myths regarding 72-cell panels

The first one is that these panels are only reliable for large-scale applications and are not used for houses. 72-cell panels, have less racking rail and require fewer electrical connections but they are good for residential areas.

Is it hard to install 72-cell panels?

Yes, it is hard to install them because they are heavier and a little bit bigger. So, you do need two or more people to set the solar panels in place.

It also requires a strong rack support for the panels. Thicker rails can be installed for these panels.

When to choose 72-cell and 60-cell panels.

The main difference is only its size. The ultimate decider of the panels is their value, cost per watt, and efficiency. Divide the price of the panel by its output power.

This gives you a price per watt. A baseline will be used to compare the panel value. If the cost per watt price of the panel is low then chose it.

Mixing and matching 60-cell and 72-cell panels

It is possible to mix both cells according to the demand of the system. If the roof size is small, then some 72-cell panels can be combined with 60-cell panels to complete the demand.

Mono vs poly vs thin film

Monocrystalline solar panels

These cells are cut from a single crystalline silicon ingot. The required composition of these cells is completely pure, and each cell is made up of a single piece of silicon. These cells are expensive. The performance level of these cells is better in heat and in lower light environments. These panels are not good for the environment and contain a uniform black look.

Polycrystalline solar panels

These cells are blended together to make multiple pieces of silicon. Small bits of silicon are treated and molded on the cell. These panels are also environmentally friendly because it creates less waste. Such blended makeup of the cells is giving it a blue color. The efficiency of these panels is comparatively lower than mono-crystalline, and these panels are inexpensive.

Thin-film solar panels

These panels are used for large-scale utility projects and for special applications. These panels are made from a thin layer of conductive material that is applied on the backing plate made of glass or plastic. The efficiency of these panels is extremely low. The manufacturing cost is low. These panels are cheaper than the other two types of panels. Such panels are also highly flexible to use in various places like RVs and boats, Cars, and Carports.

Best panels in the market

In the market, there are a lot of brands that are making solar panels. But selecting the best one is extremely important. This section will show vital information regarding the best panels on the market.

Best value solar panels:

Astronergy 365W Features

Workmanship warranty	10 years
Cost	70 cents per watt total $257
Performance warranty	25 years
Degradation	-0.7%
Efficiency	18.9%
Number of cells	72
Temperature coefficient	-0.376% Wp

Cell type	Mono PERC

This panel shows the lower cost per watt to the buyer, so it is affordable and also its features are reliable to use for long periods of time.

Best American-Made solar panels:

Heliene 320W

Features

Workmanship warranty	10 years
Cost	80 cent per watt total $256
Performance warranty	25 years
Degradation	-0.7%
Efficiency	19.26%
Number of cells	60
Temperature coefficient	-0.38% Wp
Cell type	Mono

On the American market, **Heliene** is the best choice. These panels contain a high efficiency rate. In the long run, such prices are quite competitive in the market

Best premium solar panels:

LG 375W Features

Workmanship warranty	25 years
Cost	1.36 dollars per watt total $513
Performance warranty	25 years with 90.8 efficiency
Degradation	-0.4%
Efficiency	21.7%
Number of cells	60
Temperature coefficient	-0.3% Wp

Cell type	Mono

These panels are considered space-efficient packed with more output into a 60-cell panel. The Lifespan of these panels is extremely high with only - 0.4% degradation rate per year.

Best solar panels for off-grid systems

For the off-grid system, the panels must be paired with some components and also sized properly. In the past, PWM charge controllers are used in Off-grid systems. But now MPPT charge controllers are more beneficial. Still, it is important to take string sizing considerations that are according to panels and charge controllers. It is important to size the panel's array to give sufficient charge to the batteries.

Best solar panels for Mobile and RVs applications

Off-grid solar systems are the best for boats and RVs. But require smaller solar panels. Therefore, Sol-Go 115W solar panels are used because they are flexible.

These panels are light in weight and easy to install and also efficiency is high during low light. There are also two other types of solar panels that are beneficial.

- Solarland 180W panel with price $335
- Ameresco 90W panel with price $185

Buyer's guide for solar panels

Whenever there is a need to buy solar panels that are mounted to the roof, people consider 12-volt solar panels. Because they are safe, versatile, and powerful enough to use in various applications.

The next point is that the installation of solar panels is based on the energy they produced. It is important to consider watts and volts of panels. If the value of the current is high, then you need larger circuit protection and wiring components. It is wiser to consider 12-volt solar panels because of their versatility. Such as in small areas.

But if the energy requirement is about 1000 to 5000 watts, then a 24-volt and more volt system are best. On the other hand, if the energy demand is more than 3000 watts then 48-volt system is perfect. For residential and commercial areas, 24-volt panels are considered the ideal choice. The fact is that when they are combined so they produce 48 volts. The wiring cost will be decreased, and inverter efficiency is increased.

Determining components for 12-volts and 24-volts systems

The 12-volt solar panel's system is compatible with a 12v inverter and a battery bank and if 24-volt panels are used then components need to be used that are compatible with 24-volt. But a 24volt battery is not by connecting 12-volt batteries in series. It is important to plan for the solar panel rating not to be higher than the charge controllers. This means if there are 12-volt solar panels then its amperes will be 14 and charge controllers must have at least 14 amps. But due to some environmental factors, it contains an extra 25%. Therefore, the charge controller must have 12 volts and 20 amps. It means based on your demand select the solar panels for home or commercial usage then buy them. Also, mono-crystalline panels are more beneficial to buy compared with poly-crystalline panels.

Mountings

There are two types of mountings that are used that include Ground and roof mounting. Both of these types contain its own drawbacks and benefits. Also, these mountings contain their own merits according to the specification of the project.

Ground mounted panels

Advantages	Disadvantages
It is easy to access	Its installation is extremely labor intensive
Through this mounting, panels can be cleaned easily	The installation cost of these panels are high
It is easy to troubleshoot panels	Its permitting process is also expansive
It contains a strong racking system	Decreases value of the real estate
The required system is not confined to the dimension of the roof	It requires more space
The panels temperature is low with high efficiency	
No need to remove the panels before the removal of the roof	

Roof-mounted solar panels

Advantages	Disadvantages

These mountings are less expensive	It is difficult to access the roof when it is slippery
The labor cost is low	It is hard to troubleshoot errors
It requires fewer materials to install	This mounting is increasing the temperature so output will decrease
This mounting can utilize unused space	The total size of the system will be reduced due to less space
It is easy to permit panels	While putting holes in the roof will cause problems

Best mounts on the market

Here is a list of the best solar panel mounts with specifications below.

Ideal roof mount:

IronRidge XR100

This company is leading in PV racking manufacturing and is involved in making good quality roof-mount racking. It contains various sizes XR10, XR100, and XR1000. From them, XR100 is the standard size. It can easily hold heavy rains.

If the area contains high wind, then XR1000 is reliable, and XR10 is only used for lightweight solutions. Furthermore, there is also a need for flashing and it is dependent on the condition of the roof.

Best tilt legs: Quick Mount/ SunModo

It is ideal to combine XR100 with the tilt legs.

These are paired with Quick Mount QBase low slope flashing and used for low or flat slope roofs. Furthermore, for the commercial racking systems, SunMode EZ sunbeam is reliable. With this, it is possible to gain maximum usable built space on the rooftop.

Ideal ballasted mount:

DynoRaxx

This concept is applied when there is no need for any drilling on the roof. Such mounting is useful when someone is not owning the property. Its trays are made up of fiberglass and it is extremely lightweight and will not damage the roof. This mounting is quite easy to install.

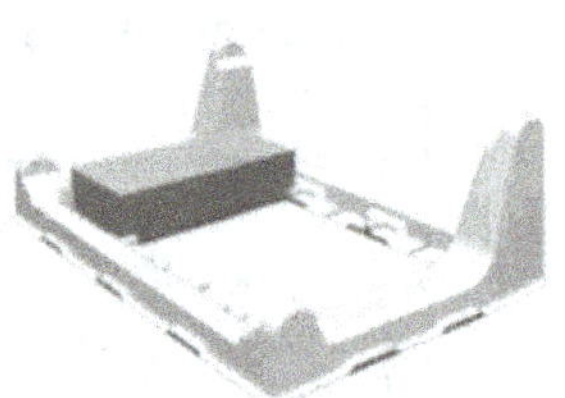

The ideal ground mount:

IronRidge SGA

This ground mount is using XR1000 railing, and it is the same one that is used for high-quality roof mounts. But for ground the rails used are only 2-to-3-inch steel pipe. It is quite easy to install a mounting system. Such mountings are important where the weather condition is extremely bad.

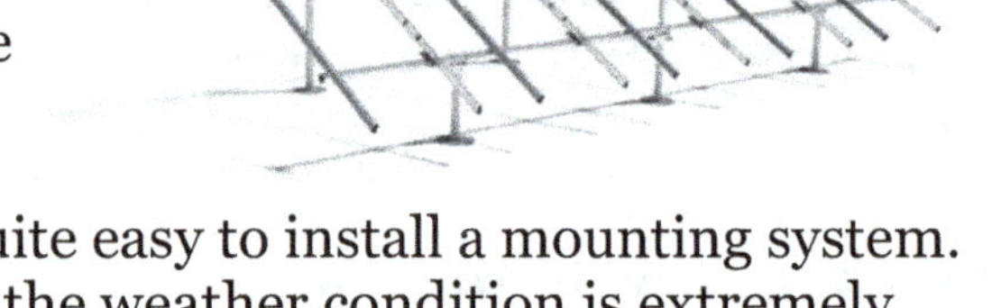

The idea pole mounts:

General Specialties

This company is manufacturing the best pole mounts. These mounts contain high quality with absolute flexibility. But the MT solar pole mounts are also a great option in the market.

The ideal trackers:

Wattsun

Trackers are considered the least-effective mounting option used. But such installation is not recommended for residential areas. But for commercial applications, a single-axis tracker is the best way to increase efficiency and save space for large utility-scale installation.

Solar panel cost calculator

There is a huge range of sizes of solar panels. It starts from 5W to 400W+ panels. Therefore, evaluating the cost-per-watt of the panels will help to compare them properly.

If the cost-per-watt is low for the panels, then its efficiency will be low also. Like, if a panel contains a total cost of 200 dollars and its watts are 300.

Now its cost-per-watt will be:

$$cost\ per\ watt = price\ of\ panels \div\ total\ watts\ of\ power$$

Now it's possible to calculate the cost-per-watt of the panels. But it is important to consider panels whose cost-per-watt is high so their efficiency and lifespan will be high too.

8-B: Batteries

Lead-Acid vs Lithium-ion batteries

In the above sections, information regarding these types of batteries has been discussed. Now take a look at the main differences between these batteries.

Cycle life

When the battery is discharged, then they are charged from the panels, and it is considered one charge cycle. The lifespan of batteries is measured through the number of charge cycles they perform. The number of cycles for lithium-ion batteries is higher compared with lead-acid batteries. With full use, the number of cycles is lower for lithium-ion batteries than for lead-acid batteries per year.

Depth of discharge

This factor is in regard to how much capacity of the battery is used during recharging. If a quarter of the battery capacity is used then its depth of discharge will be 25%. After the use of the batteries, they will not discharge completely. Therefore, it is recommended to charge a battery before reaching the depth of the discharge point.

Lead-acid batteries contain only 50% depth of discharge. If it is beyond this point, then it will affect its lifespan. Lithium batteries contain 80% depth of discharge. This means, lithium batteries have more usable capacity.

Efficiency

The efficiency of lithium batteries is high because they can store more solar power in them, and their usage is very reliable. But the efficiency of lead-acid batteries is only 80-85%. That depends on the condition and model. Whereas lithium batteries are 95% efficient. Due to high efficiency, the battery can charge faster.

Charge rate

When the efficiency level is high then its charge rate is faster. Therefore, lithium batteries have a fast charge rate.

But lead-acid batteries have a slow charge rate. moreover, the charge rate is expressed as charge rate = C/5

Like a battery of 430 Ah then its charge rate will be:

$$\text{charge rate} = 430 \div 5 = 86 \text{ charging amps}$$

Energy density

The overall weight of lead-acid batteries is extremely high and more than 85 pounds. But lithium batteries only weigh 36 pounds. But the main point is that the energy density of lithium batteries is high, which means they contain more storage capacity by taking less space. On the other hand, lead-acid batteries have less energy density.

Comparing them, it is better if someone wanted a full-powered Off-grid system, then it is important to install lithium batteries because they are extremely beneficial.

Batteries in series vs parallel

Batteries can be connected in series and parallel. This section will take a look at the pros and cons of attaching batteries in series and parallel. The main difference between the connection of batteries in series and parallel is the impact on the output voltage and its capacity. When the batteries are connected in series, then their voltages are added but when they are attached in parallel, their capacities are added.

Battery connected in series

When batteries are connected in series, then the positive terminal of one battery is connected to the negative terminal of the second battery. When two 12 volts batteries are connected in series, then they will show 24 volts.

Pros

- The required power consumed by the battery is equal to its operating voltage and the required current it draws.
- Like a battery contains 12 volts and 30 amps. Therefore, it has 360 watts. But if the batteries are connected in series, their watts will be the same but their voltage will become double.
- When batteries are connected in a series they will provide high voltage and low current. Due to this, voltage drop will be low in the system.
- The charge controllers are dependent on the current rating so charging works at the same rate.
- For large power systems, the connection in series is quite beneficial for the system.

Cons

When batteries are connected in series, it is not possible to get low voltages from the battery bank without a converter.

It is important for all the components to function at higher voltages.

Batteries in parallel

When batteries are connected in parallel, their voltages will be the same and their current will be added. It can be done by connecting the positive terminal and negative terminals with each other. Like, the positive terminal of one battery is connected with the positive terminal of the second battery.

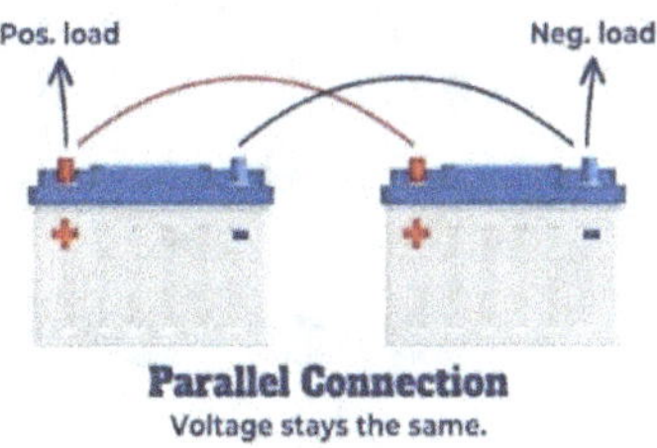

Pros

- When batteries are connected in parallel, it is possible to increase the available runtime of the system, but voltages will remain the same. But its amp-hour capacities will be added. Therefore, when two batteries are connected in parallel then it will double the runtime.
- When they are connected in parallel, then there is no problem if one battery stops working.

Cons

- Through a connection in parallel, the voltages of the system will be decreased, and a high amount of current will be drawn.

When the current value is high then there is a need of thick cables so voltages will be dropped more. It is difficult to operate high-power appliances.

The number of batteries can be attached in a series

The connection of batteries in a series depends on the requirement of the system and the manufacturer. Like, a battery from **Battle born** can easily be attached to lithium batteries one at a time and it will create a 48-volt system.

It is important to check the manufacturer of the battery before connecting in a series.

Number of batteries in parallel

There is no limit to connecting batteries in parallel. If the number of batteries connected in parallel is high then its capacity will be increased and have a longer runtime. But it will take more time to charge these batteries. When more batteries are attached in parallel, the capacity of the system will be increased. Therefore, it is important to have perfect fusing system to prevent accidents.

It is impossible to connect the same battery in series and parallel. Because of this, the batteries will be short. Therefore, a set of batteries needs to be connected in series or parallel.

Charging time of batteries

When batteries are connected in a series they will charge at fast rate. Whereas, when batteries are connected in parallel, they are charged at a slow rate. QR code: batteryguy

Connected batteries in series with different voltages

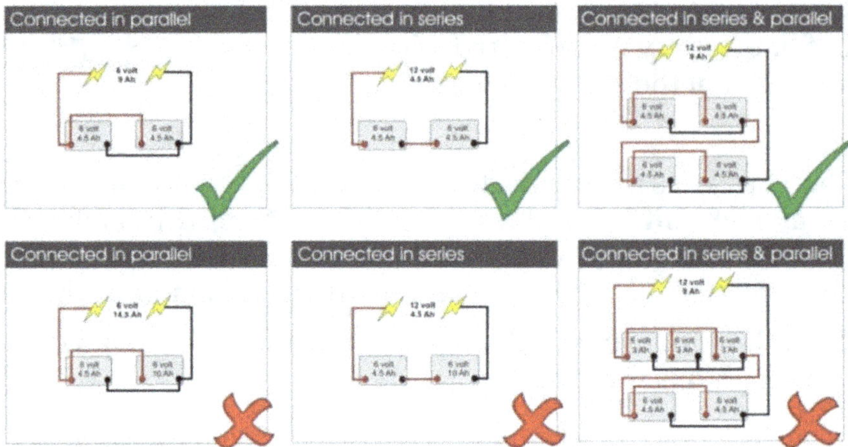

When batteries are connected with different voltages in series then it will work. But it will damage the batteries during charging and discharging cycles. If there is a greater difference present in the batteries capabilities then it will drain at a fast rate. it will also decrease the life of the batteries.

Connected batteries in series with different amp hour rating.

When batteries are connected with different amp-hour ratings in a series then it will never work. It is important to attach batteries in a series when its voltages and amp-hour capacity is the same and also manufacturing brand is the same. With different amps hours, there will be a huge risk of explosion.

Connection of batteries in parallel with different voltages

When batteries with different voltages are in parallel, this will decrease the lifespan of batteries. For the secondary batteries, it is important to use the same brand and age of the batteries before connecting them in parallel.

Connecting batteries in parallel with different amp-hour capacities

This connection is possible, and it will also not cause any damage to the battery. But it is important to take a look at some important issues. The batteries chemistries need to be the same. Like both batteries must be lead-acid or lithium batteries. If one Sealed lead-acid is connected with flooded lead-acid then it will not work. Also, double-check the voltages. The voltages with different amp-hour batteries must be the same.

Choosing the best batteries

When choosing the best Off-grid solar system battery, it is important to consider these points

Power rating

If you need higher power at home, then it is important to consider a battery with a high-power rating. This power rating is expressed in kilowatts. Overall, there are two types of power ratings that is instantaneous and continuous power ratings. But depending on the system if there is a need for power in short bursts then instantaneous is beneficial.

Battery size

The battery size is related to its capacity. It shows the amount of energy it can store. It is denoted by kilowatt-hours.

The storage capacity of a battery will tell how much it can store a charge in it to give power.

It's also recommended to check the power requirement of the home and then buy it.

Roundtrip efficiency

It is a system-level metric that will show how a battery is converting and storing electricity. The roundtrip efficiency of the battery is showing how many electricity units will be obtained from the battery. If this factor is not checked then it may create problems and its lifespan is affected.

Battery lifetime

It is related to its throughput and cycles. It is important to check how many cycles a battery can complete. If these cycles are less than 400 then the battery is useless to buy. The cycles are measuring the number of times you are charging and discharging a battery.

Safety

It is important for all solar batteries to meet the safety requirement. Therefore, they can get certified for installation in homes and commercial use. If this factor is not checked then it may create problems when used.

Chemistry

The chemistry of the battery is depending on its important characteristics. Like, the lithium-ion chemistry is different and that's why it contains more dense power and stores a high amount of electricity. It is important to consider the batteries chemistry because good chemistry batteries have high prices.

For buying the best solar battery, it is extremely important to check out these measures properly.

How to choose the best battery

The best battery is chosen through some research. There are a lot of best Off-grid batteries available in the market.

Discover 48V lithium battery

Discover Battery AES 7.4kWhr, this battery can easily keep up the power demand in an off-grid system. It is a lithium battery, so it is a premium storage option. By using this battery, it is easy to expand the system over time. Lithium batteries have the ability to increase the time period without recharging.

Best value Off-grid battery for homes

If someone is looking for a cost-effective option then Crown CR430 flooded lead-acid battery is a good choice. It is the best value battery that can be used for this system. It is easy to increase capacity by spending less for the system.

Calculation of Size and battery bank

The best way to size the off-grid battery is depending on the daily power usage at home and battery type. Like, if the power usage is 10kWh

Sizing for lead Acid battery

10kWh x 2 (with 50% depth of charge) x 1.2 (inefficiency factor)

Total battery size = 24 kWh

Sizing for lithium-ion battery

10kWh x 1.2 (with 80% depth of charge) x 1.05 (inefficiency factor.)

Total battery size = 12.6 kWh

If a lead acid 24 kWh battery is selected then with 2000 amp-hours it contains 12 volts. Moreover, with 1000 amp-hour it contains 24 and with 500 amps hours it contains 48 volts. Whereas if 12.6 kWh lithium battery 1050 amps hours with 12 volts. Its 525 amps hours with 24 volts and 262.5 amps hours with 48 volts.

8-C Charge controllers

What is a solar charge controller?

The main purpose of the charge controller is to manage the power that is transferred into the battery bank from the solar array. The charge controller will ensure that deep cycle batteries are not overcharged, and the power does not run back towards the panels. There are two important technologies of charge controllers including MPPT and PWM.

PWM

It stands for Pulse Width modulation. It is operated by making a direct connection from the solar array to the batteries. When batteries receive bulk charging, then the output voltages will be pulled down to the required battery voltage.

It means that when a 12V solar panel is charging a 12-volt battery

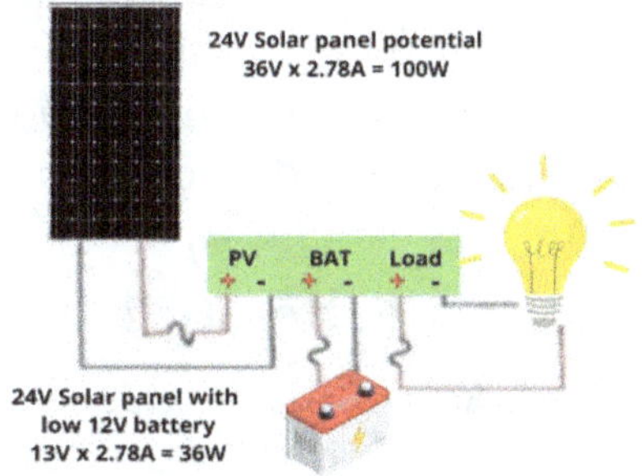

then 72W is stored in the battery. It will show the loss of only 28% But if 24 solar panels are charging a 12-volt battery then 36W are stored. It will show a loss of 64%.

MPPT

Maximum power point tracking. This charge controller measures the Vmp voltage gained from panels and converts it into PV voltage and transfers it to the battery. The power in the charge controller is equal to the power out of the charge controller. When one 12V solar panel is connected to a 12V battery then 100watts of power will be stored. If 3 20-volt solar panels are connected in series and charging a 48-volt battery, in both conditions, there is no loss.

Key features

Multistage charging of battery bank

It can easily change the amount of charge given to the batteries according to its charge level.

Protection from reverse current

It provides protection against the reverse current at night when there is no power taken from the panels.

Low voltage disconnects

The charge controller can easily disconnect from the battery during low battery.

Control for lighting

It has the ability to turn on and off the lights during the day and night. Controllers are controllable with various settings.

Display

The display provides information regarding the remaining battery value and how much time is left to charge the battery in amp-hours.

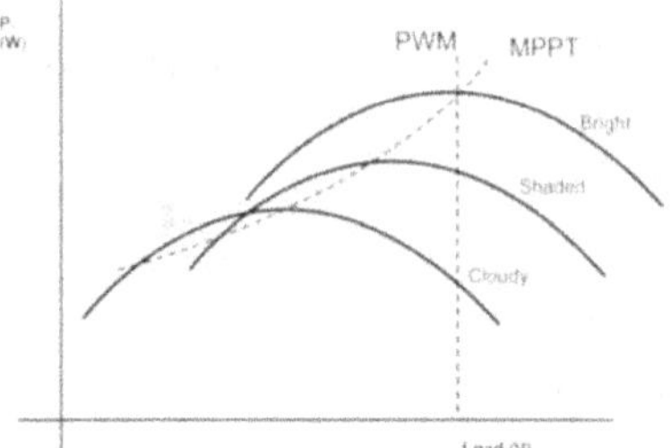

Which is better MPPT or PWM

According to a performance perspective, the MPPT charge controller is way better than PWM. The MPPT charge control is less expensive, and its highly recommended to use MPPT. But for the tiny system like less than 1kW then PWM is better. Although the MPPT is of better quality. These charge controllers are less expensive and use less energy compared with MPPT

Benefits of MPPT

These charge controllers produce more energy from the solar array in various conditions and have the ability to choose panel array voltage that will save various costs in off-grid. They are for higher quality and higher output systems. **How big should a charge controller be?**

It's difficult to size a charge controller because it is dependent on the power consumption of the system.

The size of the controller has to be big enough to send the power generated from the solar panels. The total current supplied through array is calculated through dividing the solar array power to the output voltages of the solar array.

Controller size=Solar array power / output voltages of array

This means if the solar array has the power of 1000W and its voltages are 12. Then you need an 80-amp charge controller.

What will happen if an undersized charge controller is used?

If the charge controllers are under size then it will max out the power obtained from the panels and will not be using the complete potential of the panels.

What will happen if an oversize charge controller is used?

Nothing will happen, only that you'll pay extra cost. Sometimes, panels may produce more wattage during the day. So, its good idea to have an oversized controller.

Is it O.K. to install multiple charge controllers in one system?

Yes, it is possible to have multiple charge controllers that are attached to the same battery bank. But it is important to have the same charging profile for both charge controllers. They must have the same battery setting input.

PWM charge controller

The PWM charge controller measures the voltages from the battery bank and then adjusts the power output taken from the panels and matches it with the system. Its doing it by connecting and disconnecting rapidly with the panels so it will charge the batteries safely.

While charging the batteries, the graph will show rapid pulses of varying widths. When the battery is charged fully then the width becomes narrower.

MPPT charge controller

Every solar panel or solar array contains power that depends on the required load on the panels. With the proper combination of voltage and current, the panels will produce the maximum power as possible. But this will be changing as the solar times change. The monitor of the MPPT charge controller will monitor the power output of the panels and make adjustments so it can produce maximum power. MPPT contains DC-DC inverter inside it. This converter generates maximum output and also charges up the battery bank.

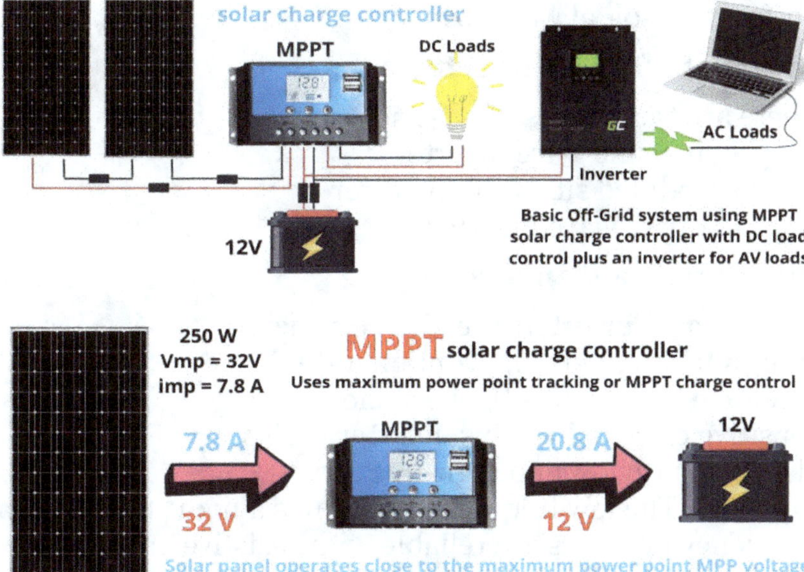

8-D inverters

Grid-tied vs off grid inverters

Off-grid inverters

These inverters work alone and unable to synchronize with the grid. They are connected with the home in place of power grid. It supplies instant power to the appliances and work over the capacity rating. In the hybrid system an Off-grid inverter is more useful.

Grid-tied inverters

These inverters are designed to connect with home and the grid. This inverter is taking solar energy from panels and transferring it to the grid. This inverter is synchronized with the grid power. This inverter is also supplying instant power to the grid.

Off-grid inverters

Connection of an off-grid inverter

The off-grid inverter is placed between the AC load and the solar panels. This inverter is not only connected with the solar panels but also with the batteries for controlling the energy supplied to the inverter from the panels. In off grid, an optional generator is also connected with it when batteries are drained off.

Off-grid inverter

The inverter is taking the DC power from the solar panels and providing it to the batteries. It also converts DC power into AC and supplies it to the load. The inverter circuitry contains capacitors and inductors that are restricting certain changes in the direction of current and provide a perfect sinusoidal waveform.

Types of off-grid inverter

There are three types of off-grid inverters
- Pure sine wave inverter
- Modified sine wave inverter
- Square wave inverter

Pure sine wave inverter

These inverters are also considered true value inverters and contain a stable sinewave output. It is the best choice for sensitive electronics. This inverter is also classified into low and high-frequency inverters. The low frequency generates a high starting current. High-frequency inverters are reliable with resistive and inductive loads.

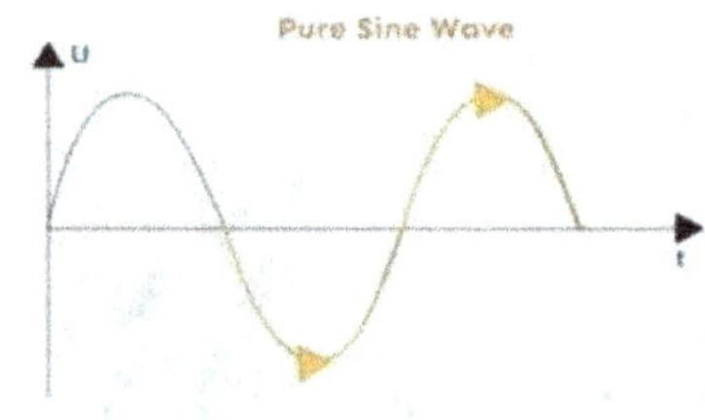

Modified sine wave inverter

This type of inverter is cheap, but it contains a distorted waveform.

It contains a time interval between positive and negative maximum points. These inverters are not recommended for inductive loads. It causes extra heat and also affects the durability of the appliances. It is only used for small appliances.

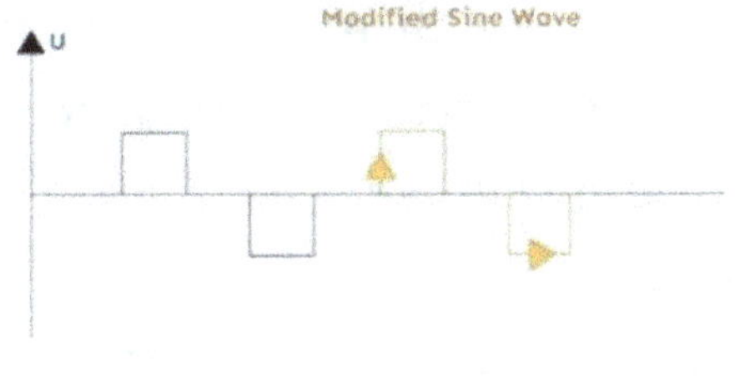

Square wave inverters

These inverters are generating poor quality unstable square wave AC output that affects the inverter and the appliances. These inverters contain a lot of harmonic distortions.

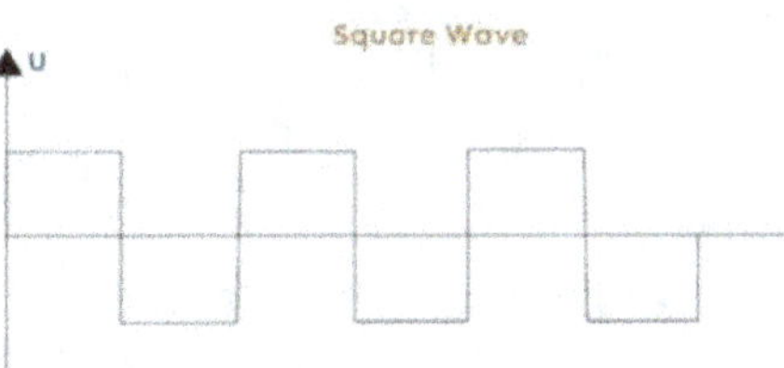

How to select an off-grid inverter for home

For home, always select pure and modified sine wave inverters. Both of these inverters are good for an off-grid system. But pure sine wave inverter is more beneficial. The selection of an inverter is based on these criteria:

- Connection with various AC appliances.
- Advance features in the inverter.
- Power consumption
- Efficiency
- Size of the Off-grid system.

Advantages

- Not connected with the grid.
- Its output can be regulated.
- This inverter is reliable to store energy in batteries.
- There is no need for any synchronization between grid and inverter.

Disadvantages

- No grid connection is available
- Not easy to install
- Contains limited backup

FAQs

Do solar inverters work at night?

No, these inverters work with solar energy but at night there is no solar energy. So, they are off.

Why sine wave is used over a square wave?

The square wave is generating a lot of harmonic so it's not reliable for the appliances.

Power outage affecting off-grid solar inverters?

No, because there is no connection with the grid.

String vs micro inverters vs optimizers

String inverter

Pros

- Cost-effective inverters
- It is easy to pair with power optimizers
- The best for residential and commercial

Cons

- When one string is suffered then it will decrease the output
- Only work properly when all arrays are connected.

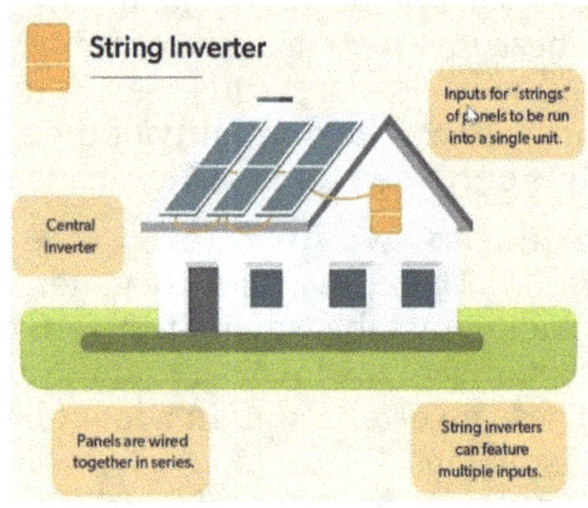

Micro-inverters

Pros

- Each array is connected with small electrical systems
- It is easy to build with various orientations and configuration
- It is easy to expand by using such inverters

Cons

- These inverters are expensive
- For large-scale systems it is not a cost-effective solution

Power optimizer

Pros

- It provides more flexibility compared with a micro-inverter system
- It ensures more production
- It can overcome and identify various defects

Cons

- Extremely expensive inverter

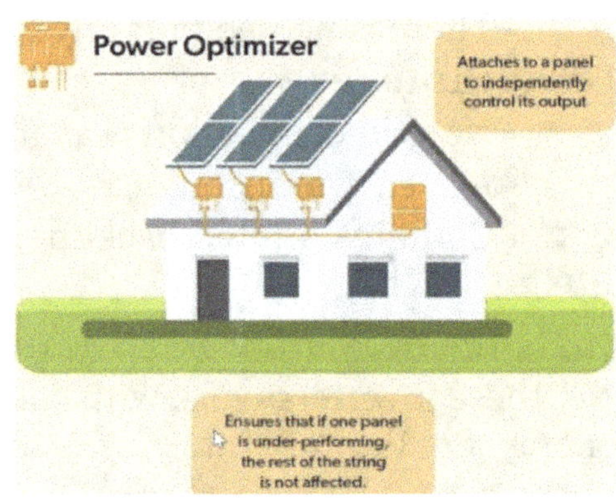

Buyer's guide

Before buying an off-grid power inverter, there are some points that must be considered.

- Think about the size of the off-grid solar system
- Always consider pure sine wave inverters instead of other types if a person wanted high durability.
- Take a look at various technical specifications of the inverter
- Efficiency
- Self-consumption
- Surge capacity
- Temperature range
- Battery charger output
- Warranty

8-E Cables and connectors

For connecting the solar panels, MC4 connectors and MC4 extension cables are used. The MC4 connectors are of two types that are male and female. The MC4 extension cable size is from 8ft to 100 ft. Solar panels are connected to the junction box.

Wiring MC4 in series

If someone wanted to connect solar panels in series with MC4 connectors, then a male MC4 is connected with the positive terminal of the first panel and then connected with the female MC4 to the second panel on the negative terminal.

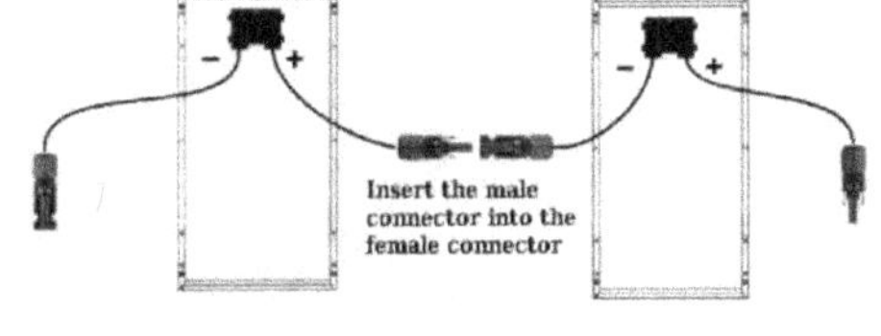

Wiring MC4 in parallel

To do this use a positive male MC4 to a panel and one is connected to the second panel positive terminal with a female MC4. The value of the current will be increased.

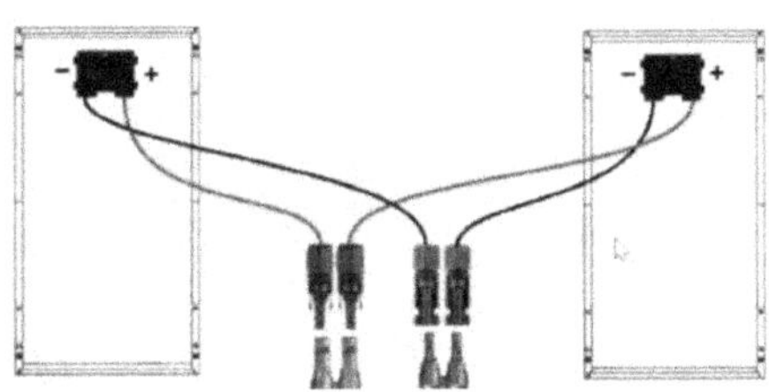

MC4 cables

These cables are expensive compared with other types of cables. These cables are similar to an electrical extension cord. The male is connected with the female cord end. The length depends on the solar panel system. While connecting in parallel, these cables are cut from the middle to get a cost-effective solution.

MC4 disconnector

This is a tool used for disconnecting MC4 cables.

Choosing the right wire size for an Off-grid system

The right size of wire depends on the required system. If the system contains a heavy current then the wire must be heavy that can carry the current easily. The chart below shows the current value and the size of wire used for a system.

2% Voltage Drop Chart						
AWG =	14	12	10	8	6	4
Capacity(AMPS)	15	20	30	40	55	70
ARRARY AMPS	FEET ONE WAY FOR A PAIR OF WIRES					
1	45	70	115	180	290	456
2	22.5	35	57.5	90	145	228
4	10	17.5	27.5	45	72.5	114
6	7.5	12	17.5	30	47.5	75
8	5.5	8.5	11.5	22.5	35.5	57
10	4.5	7	9.5	18	28.5	45.5
15	3	4.5	7	12	19	30
20	2	3.5	5.5	9	14.5	22.5
25	1.8	2.8	4.5	7	11.5	18
30	1.5	2.4	3.5	6	9.5	15
40			2.8	4.5	7	11.5
50			2.3	3.6	5.5	9
100					2.9	4.6

Chapter 9
Tools and Safety

Tool list

Tools for site assessment

- 50-100 ft measuring tape
- Compass or solar path finder
- Maps
- Digital camera
- How to use a multimeter

Tools for installation

- Angle finder
- Fish tape
- Torpedo level
- Cordless drill
- Chalk line
- Hole saw
- Drill bits
- Hole punch
- Nut drivers
- Torque wrench
- Wire strippers
- Lineman's pliers
- Large or short cable cutters
- Multimeter
- Slip-joint pliers
- Fuse pullers
- Blanket cardboard, black plastic
- Caulking gun

Additional tools to consider

- DC clamps on amp meter
- C-clamps
- Pry bar

- Large crimpers
- Conduit bender
- Magnetic wristband for holding
- Right angle drill

Battery system tools

- Rubber gloves
- Turkey baster
- Distilled water
- Voltmeter
- Baking soda
- Rubber apron
- Smart flashlight
- Hydrometer
- Funnel

The most important tools used for DIY solar installation

- Digital multimeter
- Battery-operated drill
- Hack Saw
- Flat pry bar
- Caulk Gun
- Conduit bender
- Solar panel hanger
- Measuring tape
- Wire stripper/ cutters
- Screwdrivers

How to use a multimeter

The multimeter contains three parts

- Display
- Ports
- Selection knob

For measuring the DC voltages, move the selection knob towards DC column and connect the red port with positive and black port with negative then the display will show DC voltages.

For measuring AC voltages, move the selection knob towards AC column and connect both nodes and positive and negative ends to get the results on the display.

For measuring AC or DC current, move the selection knob towards the current section.

Also, shift the black wire to the 10 Amp current meter and then attach the ports to one end and then a second end to measure the current.

For measuring the resistance, just change the knob to resistance and measure them by putting ports at both ends.

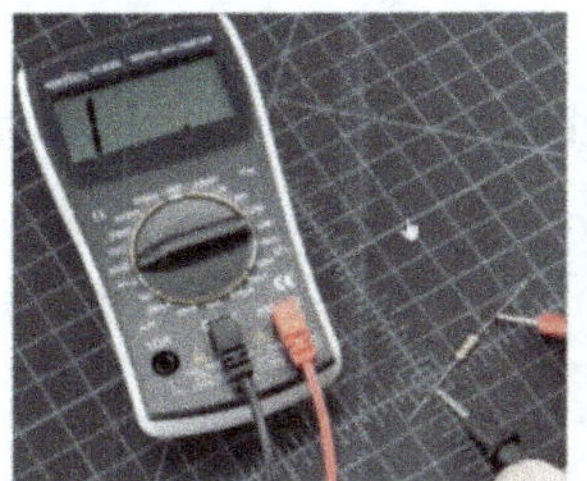
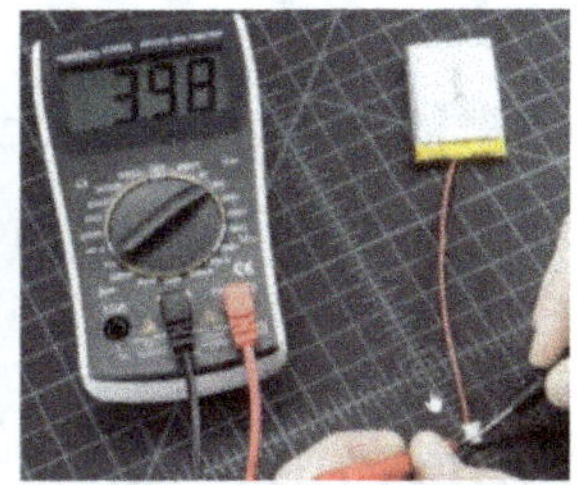

Tools used for successful solar installation

A proper basic household toolkit, cordless drill with an impact driver, basic safety gear, and other components given in installation manuals.

Safety precautions

It is quite important to minimize risk while installing solar panels. From this, some safety precautions are given below

- Whenever there is bad weather, don't even try to install solar panels because it is unsafe.

- Don't apply any kind of pressure on the panels by sitting on them because they can break and also don't spill anything on them.

- Always ensure that the home sheathing is not wet and also does not having leaks after installing.

- It is useless to install solar panels that are within 3 miles from the salty water or sea because moisture will interface with the PV panels.

- Always ensure that the whole solar panel system is earth-grounded completely.

- Do not install solar panels on rainy days and also just after the rain.

- Do not install the PV system alone and always work with two or three helpers to refrain from accidents.

- While installing panels, it is important to wear protective safety gear.

Hazard section

Some of the hazards related to solar panel installations are given below:

Lifting

The solar panels are heavy, it is not possible to lift them alone. Lifting improperly will cause strains on it and also cause injuries to a person.

Safety method

- Always two persons to lift a solar panel.
- Use gloves to protect and get an extra grip
- Always keep the load towards the body and use smooth steps.

Falls and trips

During construction, accident rates are about 39% yearly.

It is one of the most common accidents. Moreover, while falling other risks are also associated with it like broken and shattered bones, internal injuries, and other pains.

Safety method

Fall accidents can be avoided, use safety nets and a personal fall strap roof harness OSHA approved.

Electrical

The PV system contains a lot of components that conduct electricity. There are two main sources of electricity that include solar arrays and the utility company. Therefore, if the main breaker of the company is shut down but the solar system is producing power, there are some risks that include damage to muscle, nerve tissue, and also death.

Safety method

- Always use proper protection from harmful shocks.
- Always work at a safe distance from the power lines.
- Always work by turning off all power supplies so risks can be minimized.
- Under any load never disconnect any PV connectors

Ladders

In the past year, about 949 fatalities occurred, and 170 were due to falling from ladders. Due to this, a person may face serious injuries like fractures.

Safety method

- Always stand one person holding a ladder
- Always inspect the ladder before use and if it contains any defect, then mark 'do not use'
- Place the ladder on a dry surface so it has the proper grip
- Do not use vertical rails and focus on horizontal ladder rungs.
- Never carry any solar panel while climbing up the ladder.

Part-IV

Chapter 10

Building an Off-grid Solar System
A six-step process

Overview of building an Off-grid solar system

It is easy to build an Off-grid solar system at home. But you must have proper knowledge about every component and also its connection.

Step 1: Planning and designing of a DIY solar system

In the first step, design a complete DIY solar system according to the demand. It is considered the most important thing to building an off-grid solar system, is to get proper information regarding the need for energy usage per day and year. Renewable energy systems are inherently variable. It is important to understand the yearly rhythms and then arrange it according to the demand. It will take time to calculate the complete load demand.

Step 2: Choose the right place for the panels

It is an extremely important step; the whole solar system is dependent where panels are going to be installed. Many people try to install panels on the roof top and it is the best place to install them. If the right spot is selected for solar panels, try to prevent shading and provide extensive cooling for the solar panels. If the best place is chosen properly, it will increase the efficiency of the solar panels

Step 3: Ordering of solar system components

The components of solar systems are also important. After choosing the best place, it is vital to choose the ideal components.

The choices regarding the solar system components are given below.

- The size and number of solar cells of the panels.
- The choice between MPPT and PWM charge controller

- For the battery bank, choose between lead-acid and lithium batteries.
- Check the overall voltage of each leg and the type of load.
- The required rating of the solar inverter.

Step 4: Building a solar battery house

For the battery bank, it is important to make a battery room. In this room simply put batteries so they will be protected from various temperature issues. Batteries must be placed in such an area where the heat factor is low. This room must be protected from children. There are some batteries that are useless in freezing weather. Install expensive unsealed batteries. In the battery room, provide good ventilation. Also, it must have the capacity to install an inverter and charge controllers with a fusing system.

Step 5: installation of solar panels

When all the components are arranged, then it's time to install the solar panels. Firstly, install the support for the solar array. The panels must be adjusted where the power output is maximum from the sun. The panels need to be placed on a tracking system. Refer to the installation guide for details.

Step 6: Wiring up the off-grid solar

It is considered a critical point before turning on the Off-grid system. If the wiring is not correct, it may damage the system and also burn many DC appliances. Therefore, for wiring always hire a licensed electrician for wiring the system. If someone wanted to install the system himself, then it is important to have a proper understanding of electrical.

Planning and designing

There are many things that are important before designing and planning the solar power system. Like the type of panels, inverters, battery bank, and charge controller. This section will show how to make a cost-effective off-grid system.

Making off-grid cost-effective

It is not a good idea to make a cost-effective solar power system for off-grid by buying cheap components. The main reason is that it will take less time to ruin the whole system than by using the right system.

Therefore, it's a wise idea to buy the best components for off-grid and benefit from a far longer lifespan.

Cost of off-grid solar and on-grid solar

The cost factor is extremely important for both on-grid and off-grid systems. But the cost statistics sometimes are a little bit misleading when it

is related to off-grid power. The main reason behind it is that the prices regarding energy storage costs do not remain the same. This cost is included in the running cost for the system.

Data from EIA shows that the average residential power price in the US was about 13.26 cents per kWh. But in some places, the price is about 28.87 cents. Some areas of the US have 5Wh per watt of panels. You can assume that if the solar system's lifespan is about 20 years, then its cost will be 10 cents per kWh.

The main point is that an off-grid solar power system is extremely competitive with grid power over the whole life of the system. but one of the huge drawbacks of an off-grid system is that you have to pay the complete upfront price of the system.

Off-grid power provides high energy security

This system is providing complete security related to energy. This means that during a power outage there is no need to depend on the grid. Even when the sun is not present then your battery bank will complete the power and if they are drawn down, then it's your generator that will provide power.

But in On-grid systems, a person is dependent on the grid.

If any power outage happens then there will be no power.

Greater freedom through off-grid solar

If someone wanted greater freedom while using electrical power, then it will be obtained by going off-grid.

The freedom to cut the cord. An off-grid system can be applied on a small to large scale depending on the required demand of the system.

The upfront cost of off-grid will lead to high efficiency

If the upfront cost of the off-grid solar is high then it will lead towards greater efficiency. Like, if such solar panels are installed that contains high upfront cost, then its efficiency will increase with its life span. If the battery bank contains lithium-ion batteries, then the system will work for a long period of time and increasing the efficiency of the system. The tradeoff is its upfront cost being higher than lead acid batteries.

Chapter 11

Planning and Designing the System

Determine demand

It is an important step, before installing always ensure how many panels are required to complete the demand. For this, calculate the whole load of the home. Knowing the load, make a system that contains extra capacity than the total load. As the renewable resource will never remain the same the whole year. It is important to understand daily and yearly average uses.

How many kW solar panels are required

It is one of the critical steps before installing off-grid solar panels. The required energy is measured in kilowatt hours. Therefore, calculate the total energy usage at home for the whole day.

How to measure power usage

There is also a theoretical way to measure power usage at home, but it will not give accurate values. The best way is to use a 'kill-a-watt' power measuring device and measure each appliance. Each device will show how much energy is utilized. Attaching this device all day will give you complete information regarding energy usage during the whole day.

Calculating daily power usage

With the kill-a-watt meter, calculating daily power, you can add up all the energy measurements taken from the device for a whole day. It will provide complete information regarding daily energy use. Moreover, usage of energy may fluctuate throughout the year. The use of lights will increase in the winter and also the use of air conditioners will increase in summers. Therefore, just check the differences and adjust the number of hours of assumption. On the other hand, the power production through sunlight also varies the whole year. It is recommended that always oversize the system before installation.

Find out how much energy produced by solar panels

The amount of energy produced by the solar panels depends on the sunlight. Like, during

the summer days are long so solar production will be high. But in winter, the production will be low because of short days. Therefore, the number of solar panels depends on the power they are producing in the whole year. The solar panels must be higher in wattage compared with the load demand of the area because cloudy or rainy days will make for less production.

Choosing the right size for the Off-grid solar system.

It means that before installing the off-grid solar system, it is important to size the system. The required system must have the ability to produce enough power in winter and summer. The off-grid system has to produce power greater than the demand. The solar panels are not 100% efficient. Also, panels have to charge the battery bank for a whole day. Also analyze all the components and find out their efficiencies. Like, 70% is the ideal figure for the efficiency of the whole system. Calculate the energy usage and extra power for your residential area and calculate the kW of the panels with efficiency. This is done by adding the kW and dividing it by 0.7. This value will give you the number of solar panels required.

Considering battery capacity

The battery bank is extremely important for an off-grid system. These batteries are completing the demand at night when no energy is produced. Batteries are also covering the demand on rainy or cloudy days when there is no sunlight. It is important to build the battery bank according to the energy used at night with a backup of 5 days.

The battery capacity is measured in amp-hours. To obtain the value in kilowatt- hours just multiply the number by the battery voltage. For large off-grid solar panel systems, 48V batteries are recommended.

Determine the cost of the off-grid solar panel

For finding the total cost of the system, you need to work backward. After calculating the power demand, then based on that, calculate the number of panels required for the system. Based on this adjust all the other components for the system. Solar production may vary due to variations in climate and seasons. Calculating the number of panels must be based on these factors.

Determine energy usage

The energy usage at home can be determined through various methods.

Method 1

One of the easiest ways to calculate

TYPE	POWER (W)
USB1/2 (older devices)	2.5 W
USB3 (recent devices)	4.5 W (some 7.5 W)
Apple devices w/ Apple charger	5 W
Retina iPad w/ Apple charger	10 W

energy usage is to analyze the energy bill. It will provide information regarding total use of energy in the whole month. It is given in kWh and it is also given for the whole year. Then according to this, chose the highest value for both seasons and divide it by 30 for daily value and it will show the daily usage of power at home.

Method 2

For this, just consider the hypothetical off-grid energy usage of the appliances at home. Just list the heavy electrical loads at home and write their power value and then multiply it with the number of hours usage in the whole day. It will be your energy usage. Like, the power of an air conditioner is about 900W, and it is used about 22 hours in summers then its energy usage will be 5.5kWh.

APPLIANCE	POWER	TIME - SUMMER & WINTER	DAILY ENERGY USAGE
Desk Lamp	16 W	2h summer, 6h winter	32 Wh – 96 Wh
Computer	80 W	4h summer, 4h winter	320 Wh – 320 Wh
Fridge	20 W	2h summer, 1h winter	40 Wh – 20 Wh

Summer: 392 Wh/day   **Winter**: 436 Wh/day

After this, find out how much power in watts is used by the device. This information is on the manufacturer's website or placard regarding electric use. Multiplying this number with the voltage will give you the power rating in watts and enter this value in the power column.

Calculation of solar panels required

The next important step is calculating the total number of solar panels required. This depends on the total demand at home and the efficiency. The best way is to check out the solar map of the area from the US department of energy. There is a box that shows the photovoltaic solar radiation bar and check the solar radiation by months and then take the lowest number for the required area. For example, if the area selected for installation contains 2 hours or less and gains 4 hours in the summers, then the total solar panel size is found using this formula. Panel Watts = daily Kwh/sun hours/.07, then 0.7 is the total efficiency of the panels. If you require 400W in summers and 230W in winters then take the highest value and select your high efficiency solar panels. Rule of thumb, the estimated cost for the solar panel depends on the energy usage and season.

Off-grid battery cost

The next important expense is the batteries. Before calculating the cost, just figure out the total size of the batteries. The battery size has been discussed in the above section.

The formula for calculating battery storage in Amp hours.

Battery storage = daily kWh x days of storage/12

If you have 436 kWh/day and using a full day of battery storage, then 36Ah of batteries will be needed assuming 12 volts. The next point is to

consider the type of batteries and their various factors like cost, efficiency and lifespan.

After analyzing all costs of the batteries then choose the best one. The lithium-ion battery is selected because it contains the highest cycle range so its cost will be low.

BATTERY TYPE	COST (USABLE KWH)	UPFRONT COST	LIFETIME
Sealed Lead Acid	$388/kWh/1k cycles	$388/kWh	1000 cycles
Flooded Lead Acid	$240/kWh/1k cycles	$240/kWh	1000 cycles
LiFePO4	$150–$250/kWh/1k cycles	$750/kWh	3000–5000 cycles
Edison NiFe	<$10 (can last decades)	$900/kWh	10k+

Total cost of an off grid solar system

Before calculating the total cost of the off-grid solar system, you need to consider other components like panel mounting material, grounding rod, thick copper wire, charge controller, and solar inverter.

Mounting material for panels

There are some solar panels that come with mounting hardware and also contain minimal brackets. But depending on the location of installation will be a need for some additional hardware. Many people consider rooftops for installing panels but if the rooftop contains shade, then a mounting system to adjust the panels to avoid shading. It is important where solar panels are installed, and they must be supported properly. Also, put a little bit of space between the panels. The cost of mounting depends on the location and the mounting type used by the installer.

Thick copper wire

Solar panels draw heavy current from the wiring due to running at low voltages between 12 to 72V. If the amp value is high then you need thick copper wires. These wires are not cheap, and the cost is between $50 to $300 depending on the brand used by the installer. It also depends on the size of the system and the location of the panels. Also, consider the total wattage of the solar panels and then calculate the value of amps.

Also, consider the connection of panels that are in parallel or in series. If in parallel then the rated current will be high. The formula for calculating the current is given below.

Panel current = total wattage of panel / panel voltage

For example: if the panel wattage is 500 with 15Volts then its current will be 33 amps. The cost of wire is related to the length and also its gauge. This wire must be protected from the sun with insulation.

Grounding rod

You also need a grounding rod for saving the system from any lightning damage and also rapid degradation of the panels. But the cost of

the grounding rod is inexpensive and is only about $30 and it is important to ground the whole system.

Battery charge controller

The main role of the charge controller is to protect the battery from over and under charging that will decrease the life span of the batteries. There are two main types of charge controllers which are PWM and MPPT. There are a lot of points to consider before selecting the best charge controller. These factors include price, efficiency, and size of the system. PWM's price is low, and it can be applied only for small systems also its efficiency is low. MPPT must be the recommended charge controller for huge off-grid systems. But it is important that the charge controller is according to the amps rating. If a 20A MPPT charge controller is used then its price is about $80. As the amount of current is increased then its cost will be increased.

Pure Sine wave inverter

The next important component of an off-grid solar panel system is the solar inverter. The required inverter of the system depends on the power rating. If the power rating is about 4kW then a solar inverter with 5kW capacity will be recommended. The efficiency of the inverters must be considered as its usually between 80 to 90%. It's important to size up the panels, batteries, and also wires to overcome losses.The price of the inverter is depending on the wattage rating.

If the wattage rating is low then its price will be low like a 300W inverter cost $40 and a 5000W inverter cost $400. A Pure Sine wave solar inverter is expensive but reliable.

ITEM	COST
Panels (100W, 4ea)	$400
Battery (75Ah, 1ea)	$140
Wire (10 ga, 100 ft)	$35
Charge Controller (20A)	$80
Pure Sine Wave Inverter (300W)	$50
Total	$705

Summing it up

This table shows the information regarding a system with small appliances. Its total cost will be around $700

Sizing the system

This section will show various steps to size an off-grid solar power system so it will generate enough power without the grid. The size of an off-grid system is depending on the demand of the house or business.

Determine energy requirement

Before installing the solar power system, you have the proper information regarding total energy usage. Example formula (a 10 watts appliance is used in 24 hours.)

10 watts x 24 hours = 240-watt hours per day

This information is present on the data sheet or on the appliance. When an inverter is used then it is important to include its self-consumption and efficiency losses. The efficiency losses are depending on the load handled by it.

Location evaluation

It is important to evaluate your location. Check the map that shows the intensity level of the sun. According to this map, solar power production is estimated for the whole year.

It is also vital to consider the system voltages and also days of autonomy which are critical for off-grid solar systems and the energy is carried over through batteries or DC generators

Calculate battery bank size

The battery bank size is depending on the total load demand and days of autonomy of the area. When the battery bank is decided, then the number of solar panels can be determined.

If the battery bank is made from 240Wh/day and lead-acid batteries are used, check the inefficiency of the inverter and it is between 5 to 15%.

But consider the 10% inefficiency of the inverter then it will be calculated like this:

24 Wh x 1.1 efficiency compensation = 265 Wh

This is the required amount of energy drawn from the battery to run a load from the inverter. Also, consider the temperature effect on the battery. Therefore, multiply the number by 1.59 for compensating the battery temperature during the winter.

264 Wh x 1.59 = 419.76-watt hours

Now also add the amount of efficiency of the battery.

Using lead-acid batteries the efficiency will be 20%

419.76 Wh x 1.2 = 503.71 Wh

This is for a single day of autonomy, but it is better to make a battery storage system that can handle 5 days of autonomy.

504 Wh x 5 days = 2520 Wh of energy storage

The battery size is increased because of various factors like temperature and also days of autonomy. These factors will affect the size of the battery so it must be considered properly. The lead acid batteries are given in, Ah not in Wh. Through this equation, it can be converted into Ah.

2520 ÷ 12 = 210 Ah and 12 V battery bank

2520 ÷ 24 = 105 Ah and 24 V battery bank

$$2520 \div 48 = 53 \text{ Ah and } 48 \text{ V battery bank}$$

Also, consider the discharge depth of the battery. The charging depth of the lead-acid batteries is about 50%. Therefore, the total required minimum battery capacity will be equal to 2.52 kilowatt-hours.

Quantity of solar panels

After determining the battery capacity. Now the number of solar panels can be calculated. The peak sun hours are 2.5 and the per day energy requirement is 240 Wh.

$$240 \div 2.5 = 96 \text{ W PV array}$$

This also includes various inefficiencies and a 15% of inefficiency of the panels.

$$96 \div 0.85 = 112.84 \text{ W}$$

Therefore, the minimum size of the PV array is calculated. But this size must be larger than the minimum value of the PV array, then it will be reliable.

This figure is showing the information regarding the required PV array for charging the battery bank with the Ah battery bank capacity. It means that for charging 800 Ah with a 24V battery bank, the PV array must be between 4000 to 6000W

Array Size: PV Watts (STC)	Battery Bank Size: Watt Hours (@ C20 rate)	Battery Bank Ah Capacity
100-175	600	50Ah @ 12Vdc
200-350	1,200	100Ah @ 12Vdc 50Ah @ 24Vdc
400-700	2,400	200Ah @12Vdc 100Ah @ 24Vdc
800-1,400	4,800	400Ah @ 12Vdc 200Ah @ 24Vdc 100Ah @ 48Vdc
2,000-3,000	9,600	800Ah @ 12Vdc 400Ah @ 24Vdc 200Ah @ 48Vdc
4,000-6,000	19,200	800Ah @ 24Vdc 400Ah @ 48Vdc
8,000-12,000	38,400	800Ah @ 48Vdc

Planning consideration

Before planning the off-grid solar power system, there is a need to consider the important limitations of the equipment. Like, such as charge controller and solar module limitations.

Charge controller limitations

The two main types of charge controllers include PWM and MPPT. PWM is only beneficial for the system that is less than 100W. Therefore, it will give the best design at a low cost. But for larger systems MPPT is reliable and PWM will not work. MPPT also contains a DC-to-DC converter. Due to its sophisticated design, it can extract 20 to 30% more solar power from the solar module.

Limitation of solar module

According to this, each solar cell is producing about 0.5V and when more cells are added the output voltage will be high. It is important to use a charge controller with 60 to 72-cell solar panels. Without it, the battery will not charge properly, and it may overcharge. Therefore, it is important to use an MPPT controller to charge a battery bank properly.

Determine total load

It is the starting point of the calculation. It is one of the hardest steps in the whole process so it must be accurate. The main goal is to get information regarding the total power used in a day.

For this take an example DC load. Consider a flood light of 30 watts with 12V/DC.

If the light is working from night to day in winter, then it will be operated for 15 hours a day. Then a power day watt hour will be calculated like this. $\qquad 30W \times 15h \div day = 450\ Wh\ /\ day$

Now for the AC load, if two loads are working on the day of 100 and 50W. Therefore, 100W is operating for 4 hours a day and 50W is for 6 hours a day then: $\qquad 100W \times 4h \div day = 400Wh\ /\ day$

$$50W \times 6h \div day = 300Wh\ /\ day$$

The total AC load will be 700Wh ÷ day at 120V / AC.

For producing AC power from sunlight DC to AC inverter is used. Therefore, the minimum capacity of the inverter will be 150W but its efficiency will affect it. For this consider the inverter losses are about 15%. If inexpensive inverters are used then it will consume 5 to 10 watts without any load connected to it. The large inverters contain a circuit that can easily detect the load connected and reduce standby current. AC load is about 700 Wh/day. Now multiply with the inverter losses that are 15% $700Wh/day \times 1.15 = 805\ Wh/day$. When both loads are operated at the same time then:

$$24 - 6 - 18\ hours\ in\ a\ day$$

Now also add standby loss of 10W ($10W \times 180 = 180\ Wh/day$)

Total AC load will be: $Total\ load = 805 + 180 = 985Wh/day$

The DC to AC inverter selection is based on these factors. When the total wattage of all loads is added to these factors then the total wattage of the inverter is gained. From the above example, a 1000W inverter will be reliable for these loads. If the water pump is running through the inverter, then it must have enough power for the amps of the motor. Loads that are not used daily will be calculated easily. If the load is working 2 days a week, then multiply it by Wh/day and take the ratio 2/7 then it will give information regarding the average daily load.

The total demand for solar for an MPPT controller

The demand for solar panels for MPPT controllers can be found through this formula.

Load x recharge factor x MPPT controller loss ÷ Sun hours = total array size

The recharge factor will give information regarding the probability of a clear day. If the day is cloudy then solar panels are unable to charge the batteries.

There are three recharge factors that can be used that include 1.15, 1.2, and 1.3. From these factors, 1.2 is reliable because it will provide a good design system that can easily operate all year long without fail.

MPPT controller losses

If the MPPT controller contains losses of 1.10 then it is reliable to use for the Off-grid system.
The location is also a vital factor.

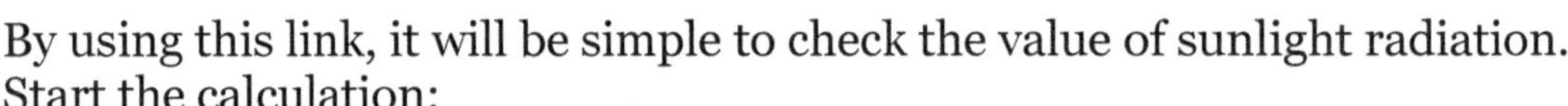

The information regarding the location of sunlight is provided at :

By using this link, it will be simple to check the value of sunlight radiation. Start the calculation:

load x recharge factor x MPPT controller loss ÷ Sun hours = total array size

985 Wh/day x 1.2 recharge factor x 1.1 MPPT loss = 1300.2Wh/day

1300.2 ÷ 3 sun hours = 433.4 watts of solar module

If a 280W module is used then 2 solar modules are added in series.

Sizing the battery bank

It is extremely important to size the batteries properly. The batteries are storing complete energy. If the storage capacity is not good then it may create problems. For this, use this formula.

Load Wh/day ÷ Base battery voltage = load Ah/day

For days of autonomy

load x days of autonomy ÷ Max DOD ÷ Cold temp factor = AH battery bank

Base battery voltage

The required nominal voltages of the battery are about 12V, 24V, and 48V. If the value of voltages is high then the current will be low. If the amps rating of the charge controller is about 50 amps then it is possible to get more power from the same controller.

$$50A \ x \ 12 = 600W$$

$$50A \ x \ 24V = 1200W$$

$$50A \ x \ 48V = 2400W$$

Like, if the AC load on the solar inverter is more than 4000W then always use a 48V battery bank to overcome voltage loss. For small AC volts, 12V battery bank is suitable. For mid-size AC loads 24V battery bank is reliable.

Days of autonomy factor

It is an important factor to consider while sizing the battery bank. The battery bank has the ability to withstand 5 days of backup.

Max DOD

It stands for maximum depth of discharge. When a battery is discharged and recharged then one cycle is completed. For example, if the battery is only discharged 10% and contains 90% of the power then it will contain 5000 cycles. Therefore, the total life of the battery will be:

life span of battery = cycles ÷ number of days in a year = 5000÷365 = 13.7 years

When the same battery is discharged at 50% then 1250 cycles will be completed so it will last only 3 years. Therefore, the battery bank has the ability to retain 5 days of autonomy with 80% max depth of discharge, then it will last for 8 years.

- 80F = 1.0
- 60F = 0.95
- 40F = 0.88
- 32F = 0.80
- 20F = 0.77
- 0F = 0.60
- -20F = 0.40

Cold temperature factor

This factor is also important because batteries are not working properly in cold temperatures and their capacities will be reduced. The battery capacity with temperatures is given in the figure here:

It is important to check the battery chart. There are many batteries that are operated in these temperature ranges. If the temperature is greater then it affects its lifespan. Taking the load value and base voltages of 24 V

$$965Wh/day ÷ 24V = 41.04\,Ah/day$$

load x days of autonomy ÷ Max DOD ÷ Cold Temp Factor = 41.04 x5 ÷ 0.80 ÷ 0.80 = 320.6 Ahat 24V battery

In the market, 120Ah batteries are available then:

$$320.60\,Ah ÷ 120Ah = 2.67\,batteries$$

It means 3 batteries are required that are attached in parallel. The battery is 12V so you need 6 batteries in which 2 pairs of 3 batteries are in parallel and attached together to get 24V with 360AH.

Getting started with solar system sizing

Before sizing the solar system, it is vital to figure out the main constraints. These constraints refer to budget, energy offset, and space constraints. It will be beneficial if the required system is under the target budget. The factors that affect the size of the solar power system include local level of sun exposure, future expansion plan, orientation of the array, product efficiency rating, and degradation of the components.

Estimating the energy usage

It is important to estimate the total amount of energy used at home before sizing it.

Calculate kWh usage

There are various methods to calculate kWh usage as discussed in previous chapters. Getting kWh usage from the electric bill. Average out the monthly kWh usage. It can be found by dividing it by 12. Another method is to find out daily kWh usage, dividing it by 30.

Look up peak sun hours

Over the whole year, the average peak sun hours will vary depending on the location and season from the sun hours chart for the information regarding the location and also the total months.

Calculate the size of the solar system

To find out the size of the solar power system, take information regarding daily kWh energy requirement for the whole day and divide it with the peak sun hours value with the efficiency factor of panels.

(daily kWh) ÷ average sun hours x 1.15 efficiency factor = size of solar panels

Take an example, with 33kWh total energy consumption, with 6.1 sun hours in summers.

$$33 \div 6.1 \times 1.15 = 6.2 \ kWh = 6200 \ watts$$

It means the panels must be connected in series in such a way to make more than 6200 watts.

Fine-tuning the estimated system design

After estimating the solar power system size, then decide on the perfect roof mounting, the direction of panels, and also the appropriate size of panels.

Select mount type

If roof mounting is selected then it is the cheapest way to support the panels. Check out the location where panels are going to be installed. Ensure that the panels must face south while installing them on the roof. If the south angle is not available then add more panels to complete the demand. Also, ensure that there will be less gap between the panels and also the other components. If there is no option on the roof then go for ground mounting.

Chose the panels

If the size of the roof is small, then it is important to consider solar panels with a greater number of cells.

If the roof contains enough area, then install more panels to obtain the required output from the panels.

But if the roof area is small then using panels with a high efficiency ratio, it will be costly but a cost-effective solution.

Calculate solar output

After adjusting the best location for the solar panels and also the angles. The next step is to calculate the PV watts of the panels. For this go to PV watt calculator and follow these steps

- Enter the address and also hit the orange arrow to the right.
- When the system info page is opened then add the value of DC system size.
- Select a standard module
- For the required array time, select fixed for roof and open for ground mounts.
- Add the system losses of 15%
- Enter the value of slope of the roof and the azimuth. It is obtained from this QR code
- By clicking the right arrow, it will give information regarding monthly solar system output.

Appliance table

Off-grid load calculator

Off-grid solar system size by using the calculator.

This particular calculator will estimate the system size. There are three main steps used to calculate the size of the solar power system.

- The user has to enter the zip code
- Then fill up the load calculator for each appliance at home
- Then click on calculate, it will give information regarding off-grid system size.

Various calculators

There are some other off-grid sizing calculators are given below. A person can get them by the QR links

Solar panels output

For calculating the solar panel output, it is important to consider the important factors regarding solar panel output.

- Efficiency of solar panels
- Location of the panels
- Direction of the solar panels

There are also other variables that change the value of the final output. For this, take an example, if there is a solar panel of 250 watts and the average sunlight value is 5 hours a day. The efficiency of panels is about 75%. Therefore, it is given this:

$$250 \; x \; 5 \; x \; 0.75 = 037.5 \; Wh = 0.937 kWh$$

Through this, it is possible to calculate the total size of the solar panels required for the solar output.

Appliance	Watts	Appliance	Watts	Appliance	Watts
Kitchen		**Living Room**		**Tools**	
Blender	500	Bluray Player	15	Band Saw – 14"	1100
Can Opener	150	Cable Box	35	Belt Sander – 3"	1000
Coffee Machine	1000	DVD Player	15	Chain Saw – 12"	1100
Dishwasher	1200-1500	TV – LCD	150	Circular Saw – 7-1/4"	900
Espresso Machine	800	TV – Plasma	200	Circular Saw 8-1/4"	1400
Freezer – Upright – 15 cu. ft.	1240 Wh/Day**	Satellite Dish	25	Disc Sander – 9"	1200
Freezer – Chest – 15 cu. ft.	1080 Wh/Day**	Stereo Receiver	450	Drill – 1/4"	250
Fridge – 20 cu. ft. (AC)	1411 Wh/day**	Video Game Console	150	Drill – 1/2"	750
Fridge -16 cu. ft. (AC)	1200 Wh/day**	**Lights**		Drill – 1"	1000
Garbage Disposal	450	CFL Bulb – 40 Watt Equivalent	11	Hedge Trimmer	450
Kettle – Electric	1200	CFL Bulb – 60 Watt Equivalent	18	Weed Eater	500
Microwave	1000	CFL Bulb – 75 Watt Equivalent	20	**Misc.**	
Oven – Electric	1200	CFL Bulb – 100 Watt Equivalent	30	Clock Radio	7
Toaster	850	Compact Fluorescent 20 Watt	22	Curling Iron	150
Toaster Oven	1200	Compact Fluorescent 25 Watt	28	Dehumidifier	280
Stand Mixer	300	Halogen – 40 Watt	40	Electric Shaver	15
Heating/Cooling		Incandescent 50 Watt	50	Electric Blanket	200
Box Fan	200	Incandescent 100 Watt	100	Hair Dryer	1500
Ceiling Fan	120	LED Bulb – 40 Watt Equivalent	10	Humidifier	200
Central Air Conditioner – 24,000 BTU NA	3800	LED Bulb – 60 Watt Equivalent	13	Radiotelephone – Receive	5
Central Air Conditioner – 10,000 BTU NA	3250	LED Bulb – 75 watt equivalent	18	Radiotelephone – Transmit	75
Furnace Fan Blower	800	LED Bulb – 100 Watt Equivalent	23	Sewing Machine	100
Space Heater NA	1500	**Office**		Vacuum	1000
Tankless Water Heater – Electric	18000	Desktop Computer (Standard)	200	**Note**: TVs, Computers, and other devices left
Water Heater – Electric	4500	Desktop Computer (Gaming)	500	plugged in but not turned on still draw power.
Window Air Conditioner 10,000 BTU NA	900	Laptop	100	**To estimate the number of hours that a
Window Air Conditioner 12,000 BTU NA	3250	LCD Monitor	100	refrigerator actually operates at its maximum
Well Pump – 1/3 1HP	750	Modem	7	wattage, divide the total time the refrigerator is
Laundry		Paper Shredder	150	plugged in by three. Refrigerators, although
Clothes Dryer – Electric	3000	Printer	100	turned "on" all the time, actually cycle on and
Clothes Dryer – Gas	1800	Router	7	off as needed to maintain interior temperatures.
Clothes Washer	800	Smart Phone – Recharge	6	
Iron	1200	Tablet – Recharge	8	

Chapter 12

Choices, Choices! -Site Survey

Site survey

If the right site is chosen for the panels, then the system will be extremely efficient. Therefore, the rooftop is the best site to adjust solar panels. The perfect site for panels is where the shading effect is zero. The required place must be reliable for passive cooling. The efficiency of the panels will be double over their lifetime.

Where to put solar panels

The best place to install solar panels is the roof top. The reason behind it is that it can be accessible, less shading effect and easy to adjust direction.

The location of panels must be at proper angles

The angles of solar panels are an important factor. If they are not placed at the right angle then panels are unable to gain maximum output.

It means that a lot of power will be lost when solar panels are not facing south and also if they are not angled properly. It's extremely important to adjust the tilt angle for panels for maximum output power.

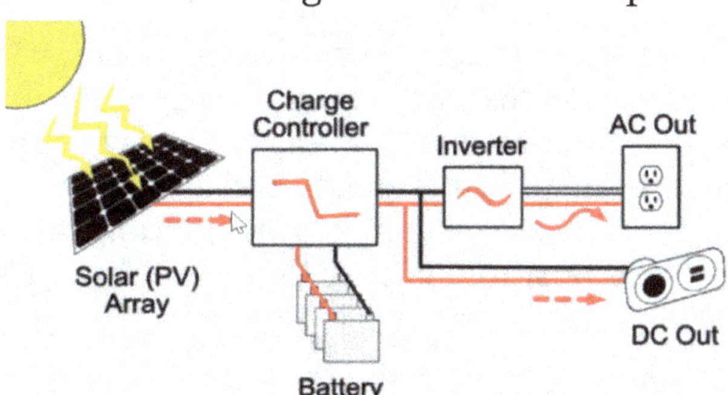

Avoid solar panel shading

If solar panels are facing the south and also their angles are perfect, but they are installed in shading then all factors are useless. While installing panels, also consider this factor and avoid shading. If the shading value is 10% then it will affect the power output by 10%. Depending on the wiring, the shading can reduce the power of whole array. Shading a cell has an effect on the whole panel.

Calculation for row spacing

For row spacing, it is important to perform shadow calculations. Before designing a solar system, it is vital to understand the time of shadow. Plan for row spacing between the solar modules. Consider that sun travels in an arch across the sky. Know your attitude position and also the azimuth for finding the length of a shadow.

The sun's path will follow the image of a shadow caused by a tree or branch throughout the day.

It is important to know the shape of the shadow caused by the sun changing its attitude and its azimuth. The center line is showing the information regarding solar noon. This shadow length is taken after every 30 minutes.

If the solar panels are going to be installed on a commercial roof and it contains a 4ft tall HVAC unit then it is important to know how to position the solar module with no shade.

After this, the next step is regarding scaling of the shadow length template regarding height of the object.

Then the shadow line is placed on the corner of the object. After this, just remove the shadow line that are not applied and outline the object shadow. It will be easy to know the best place to install solar panels for optimum performance. You can get information regarding the suns position data by following this QR code

With these calculations create a drawing template of the required area. This figure shows the shadow drawing template for 21st December with 2.1 ft long shadow and 1 feet tall object. For designing the system, use 10 am to 2 pm for the solar window to avoid any kind of shade.

The panels must be accessible

If there are any defects in the panel, it is important to repair them as soon as possible. The panels need to be accessible to solve the issues and the panels need to be clean to maximize efficiency.

   Hence, panels must be installed where it is possible to access them without any difficulty.

The panels must be cool as possible

The solar panels are black, and their temperature is high. When panels are overheated then they will produce less power and their efficiency is affected. A proper setup for the panels must have a 6-inch space behind the panel. In this space, the air can pass freely and cool them down.

The rooftop is not the best place because it is hot but through mounting racks, the ventilation will be increased. Always ensure that there must be less induced heat when energy is produced from the panels.

SunPosition output complete.
Latitude is 40.7 degrees north
Output angle units are degrees

PVeducation.com

Date	Time	Sun Altitude (degrees)	Sun Azimuth (degrees)	Unit of Shadow Length of Shadow for a One Unit Tall Object	Sun Position	Minimum Row Spacing
21-Dec	7:30	0.39	57.96	147.0	Sun Rise	78.0
21-Dec	8:00	5.08	52.91	11.3		6.8
21-Dec	8:30	9.45	47.56	6.0		4.1
21-Dec	9:00	13.45	41.84	4.2		3.1
21-Dec	9:30	17.01	35.74	3.3		2.7
21-Dec	10:00	20.06	29.24	2.7		2.4
21-Dec	10:30	22.54	22.34	2.4		2.2
21-Dec	11:00	24.37	15.11	2.2		2.1
21-Dec	11:30	25.49	7.62	2.1		2.1
21-Dec	12:00	25.87	0	2.1	Solar Noon	2.1
21-Dec	12:30	25.49	-7.62	2.1		2.1
21-Dec	13:00	24.36	-15.11	2.2		2.1
21-Dec	13:30	22.54	-22.34	2.4		2.2
21-Dec	14:00	20.06	-29.23	2.7		2.4
21-Dec	14:30	17.01	-35.74	3.3		2.7
21-Dec	15:00	13.44	-41.84	4.2		3.1
21-Dec	15:30	9.44	-47.55	6.0		4.1
21-Dec	16:00	5.07	-52.91	11.3		6.8
21-Dec	16:30	0.39	-57.96	147.0	Sun Set	78.0
				1/TAN(C31*3.14/180)		(E31)*COS(D31*3.14/180)

Chapter 13
Building the System

Building your battery house, solar shed, or solar closet

Now the next point regarding the installation of a solar power system is you need to make a complete battery room and or a solar utility room that contains all batteries, inverter, and charge controllers for the off-grid system. This room might be a separate shed. The location of this room must be near the solar panels and near the home.

Do battery banks need to be heated?

If the battery banks get hot then their efficiency will decrease. It is important to place the battery bank where heat is at a minimum. If the temperature is approaching freezing, this too is not good for the battery's efficiency. Using a charge controller will increase the lifespan of the battery bank.

It is useless to use lithium batteries at freezing temperatures and also when the heat is high.

The best way to save batteries from overheating is to use an insulated box. Also, a heating pad is connected with a thermostat and to the charge controller.

It is possible to use nickel ion batteries at low temperatures and provide extra benefits in high temperatures.

Venting the battery compartment

For the batteries that are open like nickel-iron and flooded lead-acid

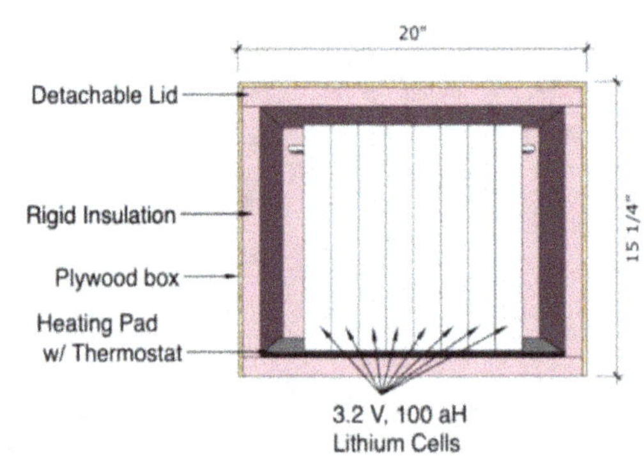

batteries, they produce hydrogen gas. This gas must be vented. But the sealed batteries and lithium-ion batteries do not contain such gases so there is no need for any ventilation in the battery compartment. Hydrogen gas is explosive, so it is impossible to put it in a closed space. This ventilation can be accomplished with a vent pipe attached to the battery room.

Solar battery installation

The three main types of batteries are used for the solar storage system.

- Sealed lead-acid battery
- Flooded lead-acid battery
- Lithium lead-acid battery

Before buying the batteries, it is important to consult the manufacturer along with the installation instructions and datasheets. Read the safety precautions before installing them.

Wiring battery banks

Before wiring up the battery bank, it is important to know the load demand of the system. If you have a high current rather than high voltage, then batteries will be wired parallel. On the other hand, if you want high voltage, then batteries are connected in series. In the previous section regarding parallel and series connection of the batteries, you will find the information about how to wire batteries in series and parallel.

When wiring the batteries, it is important to balance them. This means that at normal operation, various batteries can be connected in series then their power will be used up unevenly. Therefore, they are charged at various levels of charge. This is a big problem because charge controllers are working according to the current ratings of the batteries. The battery bank can be balanced by fulfilling these points properly.

- Discharge the batteries completely towards safe discharge point.
- Disconnect the battery bank from the panels
- Connect all batteries in parallel for about 24 hours and

Then again reconnect them in series.

It is important to check the voltages of a battery through a multimeter then it will be simple to ensure that the batteries are maintaining balance all the time.

Off-grid battery bank

The off-grid battery bank is an extremely important component to consider. For selecting the best battery bank for off-grid solar power systems some vital factors need to be considered, which include, battery type, lifespan, depth of charging, efficiency, and the total load demand.

Installing solar panels and support structure

It is the main step for off-grid solar power systems. if the solar panels are not installed properly then they will not have the required power output. The panels are depending on the total load of the home and also the battery bank capacity. After calculating all the wattage and considering efficiencies the required wattage will be obtained. Then order these panels and installed them.

If panels are going to be installed on the rooftop, then mounting will be light and inexpensive. But for ground mounting thick racks will be used and they are pricey. The support system is selected by checking the size of the roof and other factors like the direction of sun and the tilt angle.

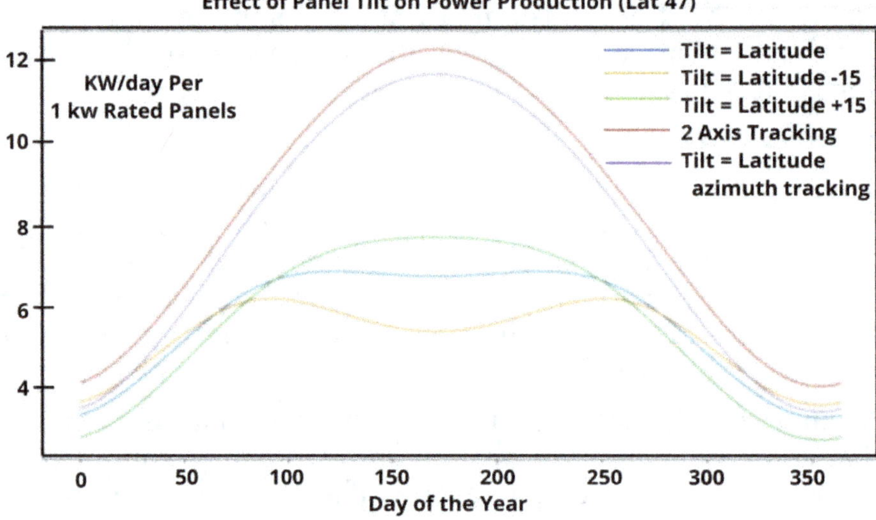

Which direction is used to install solar panels?

The ideal direction to install solar panels is when they are facing due south and also tilt at proper angle.

If the solar panels are tilted at a fixed angle, tilting them at the same angle will be maximizing the yearly output. Therefore, the required tilt angle must be about 47 degrees. The information regarding tilt angle will be obtained from your zip code. To get more production in the seasons then tilting down by 15 degrees for summer and up by 15 degrees for winter will increase the output value of the production.

Solar panels tracking

It is extremely beneficial that solar panels are facing the sunlight without any shading. If panels are facing the sun all the time, then it will get the most possible power, but this is difficult to accomplish. Therefore, full tracking setups for solar panel mounts are available on the market

but they are a bit expensive. Hence it will be cheaper to add extra solar panels rather than such complex movable mounting systems. The best alternative to initialize the tracking system is the manual tilt adjustment.

If manual tracking is performed four times a year after each season this will increase the productivity level by 40%.

Solar panel ventilation and cooling

The ventilation and cooling of solar panels are very important. If solar panels are not cooled properly then their efficiency will be affected. It's important to allow ventilation on the back side of the panels. On sunny days, the temperature of the panels will increase, and it will reach 100 F. Because of this, output power from panels will be decreased and also a decreased lifespan. Ensuring an air gap between the panels will help with cooling. If panels are installed on the rooftop, then it's important to maintain a 6 to 8 inches gap from the roof for proper ventilation.

Mounting your solar panels

For mounting solar panels, two types of mounting can be done. Roof mounting and ground mounting. It is important to consider roof mounting when someone has proper space on the rooftop, because it is less costly and is an easy install.

Installing roof mounts

If a person has decided to apply roof mounting, then it is important to follow these steps:

- Locate and mark all roof rafters properly
- Attach roof attachments for securing all rails on it.
- Attach all racking rails on the roof
- Lift solar panels on the roof according to tilt angle
- Mount panels on the rails.

If the solar panels are going to be installed on the cabin or tiny rooftop then apply these steps to gain perfect results. On a tiny roof just mark all roof rafters properly and secure all rails on it. Then lift the panel and mount them on the rails.

Wiring up the off-grid solar system

With the solar panels installed along with the battery bank. The next step is the connection between all the components of the system. The low

voltage solar systems are safe, but as the voltage value rises then it will rise to various troubles while installing. It is important to have a good understanding of electrical before wiring.

Wiring the solar panels in series or parallel

The first important question is regarding wiring the solar panels so that will be attached in series or parallel.

Is there high current rather than voltages? I so then panels will be connected in parallel. But if there are high voltages rather than current, then they are connected in series.

Wiring panels in series

The solar panels connected in series are the best option because it is saving the wire cost. The negative end of one panel is attached to the positive end of the second panel. When panels are attached in series then their voltages will be increased. The solar voltages can be increased from battery voltages when a charge controller is present.

Wiring solar panels in parallel

If a PWM charge controller is used, then the wiring of the panels must be in parallel, and it is the only option. When the wiring is in parallel then it will provide better performance in the shade. The parallel wiring of panels will increase the current. If the current of one panel is 5.5 amps then if two panels are attached in parallel then its amps value will be 11.

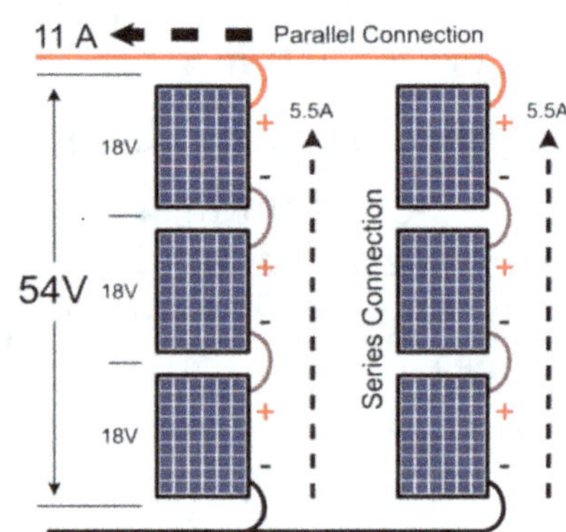

Solar panel wiring in series and parallel

This type of wiring is applied in large systems. You have too many panels to connect in series which will increase the input voltages of the charge controller. With such wiring, it will save money compared with a parallel wiring option. From the above image, the three panels are attached in series to make an array of 54V with 5.5 amps. Both of them are connected in parallel to achieve 54V and 11 amps at the output. It is important that every string contains the same voltages as the panels.

Can different types of solar panels mix?

It is not recommended to mix the different ages and types of solar panels. If one bad panel is present in the string of a series of connected panels, it will affect the whole string. Various brands of the panels contain maximum power points that are reducing the efficiency of the MPPT charge controllers by decreasing the maximum power point. It is only possible to mix different panels when they are connected in parallel.

Grounding

If there is any exposed metal part present in the solar array then it must be grounded for enhancing the safety of the system. It can be done by bolting a copper cable with the isolated metal frame and attaching these wires together with the grounding rod. Only the experienced electrician knows how reliable grounding is for the required area.

Running wires from the solar panels to battery

The wires taken from the solar panels and attached to the batteries are extremely unsafe. The main reason is that these wires are exposed to the sun. After some time, the efficiency of the wire will be affected. Hence it is important to use wire that can easily be exposed to sunlight without affecting it. For solar arrays, direct bury wire is considered the best option. But it is important that the wire must be rated according to the system.

Wiring up battery bank

The wiring of the battery bank is the same as the panels. If multiple batteries are going to be attached, then they may be in series or parallel depending on the demand.

The series connection of batteries will increase the voltages and the parallel connection will increase the current.

Batteries, series vs parallel

When multiple batteries are connected with each other then it will be according to their DC circuit voltages. These voltages will be 12, 24, and 48 volts. Whenever you need high voltages, then batteries will be connected in series. If you need high current from the battery bank then they will be attached in parallel. According to the required capacity, the connection of batteries will be organized in series or in parallel and complete the capacity demand. In parallel connection of batteries, the amp hours will be increased.

Battery balancing

When the batteries are wired, then it is vital to balance the batteries. It means that at normal operation, various batteries can be connected in series then their power will be charged up unevenly. Therefore, they are charged at various levels of charge. Due to this fact, there is a huge problem because charge controllers are working according to the current rating of the batteries. The battery bank can be balanced by applying these points properly.

- Discharge the batteries completely towards a safe discharge point.

- Disconnect the battery bank from the panels

- Connect all batteries in parallel for about 24 hours and then again reconnect them in series.

Battery management system

If lithium-ion batteries are used in the battery bank, then it is important to perform manual leveling. But it can be done by installing BMS on a battery bank. The main reason is that lithium batteries fail catastrophically when they are performing under low voltage. Leaving the batteries even is the best idea. The main purpose of the BMS is to monitor the voltage of the battery bank. There are some BMS that is self-leveling. Moreover, they also apply emergency disconnect whenever any battery gets too far out of the limit. The required chosen BMS must have proper voltage ratings. Also, each one comes with a proper number of wire connections.

It is important to connect the ground connection with the battery bank ground. For emergency disconnect, it is important to wire the battery bank output through BMS.

Wiring solar charge controller

Setting up the charge controller is the most important part of building an off-grid solar power system.

Wiring up safety switches

It is important to cover the solar panels by using thin sheets, traps, or blankets to ensure that they are not producing any power. Work with discharged batteries. While wiring the whole system it is important to follow all safety precautions and don't touch any electrical connection. It is also recommended that always install a circuit breaker on the positive side of the solar panels and other components like battery bank, inverter, and charge controller. It will be easy to protect the system against any defect and safety will be increased. Like if there is any fault in the solar panels then it will never cause problems to the other components. It is recommended to use a circuit breaker switch combo with various current ratings.

Connecting the charge controller

After installing all the circuit breakers, then power up the charge controller. The charge controllers are labeled with positive and negative terminals for power sources coming from the solar array, battery bank, and also load terminals. After this, connect the positive side of the solar array to the positive terminal and the negative side with the negative terminal like for the battery bank. After this, remove all covers from the panels and turn on the switches.

Choosing the correct charge profile

Different charge controllers contain a number of charge profiles that is according to the battery's chemistry.

For this purpose, read the complete manual regarding the charge controller and then make a proper connection. Important recommendations are also provided by the battery manufacturer when input is applied for the first time.

Temperature compensated charge controller setup

Many charge controllers have temperature compensation features. According to this feature, the charge controller can easily adjust the charge profile of the battery bank based on its temperature which extends the life of the battery bank. It can also cut off the power from batteries under certain temperatures that are damaging the batteries. If the charge controller does not have this feature then it will come with a plug labeled temp for compensating temperature.

How to connect more than one charge controller with the bank

When there are multiple charge controllers present, then connect each on the separate solar array. It is important to make sure that the charge profile of multiple charge controllers will be the same otherwise it will cut off. Then wire them with the battery bank in parallel. If the controllers contain load connections, then they will be attached in parallel

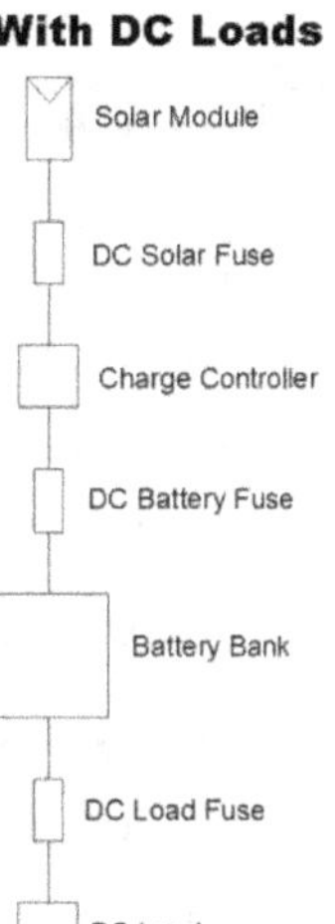

Wiring off-grid inverter and DC loads

When all solar panels are attached and also the battery bank with the charge controller and inverters, it's time to apply it with DC loads.

A diagrammatic idea

Low voltage disconnects

When loads are not applied to the charge controller, then it will get more current from the batteries than the charge controllers. You will need a low voltage disconnect. This particular device monitors battery voltage and will cut them off. A low voltage battery is the best choice that contains 12 or 24 volts with 20 amps.

The wire is disconnected from the battery bank and the fuse box then connects with the ground to the negative and positive terminal of the battery and the fuse box positive terminal.

DC power circuits and fuse box

For large systems, it is recommended to add a fuse box to the system. The main purpose of this box is to cut specific circuits when it is required and will increase safety. For large, 20 amps rating, a fuse box is recommended. An automotive/ marine/ RV fuse box works well according to the rating and specific needs.

The fuse box will be wired by connecting the load positive terminal with the box common lead that is at the top center. After this, label each fuse socket properly and connect it with the positive terminal of the appliance. Then all negative terminals are connected together and add the properly rated fuse in the circuit to enhance protection.

Inverter wiring

If someone is going with an AC-only system. then its inverter will be the only load. There is no need for any fuse boxes. You only need to wire the inverter with the load sockets present on the charge controller. At the input side of the inverter, it is important to install a fuse box because it will prevent DC power. On the AC side of the system, the required wiring is the same as home wiring. The large inverter is providing a current of over 20 amps. Due to this, a traditional circuit breaker is used to protect electrical appliances.

12V and 24V power connectors

The DC power system contains a lot of options for whole power plugging. As for the AC power system, there are no connectors on the plugs for DC appliances.

It is important to attach your own plug with the wires. There are three important types of DC power connectors that are used in the market.

- Anderson Power pole

- Cigarette lighter socket

- XT60 connectors

From them, the most vital DC power converter is the USB controller that is used on phones and smart devices. Moreover, 12 and 24 USB converters are used.

Hooking up solar panels with battery bank

For hooking up the solar panels to a battery bank, take a look at this video. This video is showing how simple is to attach the solar panels to the battery bank. If someone is interested in hooking up their solar panels with a battery bank then this video is excellent for providing accurate results. QR code:

A visual guide of the design

Key decisions to make while wiring the off-grid solar system

There are some important choices that must be made by installing an off-grid solar panel system. For this, there are some important points that are required to be decided properly.

- The number of panels and the output voltages of the solar panel array.
- Overall voltages of the system that are according to the battery bank and energy usage.

Wiring of solar panels in a solar system

There are three types of wiring used on solar panels.

- Series wiring of the panels
- Parallel wiring of the panels
- Mixed wiring with parallel and series combination

The wiring of solar panels is dependent on the requirement of the system.

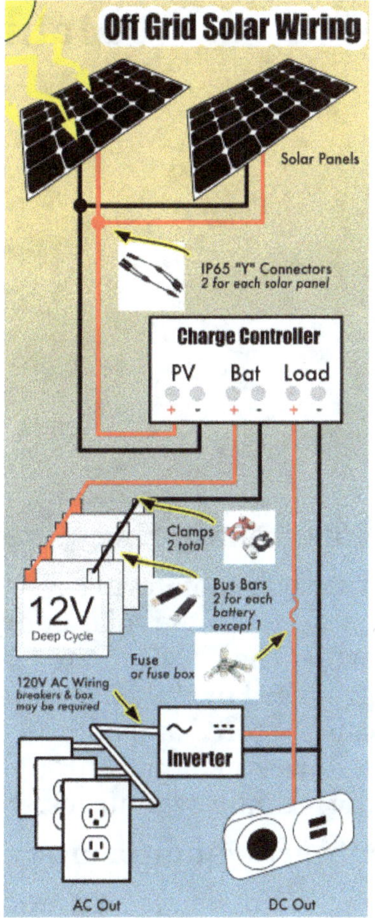

Chapter 14

Maintenance and Upkeep

Solar monitoring systems

The solar monitoring system is extremely important to measure the efficiency of the solar panels and also the energy production from the solar array. The solar monitoring system is involved in measuring the total energy produced by the solar panels. There are a lot of ways through which the data can be stored and addressed like internet connectivity and also some cellular functions. Through this, it will become possible to monitor the data during internet outages.

Off-grid monitoring system

For an off-grid monitoring system, it is important to optimize the lifespan of the battery so it will become simple to run the system efficiently. The monitoring system is measuring the state of charge of the battery.

Therefore, it will give reminders whenever you need to charge up the batteries.

The best off-grid monitoring systems

Here are the five best off-grid solar monitoring systems and they are given below:

Magnum

This monitoring system is offering both wireless and ethernet-enabled systems. With MagWeb products it is possible to add on more products.

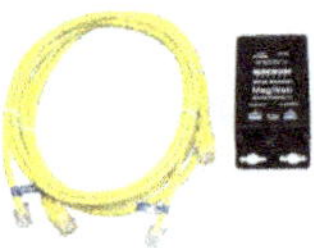

ME-MW-E MagWeb

Magnum Ethernet MagWeb Web based monitoring kit - ME-MW-E

Midnite

Midnite makes it easy to monitor any of Midnite's classic line of products like Midnite solar classic by the help of an ethernet connection

Classic 250 MPPT

Midnite Solar Classic MPPT Charge Controller 250V

Morningstar

This accessory enables communication between a PC and the Morningstar charge controller. Making it simple to remotely monitor the Morningstar controllers that contain meter bus connections.

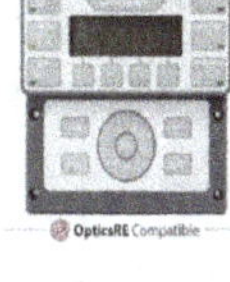

MATE3s

Outback MATE3s Digital Display & System Control

Outback

If there is an outback power system for the off-grid solar power system, then it includes Optics RE monitoring by using an ethernet connection. The MATE3s allow changes to the system's settings remotely.

Schneider

The Schneider context gateway is providing live monitoring and also local system configuration for monitoring and managing solar products. It contains wireless and ethernet connectivity.

Conext Gateway

Schneider Conext Gateway Pro

General maintenance guide

This section will provide information regarding the general maintenance guide for the off-grid solar power system.

Tips for maintaining off-grid solar system

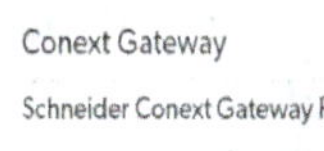

TriStar TS-MPPT-60

Morningstar TriStar Charge Controller, TS-MPPT-60

The best tip for maintaining an off-grid solar power system is to take care of the battery bank. It is the only component that contains the least lifespan. Therefore, if proper care is applied then it will increase the lifespan of the batteries and also increases the long-term cost of the system.

Check the charge level

The depth of the charge shows how much battery is discharged and the state of the charge. Therefore, if DOD is 20% then SOC will be 80%. If the battery is discharged by more than 50% on a daily basis then it will decrease its lifespan.

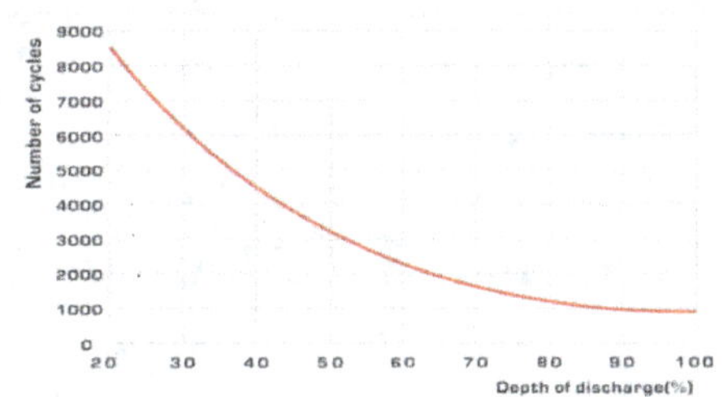

Always ensure that the battery is not discharged beyond 50%. Checking the MPPT will provide complete information regarding the batteries.

Equalize the batteries

Batteries have several cells. After charging these cells they will vary in specific gravity. Equalization is the best way to keep all cells of the battery fully charged. It is important to equalize the batteries every six months. If it is not possible to equalize the battery bank, then program the charge

controller to perform this task. There is also a manual way to measure equalization through a hydrometer.

Check the fluid level

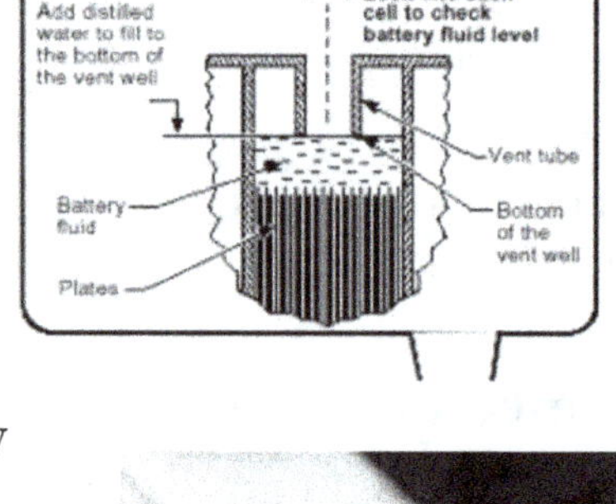

In the flooded lead-acid batteries there is a mixture of water and sulfuric acid. When the battery is charged, some of the water will evaporate. But this problem is not related to the sealed batteries.

Therefore, over time it is important to add some distilled water into the cells until no metal lead surfaces are visible. It is important to check the fluid once a week for new batteries.

Clean the batteries

When the water is escaping from the cap, then it will leave some condensation on the top of the batteries. This fluid is electrically conductive and also slightly acidic. Therefore, it will create a small path between the battery posts and pull more load than is required. For cleaning the battery terminal, the distilled water is mixed with baking soda and apply it with a brush. Rinse the terminals again and ensure the connections are tight. After this, coat the metal components with a sealant and also high-temperature grease.

Do not mix batteries

When a battery is going to be replaced then change the whole batch. If old batteries are mixed with the new ones, then it will reduce the performance and also degrade quickly. If the battery bank is maintained properly, then it will increase the lifespan of the off-grid solar system.

Maintenance and cleaning of solar panels

Solar panels are a huge investment and the whole solar power system is depending on it. If solar panels are not maintained properly then their life span will be decreased and also their efficiency suffers.

It is important to clean the solar panels regularly for efficient energy production.

Solar panel cleaning

Cleaning times of solar panels depend on the location and climate. For residential areas, regular rainfall is enough to clean them. But it is also

important to clean the panels manually if there are bird droppings, dirt, and tree debris present on the panels by rinsing the panels with a hose. Then wipe them using a small amount of dish soap and a soft sponge. Everything used for cleaning the panels must be soft.

For winter

In winters, brush excess snow off the panels for maintaining efficiency. Use a soft-bristled broom to perform the job properly. Abrasive material can damage the glass.

Solar panel maintenance

Solar panels are maintained by cleaning them on regular basis. All other parts of the system will benefit from a regular checkup and maintenance also.

Wiring

It's important to inspect the electrical wiring of the solar panels once in a year.

The ground conductors, fittings and electrical conduit need to be examined. Also, inspect PV cables and ensure that they are not touching the roof and are secured.

Racking

Once a year, it is important to inspect all racks properly. During bad weather conditions, they do get rusty so maintain them by applying an anti-corrosion spray.

Battery maintenance

It is important to set up a regular battery maintenance schedule for maintaining batteries, which will be different based on the type used. Charge controller, program voltage & set points. Then the battery bank will be charging properly.

Always refill lead-acid batteries after 2 to 4 weeks. Check the battery state of charge regularly and apply an equalization charge after every 90 days. The terminals of the batteries must be cleaned to prevent corrosion.

Part-V

DIY Off-Grid projects

Basic portable solar power system

This section will show how to build a portable solar power system that can be used on boats. This type of setup can also be used for camping, and RVs. All the parts are purchased from eBay for about $200. An old car battery will be used for storing the power. The solar panel wattage is about 40W. This system is used to power the fish finder, GPS, lights, radio, water pump, and also 240V appliances like the refrigerator. The solar inverter has a 100W capacity that converts 12V DC into AC and is stored in the car battery. I'm adding 100-amp circuit breakers to prevent overcurrent. A 12V relay is also connected with the inverter for running AC appliances. From the video link below, let's connect the components of the system.

QR Code - Build system Video

All-round 12V system for off-grid

The 12V system is producing power by connecting one panel with 12V ratings, a battery bank. In place of the MPPT charge controller, PWM is used because the load demand is less than 100 Wattage. Adjust all the components on the board and wire them properly by AC wire for AC connection and DC wire for DC connection.

Minimalist on a budget

It is the best option for an off-grid solar power system installed on a minivan, off-road truck, or van with limited roof space. This is a lightweight setup that is aerodynamic when planning to run small appliances like a USB charge, a laptop, and LED lights.

Components

- SLA deep cycle battery with 35-100 amps

- Solar panel of 100 to 200 watt

- 30-amp PWM

- Inverter with 200-1000 watts.

The estimated cost will be:

- Solar panels cost $80-200
- Charge controller cost $35
- Lead batteries price range $70 to 269
- Inverter prices are 20 to $84
- 40$ for the branch connectors like connectors and fuses
- 50 to $150 for the tools with high-quality

The estimated cost with cheap components = $295

The complete system with high quality components = $748

Small cars and minivans

The required system is going to be installed on minivans, cargo trucks, and off-road trucks with limited roof space.

Components

- SLA deep cycle battery with 100 amps
- Solar panel of 100 to 200 watt
- 20-amp MPPT
- Inverter with 750W.
- The estimated cost will be
- Solar panel cost $130-260
- Charge controller cost $125
- Lead batteries price range $200-$1000
- 280 for lithium batteries $950
- Inverter prices is 20 to $170
- 40$ for the branch connectors like connectors and fuses
- 50 to $150 for the tools with high quality

The estimated cost with cheap components = $1075

The complete system with high quality components = $1745

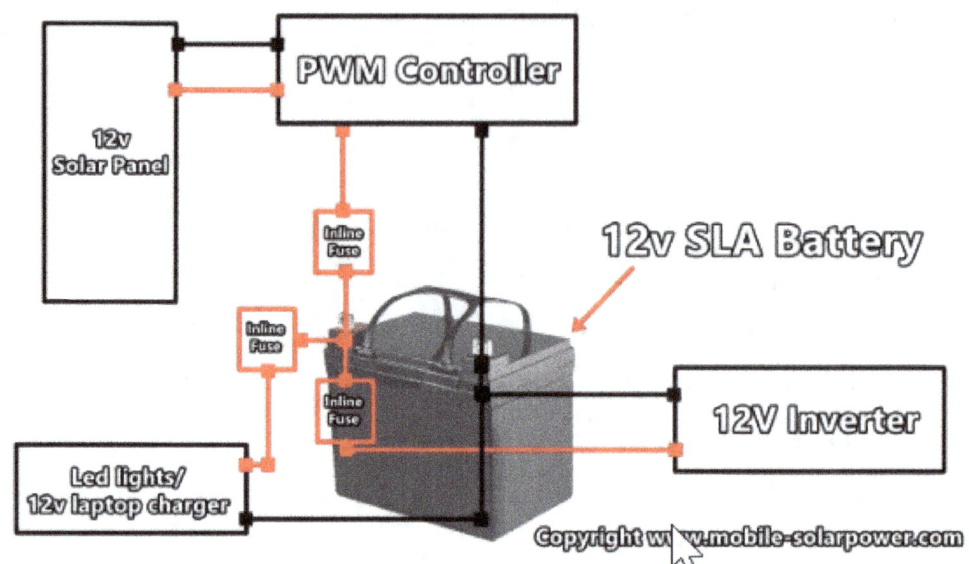
PWM Controller
12v
Solar Panel
Inline Fuse
Inline Fuse
Inline Fuse
12v SLA Battery
12V Inverter
Led lights/
12v laptop charger
Copyright www.mobile-solarpower.com

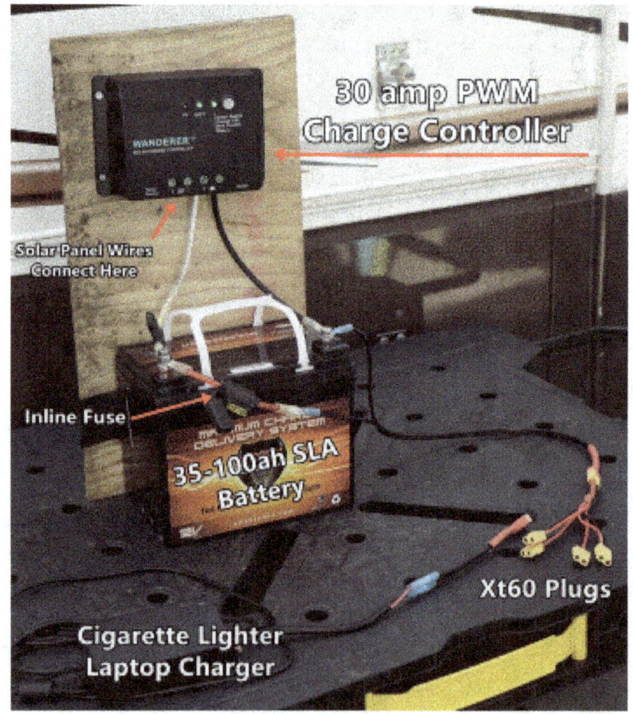
WANDERER
30 amp PWM
Charge Controller
Solar Panel Wires
Connect Here
Inline Fuse
35-100ah SLA
Battery
Xt60 Plugs
Cigarette Lighter
Laptop Charger

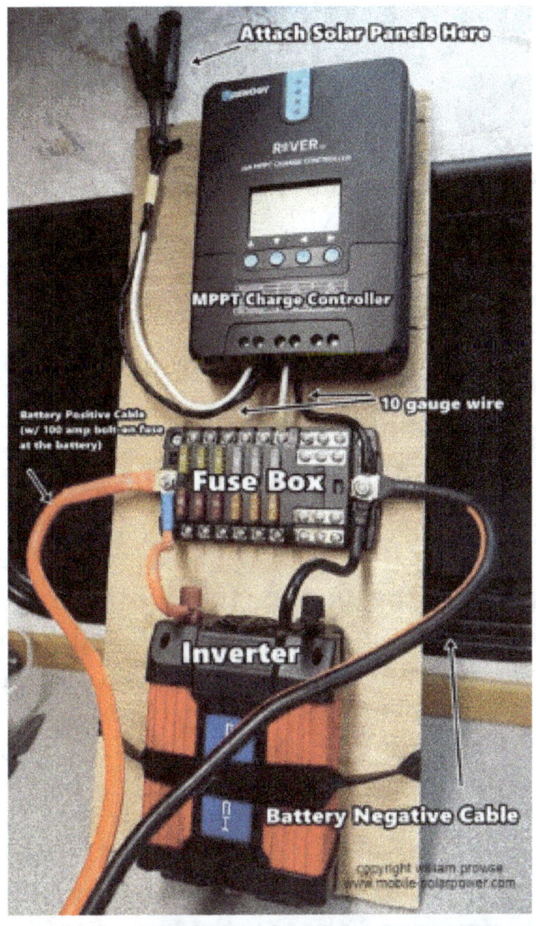
Attach Solar Panels Here
MPPT Charge Controller
RIVER
10 gauge wire
Battery Positive Cable
(w/ 100 amp bolt-on fuse
at the battery)
Fuse Box
Inverter
Battery Negative Cable
copyright william prowse
www.mobile-solarpower.com

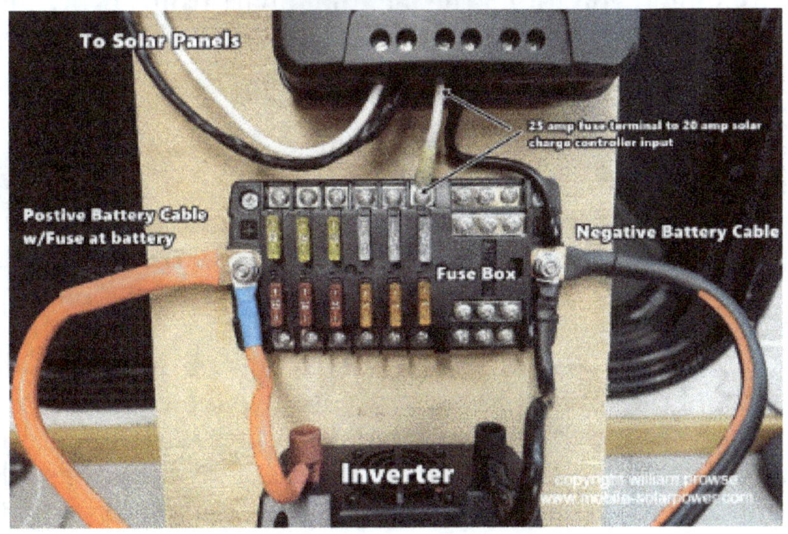
To Solar Panels
25 amp fuse terminal to 20 amp solar
charge controller input
Postive Battery Cable
w/Fuse at battery
Negative Battery Cable
Fuse Box
Inverter
copyright william prowse
www.mobile-solarpower.com

Advanced

Introduction:

"The sunlight ... that strikes Earth's land surface in two hours is equivalent to total human energy use in a year. While much of that sunlight becomes heat, solar energy is also responsible for the energy embodied in the wind, hydro, wave, and biomass, each with the potential to be harnessed for human use. Only a small portion of that enormous daily, renewable flux of energy will ever be needed by humanity"

- Christopher Flavin,
Former President of World watch Institute

Have you ever thought to yourself, what if I too decided to make a change? How hard is it to be self-sustainable? Producing food for yourself, by yourself. No, I'm not talking about democracy. What would it mean for you to drive yourself away from this economy and society that does not let you make your own decisions? It cannot be that hard, can it?

There are so many reasons for people choosing to live off-grid these days. More than freeing themselves from the shackles of society, it is about living sustainably. Wisely, even. Being in proximity with mother nature. Understanding it. Respecting it. It changes your whole perspective about this world and your contributions to it. Trust me, there is nothing better than self-reliance.

You must be wondering that all these revelations might feel good and all, but surely there must be something more to going off-grid? Of course, there is. Why should you forget the fact that apart from revolving around self-sustenance and self-reliance, off-grid is one of the most financially feasible options? Shocker, right?

I will be honest here. There is so much talk over off-grid being an option that contributes to the environment in such a positive way. That is all true and extremely respectable, of course. However, off-grid being an environment-friendly way of living has little to do with the reason people have been embracing this concept. Surely, it has contributed to this idea's popularity but is hardly one of the primary reasons for people embracing the concept and officially going off-grid.

But, let me give you some insight into how off-grid is all about going green. The fact of the matter is that most of the people who go off-grid are usually found to be settled in places that are pretty close to nature. They form a connection with it mostly due to the fact that they are so dependent on it. The sun and the winds are truly what accelerate and strengthen their life.

Once you really take a step back and see for yourself how much of a "consumer" you are, your perspective really does shift. People nowadays are consuming so much, too much even. How does the idea of a big luxurious house and a garage full of cars sound to you? Amazing, right? Even if gives the earth some lung cancer with its fumes!

Living off-grid has made it evident that people rarely use a vehicle when living out in nature and since they do not move into huge mansions with heating and cooling systems, the energy consumption is way less.

Off-grid is as much about going green as it is about managing your finances. Giving away your properties to move deep into nature. You could live anywhere you want; it could be a smaller house, or you could decide to really get the experience by living in a Recreational Vehicle (Rv). As they say, go big or go home. Ecological? Yes. Expensive? No.

The people doing this are less driven by the fact that they are putting less pressure on nature and more by the fact that it has been a huge relief for their economic and financial matters. Growing your own food and producing your own energy, whether from the sun or the winds, is not easy. This notion of going off-grid has been pretty glamorized. It is doable, of course. But that is the thing, isn't it? You have to do things. You have to put in the effort to sustain yourself.

There is this widespread belief that you can just go off into nature and start living off-grid. Yes, you could do that if you were a sheep. Unfortunately, you are all human beings, so you are going to need a little more than just an "idea" to start with your plan. So, let me debunk this myth really quickly. You need some land. That's it, no questions. How much? At least half an acre. And the right acre. For example, you cannot just go and get settled in the middle of the Sahara Desert. You don't need over 50 acres of land. Just get settled into your half an acre and buy yourself a laptop and some solar panels. Since my previous book was all about solar energy, you can take some notes from it and I'm sure it would be of significant help to you.

Trust me when I say this, off-grid living is much easier and more convenient at this time. Your generation has so many facilities that can make your experience an enthralling as well as a practical one. The Internet is something that can truly aid you as you navigate this concept of living. There are numerous websites that aim to provide you with DIYs as well as lessons for you to live off-grid successfully and happily and even have programs to provoke a sense of community for you to tackle any feelings of isolation; both physically and emotionally.

As I mentioned before, this book is a sequel to the previous one which centered around solar energy for beginners. It's called "Off-Grid Solar Power Systems for Beginners." The book constitutes solar power and its electrical as well as circuitry basics. Not only this, but it also discussed the primary components of a solar energy panel. For all the readers going off-grid and not knowing the primary ABC of solar energy, I got you covered because my

previous book provides you with a 6-step process to get you to build your own off-grid solar system! From planning to designing, you will be given all information.

However, this must trigger you to think why not just read the previous book, right? Well, not exactly. The previous book does give you all the information about the building process and the basics of solar power, but this book truly caters to all your doubts regarding off-grid. Your confusion and fears of planning. Not knowing the sizes for various aspects? No problem, I will tell you everything. I'll list suggestions for buying the right components or even full kits. However, the true essence of solar energy is still preserved in this book because I aim to provide a bigger, in-depth knowledge of solar power systems along with their components.

Talking about building solar systems for yourself in order to lead a self-sustainable lifestyle whilst simultaneously providing relief to the environment is easy. But really applying all the information to your life and getting to work is hard. As a self-taught solar energy and system enthusiast, I can totally understand the frustration and confusion that comes with trying to build and design your own system.

One of the most constant problems that people face throughout trying to build a solar system is the confusion they have regarding sizing. You're lucky when you come close to finally nailing down the basic design of your system but then come the days when it's easier to drive a nail into your own head rather than decide the perfect size that will meet all your requirements. You go back and forth and still you remain unsure. There is a sun-sized cloud looming over your head constantly. Trust me, I can imagine. Aiming to build a system that can allow me to power my laptop but turns out it can hardly get my fan to swing.

Most of you have been triggered to pick this book because you're at a point where you just don't want to waste your time designing a system that will not even align with your basic needs. Imagine, all that energy going to waste. Literally. This frustrates you whilst choosing the right components. Panels, batteries, inverters,
which is the best for you? Which one will last the longest?
Which one will give the best performance?

All these questions are valid. And I can relate to the fact of how frustrating it can be since I've been in the same boat. Nobody wants to spend their hard-earned money on substandard equipment that isn't even a right fit for their design, right?

Most people find out later on that government rebates are applicable to solar energy systems. Many of you find this feature pretty endearing but it also raises a lot of questions as well as confusion. People are not clear as to exactly how much deductions or savings they can get for their systems.

If you can relate to all the problems above, or even more, then you're in the right place because this is precisely what this book aims to tackle.

With my experience coupled with my enthusiasm for the subject, I will provide you with all the tips and tricks for you to successfully make decisions for your solar energy systems.

From 7 important considerations that could make or break your plan to go solar to all the information you need regarding the existence of the government rebates as well as incentives for off-grid alongside grid-tied systems, I'll be providing you with all. Furthermore, when it comes to the actual components of the solar system, I will erase all your confusion and apprehensions by giving you a highly detailed guide covering the following aspects:

- Solar panels
- Mounting systems
- Batteries
- Charge controllers
- Inverters
- Monitoring systems
- Wiring calculations and basics

I'll be your buying guide as well. From detailed comparisons between complete kits to their components, you've been saved. Plus, I will solve your biggest problem by explaining the sizing of your system. You'll be given various sizing options to help you understand what you can run on 1kW, 2kW, 5kW, or 10kW systems. Alongside this, this book will also be elaborating on sizing variables for tiny homes, typical homes, RVs, campers, and boats.

Since you've come this far, I only find it appropriate to share my hidden identity with you and bring you out of the darkness (Did you see what I did there?). Anyways, to sum it up, I am an avid DIYer who is extremely enthusiastic about self-sufficiency and self-reliance. I'm self-taught when it comes to solar power but that doesn't mean that you can underestimate my knowledge. I've been studying renewable energy extensively for many years, which is one of the reasons that I feel enthusiastic to share my views as well as all the techniques I have gathered up my sleeve. Since I myself have experienced the joy of being independent it is only fitting that I share those benefits.

This book is information-rich but not just with any kind of information, but especially the one that you need. You will finish this book and be able to make informed decisions regarding the sizing of your solar power systems, the very reason you have grabbed this. This will aid you in the designing process in order for you to get the best components and the right services that meet and align with your energy needs. What more could you want? So read up and solve all your problems!

Chapter 15

Breaking Down the Solar Basics

Let's start from the absolute basics and build up to the further complexities of this journey. This lifestyle demands a certain level of commitment. The fact is, no matter how much you have been taught about solar power, or how much you have researched, you haven't been told the full story. None of the common strategies and research you have accumulated will ever give you the instant solution you need, without initially understanding the basics of what you've been taught, in my previous publication.

However, I will give you a glimpse of what I narrated in "Off-Grid Solar Power Systems for Beginners." I compiled this book to help people who are looking to shift to an off-grid life, tap into the prerequisites and basics of the process.

It's true; Solar energy is a beneficial investment. It is an indispensable strategy that is mastered by people living off-grid in various places. As we know, solar energy is generated by the sun, which is converted into electricity, through the photovoltaic effect. Therefore, the most vital component of the process is a solar power system.

This is the foundation of the book and the major component that will be explored in the upcoming chapters.

What is the photovoltaic effect?

Great question!

Let me preface this by explaining that the science behind this is complex but important for your understanding. It plays a major role in the implementation, and value, of the system altogether. A photovoltaic effect demonstrates the conduction of electricity that is produced when sunlight hits the solar panels.

In an elaborate stance, the photovoltaic effect is tied closely to the generation of voltage and current in a panel exposed to sunlight. This physical and chemical phenomenon is closely linked to the photoelectric effect.

The free source of energy is taking over the contemporary needs for electricity. You are not only getting clean and renewable energy but also inexhaustible energy, which is resourceful and will be useful as long as the sun shines.

The accessibility, usage, and installation of these small panels on your roof eases your burden of bills. However, the grand strategy behind this is associated with the photoelectric effect.

Added information– The discovery of solar power dates back to 1839. French scientist Alexandre Edmond Becquerel discovered that a metal when exposed to sunlight can spark electricity.

However, this was not affirmed and explored until the 20th century. The first recorded discovery, which I am sure you must have read about, is of German physicist Heinrich Rudolf Hertz, dating back to 1887. He accidentally stumbled on this effect while experimenting with radio waves.

Understand the basic phenomenon, but don't let the complex terms confuse you.

The terms used to describe each aspect or composition of the effects can be simplified to the basic atomic science which includes the study of electrons and protons.

In the photoelectric effect, electrons are ejected from the exterior of metal, when it comes into contact with sunlight. Any material that reacts to sunlight is called photo emissive material, and the ejected electrons are called photoelectrons/photons.

You would be surprised by the complexity of this method which seems so simple to most people. Studied by scientists such as Albert Einstein this phenomenon was termed the photoelectric effect.

Einstein denoted a formula encoding that energy carried by each particle of light is correlated to the light's frequency. This is shown through the formula: **E = hv**

Where h = Planck's constant = 6.6261 × 10-34 Js.

The formula states that light is emitted in a bundle of photons, which then falls on the surface of the photo emissive material. The entire energy of the photon is transferred to the electron.

In fact, kinetic energy plays a vital role in this aspect. While part of this energy is used to remove the electron from the metallic atom's grasp, the rest of the energy is transferred to the ejected electron. Thus, during a collision, these electrons lose kinetic energy. This kinetic energy is used by the electrons to collide and aid in the generation of electric current. Not to our surprise, with the progression and revolutions that amazed the world and continue to do so, scientists created the first photovoltaic cells out of selenium. In fact, in 1950, Bell Labs developed a PV cell with silicon that could meet solar needs. Surprisingly, the silicon PV cell achieved a 4% energy conversion, which was a groundbreaking invention.

To illustrate the importance of this I will give you a brief historical reminder of light and the study of light.

We have come a long way from the traditional studies of light revolving around the vision of our eyes, the description of rays that conformed to the microscopic study of particles, waves, and their nature.

I have always been intrigued by the history behind the phenomenon, and the struggles procured by the older generations, in determining what we can now articulate easily.

While tracing the historical ideas that shaped our gradual understanding of light, its nature, and its properties, I realized that the determination, and quantification of the notion, was geographically spread. The history of light flutters from four different eras.

Let's explore the eras together.

The first era, with Athens at the center, belonged to the Greeks. Followed by the Islamic civilizations in Baghdad and Cordoba. Furthermore, the third era started around the dark age of medieval Europe. Finally, the last era started in the 20th century that dived into the revolutionist theories of Physics, along with communication technology. This historical film is continued even in this time since science is always digging deeper.

On a lighter note, solar cells were a unique invention. What makes a solar cell? Why is it important? I am sure you care less about the what than the why, but I am always looking for the intricate details that make the equipment. It helps me understand the role, importance, and sensitivity of the component.

Solar cells are made up of semiconductor materials such as silicon. The secret is that, for solar cells, the thin semiconductor wafer is treated to form an electric field containing a positive side and a negative side.

This is the base for electricity generation.

When the light hits solar cells, the grasp of the atom loosens, which initiates an electrical circuit, and the electrons are captured in the form of an electric current. This electric current is used to power a load, such as lights or appliances.

Also, might I add, that there are different types of solar cells.

Single-Crystal cells are initially made from long cylinders of silicon and then sliced into thin layers of wafer. Precision and a high-efficiency rating of 23% are the key here.

Subsequently, Polycrystalline cells are made from molten silicon castes which are sliced into thin squares. The process is inexpensive; however, the energy conversion efficiency of 20% is lower compared to the single-celled one.

Lastly, the thin-film solar cells are 100 times thinner compared to the other two. They are made from cadmium-telluride (CdTe) or copper indium

gallium diselenide (CIGS). The biggest advantage of this cell type is lightness and flexibility as it can be backed by material such as plastic or glass. Yet, the efficiency decreases to 7-12% which is the lowest.

That is to say, energy conversion efficiencies can impact your choice of a solar cell. You should be informed about the efficiency problems that occur in these cells.

At this point, if you are anyone like me, you would have heard about the Shockley-Queisser Limit, which I have dealt with in detail, in the Beginner's Guide. If you haven't heard of this, let me explain.

According to theoretical maximums, the solar cell efficiency is limited to 30%, however, we are only able to maximize 20% through a single cell. Here's why– sunlight has different kinds of photons. If you search the electromagnetic spectrum, you can actually see that light comes in different varieties, many of which are not visible to the naked eye. Aside from this, higher resistance of the electrons also causes loss of energy.

So, what can be done?

Honestly, not much– but some manufacturers stack solar cells that are developed from various materials having different energy band gaps. This multi-material stack-up permits more frequencies of photons to be absorbed thereby increasing the efficiency. A comprehensive understanding of solar cells can help you make the right choice for yourself.

Let's be honest, there are positives and negatives to everything in the world. But often some positives outweigh the cons of a system. For an off-grid choice, one of the major advantages of solar technology is the ability to generate electricity on an as-needed basis.

A solar panel planted on the roof of a house can produce electricity right where it's required. Solar panels are the perfect balancers of energy, want to blast your AC on a hot summer morning? Go ahead. You will have your immediate energy needs met, which would in turn reduce strain on transmission grids. All in all, fewer blackouts, and a system less dependent on a single power source. On an industrious level, solar technology can benefit modular structures. When single solar panels are damaged, the rest of the systems continue to work effectively.

On the contrary, solar energy is expensive. For instance, when your house appliances will not consume all the power generated from the solar system, the energy will have to flow back into a grid through 'feeder' lines. Installing these lines can be expensive for companies in the future. Moreover, there is a loss of energy in solar farms as any material current travels on, causing a loss of energy. This inevitably causes a loss of energy in the transmission process. Lastly, the major challenge is the inconsistency of sunlight. Energy generation is low on a cloudy day, which is why utility companies have hybrid options for solar grids, to balance the day-to-day demand.

In retrospect, solar panels are the future. Slowly and gradually, they are taking over the modern forms of electricity. One does wonder about the future of solar technology.

In the last 10 years, the price of solar technology has massively decreased, thereby making an expensive technology cost-effective. Since science is always advancing, solar efficiency is on the list for scientists. For instance, the scope of perovskite solar cells is an interesting innovation.

This cell is designed to be cheaper than silicon cells while being equally efficient. The material that it is manufactured from is called calcium titanium oxide crystalline. Researchers say it would take 5-10 years for the perovskite to be ready for its installation. The future will be something else.

As mentioned in great detail in the Beginner's guide, the main components that make the power system are.

Solar panels, Inverters, Racking's, Batteries, Charge controllers.

Nevertheless, even though I have explored the pros and cons of going solar in the Beginners guide elaborately, I'll touch on this area a little.

The choice of going solar gives you energy independence thereby reducing or even eliminating electric bills. In fact, it is a profitable, one-time, investment that also encases strong governmental incentives.

Yet, many will argue that it is expensive upfront. True, but look at the bigger picture here– would you spend the rest of your life paying off highly taxed electric bills or save yourself some money and go on that vacation you've been planning for so long? I think we all know the answer here.

Moreover, the solar systems are low maintenance, and sustainable, thereby improving property value. It does, however, take up space and cannot be installed on every property.

Due to the excess batteries and controllers, off-grid systems cost more compared to grid-tie systems.
However, they are an excellent and long-term investment.

The reality is that shifting to a space that is not forwardly connected to the main supplies of utilities can be expensive at first. Yet, the grid-tie systems ensure that you receive power during the night as well, which is covered through the net metering systems of the solar companies.

Therefore, the 1st step is to consider which type of griding suits you best; grid-tie systems, hybrids, or off-grid systems.

That's a wrap on the brief overview of the Beginner guide. As you can see, the potential to harness the power of the sun is limitless – but there is more to it than simply storing the energy and using it for your personal gains. And this is where a distinction emerges.

Let's explore the three kinds of solar power systems and how each design can be beneficial for you and your house.

Chapter 16

The Power of Three

Selecting a solar power system can seem exhausting. So, to make it easier for you these are the three types of power systems you should be considering during your research:

- Off-grid Solar Power System
- Grid-tied Solar Power System
- Hybrid Solar Power System

We are going to look at these three types of systems so that you can make the right decision for your roof and power supply.

There is an obvious distinction between the three; however, each is equally effective and efficient. The choice to buy whichever is yours to make, therefore research is key in this situation. If you consider the many benefits of solar, understanding the types of solar systems currently available, you can choose the one best suited for your home.

During my journey, I wondered which one of these systems is the best. I did so, to choose the best power for my utility. But I was absolutely wrong. The thing that I realized was that every house, lifestyle, and location requires a different type of power system.

Let me put this in perspective for you, in order to maximize your power needs, using a solar system, you would need to ensure that the sunlight is always hitting your solar panels.

For rural land with large acreage, the installation of multiple off-grid solar power systems would make sense. But this can be difficult to achieve in a near to city or urban household. Therefore, it becomes imperative for you to understand the types of power systems, weigh their pros and cons, and decide accordingly.

Ok, let's get busy; here is a comparative analysis of each of these systems that you can use to guarantee your own power and supercharge your utilities. Following is a summarization of the types of solar systems available.

- Off-Grid Power Systems: It is an independent solar system that has no connection to the grid, but the home runs completely off of the energy generated by the grid.
- On-Grid Power Systems: These are the most popular systems for small businesses and houses. The homes are connected to the grid so that it can make sure there is ample provision of electricity from the main utility when solar panels are not exposed to sunlight.
- Hybrid Power Systems: Alternatively called 'solar-plus-storage systems,' these make use of the batteries and sunlight to make electricity. The homes are also connected to the grid.

Grid-Tied/On-Grid Solar System

What makes this unique?

The connection of the solar power system is tied to the house and the local electricity grid.

However, this system does not have any storage battery included. The duality of this system makes it powerful and popularly demanded by the people.

We know that the energy generated by the panels is immediately consumed by the appliances. However, in case the system generates more power than the net requirement of the house, the excess power is sold back to the power company under net metering.

This conforms to a balance when the grid is not producing enough power, appliances draw energy from the utility grids.

Advantages of On-Grid Power System

1. Cost-effective purchase, since these systems require less equipment than other types of solar power they are cheaper to buy.
2. Long warranties are a plus point. Given that the operating cost of on-grid systems is low, they are easier to maintain and have a 20–25-year warranty.
3. There is no downtime without electricity and the system is simple to use thereby having increased reliability.
4. You will have the ability to design your system with batteries which is an alternative energy source and a utility source. This way your needs are met in the future.

Are you looking to save money and shift to a renewable energy source? A Grid-tied power system can become your best friend. It not only saves your money from extensive bills but also powers your appliances with a renewable energy source.

The disadvantage of the On-Grid Power System

Despite the gleaming positives, there are certain challenges that you might want to consider–

1. Once the sun goes down you are unable to use the energy produced by the solar panels.
2. There will be power storage when the electric grid goes down since solar panels will shut off automatically. This will influence your daily life and routine.

Off-Grid Solar Power System

As the name suggests, this system is not connected to the main utility grid. So how does it work? Easy, solar panels.

Solar panels are the only source of energy in an off-grid system, which is why they are popular amongst rural homes. The energy is either utilized or stored. They are perfect for remote rural use and especially in places where other power sources cannot be installed.

Advantages of Off-Grid Solar Power Systems

1. There is no dependence on utility companies. This freedom allows you to relieve yourself from the terms and policies of a multinational company.
2. In a rural setting, where people have no electricity, your home will not experience a blackout. This remains an important prospect for health appliances such as heart monitors or refrigerated medicines.
3. Freedom from electricity bills. Since you will produce your own electricity you will not have to pay bills to a utility company.

Do you have a cabin in the woods? Or a land far away from the city? Off-Grid systems ensure you have electricity that you won't have otherwise.

Disadvantages of Off-Grid Solar Power Systems

Of course, there are downsides to this system
1. Excess energy production with sun exposure requires extra batteries which are expensive.
2. The initial cost of purchase and installation is higher compared to the on-grid option.
3. You might experience energy storage shortages during cloudy or rainy days. There would be limited storage of solar energy.
4. Considering that this system requires ample sun exposure to work, energy efficiency can become an issue. You may not have enough energy to power your whole house.

Hybrid Solar Power System

This is underrated but a personal favorite. Hybrid solar systems make use of energy storage that is similar to an on-grid system but also has battery backups for the same. These systems have been becoming increasingly popular despite their high cost. One of the most attractive things embedded in this system is its reduction of energy wastage, as the

excess power is utilized to charge batteries, and stored for future use. During a shortfall, the same stored energy is used to strike a balance.

In short, a well-structured system provides dual benefits. For example, it reduces your electricity cost but also gives you the comfort of having a backup during power shortage. This system is expensive due to the added components in its structure compared to the other two solar power systems.

Advantages of Hybrid Solar Power System

1. Let's get this right: With this system you are not going to experience a complete blackout unlike your neighbors. If somehow the system produces excess energy that is not completely used by the house, it is stored within the battery of the system. Therefore, during no sun exposure, you will still have power. In fact, during a power outage your electricity will last from hours to a few days depending on your battery bank.
2. Even though, up front, the system looks expensive, having a battery can give additional opportunities to save money since you will make sure of the stored energy instead of using power from the grid.

Disadvantages of Hybrid Solar Power System

Regardless of its dualist impact that makes it outshine the other systems. There are certain downfalls that you should consider as well.

1. It is not budget friendly, that is not to say that it is not a great investment but, if you are in a budget crunch during the initial purchase then a hybrid system is not a suitable option. This is because of the additional components such as PV array, battery banks and an inverter. The batteries need to be changed regularly as well.
2. Hybrid solar power is a complex system therefore you would require an expert team to install the system. This would require additional cost.

There you have it— a detailed and unbiased account on all the three systems. Let's move forward to the operation of these systems, respectively.

This is the interesting part!

Fundamentals of On-Grid Systems

There are two basic modes of operation when it comes to on-grid systems. These operations depend on how much solar energy is generated, and what is the requirement of your house.

Mode 1: Surplus Solar Method

This mode ensures that any excess energy that is not used by the house appliances is transferred back to the grid. Thus, when there is more solar than needed, surplus solar (i.e., excess solar) is exported back to the

grid. This excess solar flows through your meter recording how many kWhs are exported to the grid. This in turn keeps a tally on the digital counters that you can revise from your meter's LCD (liquid crystal display).

Mode 2: Not enough solar

This method is used when your system is not generating enough solar energy to meet your house's needs. Thus, your switchboard imports electricity from the grid to balance the shortfall. This is managed by importing energy through your meter, after which, you are charged for the sum you imported.

However, this only measures your grid imports and not your total electricity consumption.

Components of Off-Grid Solar System

Even though the off-grid system is similar to an on-grid system, there are additional components that are required that you will need.

For instance, a battery inverter converts DC voltage into AC for your appliances. You will also need a battery bank, which is also called a feeder, to store excess energy produced that is not required by your appliances. This energy is stored and utilized during power shortages. Lastly, you will also need a generator for backup so that, when your batteries are drained or the sun is not out, you have access to power.

Basics of Hybrid Solar Power System

This system is configured to charge the batteries with any excess solar energy produced throughout the process. Is this efficient? Well, it is the cheapest form of energy you will get.

I understand that it sounds expensive and even looks extravagant, but it's convenient and resourceful. In fact, let me hint at an incentive— the excess solar energy can be sold to the grid which may earn you an income!! Furthermore, when there isn't enough energy to power your appliance, the battery inverter will do its best to provide power from the battery. Hybrid solar systems, and their batteries, are sized to get you through the nightfall but not through an avid power failure.

So, this begs the question: Which system do I buy? I can answer this shortly, but it is important to understand the reason why my answer is not an exact one.

My answer: Buy whatever suits you best. You would be wondering 'Well, this didn't help me much.' I know this is frustrating, but I can only compile the knowledge. I can make suggestions.

There are a few limitations when it comes to the residential and commercial use of solar systems. While location really has little impact on the installation and feasibility, there are certain factors you should consider.

For instance, rural residents can make the best out of the off-grid systems, as they have plenty of space to install a ground-mounted solar system.

Whereas urban residents should consider grid-tied or even hybrid solar systems. This is because hybrid or on-grid systems would already be connected to the power grid.

Since urban residents have small spaces such as their roofs, they will be unable to tap into the resource completely.

With the types of systems in mind, the next step is implementation. Getting started with implementing a system, however, requires you to take care of some finer things, especially when you need to identify your energy needs to implement the right system, and this is where things get interesting.

Let's take a look at how you can do your homework and plan for a solar power system installation...

Chapter 17

7 Considerations Before You Go Solar

I am sure by now you would have a comprehensive understanding of the basic principles of solar power systems. If yes, let's dive into the 7 important considerations that you take into account before going solar. Each of these considerations has its own importance. I personally panned through these points before designing and installing my solar power system, so I figured It would be helpful for you as well. These points also augment the process of planning and designing, thus drawing in depth from the sections mentioned in the Beginner's guide.

There are numerous steps one should follow when planning to utilize solar energy. After choosing the option of a solar power system that suits you best, you can follow these steps that apply to you. In fact, your solar energy installer and local utility company can provide more information on the steps required.
You must wonder, why are these steps even important?

Planning eases the process of installation. You are able to customize your power needs, and solar system sizes and understand the limitations of your property. It also allows you to have a comprehensive understanding of the relative estimations, monetary investment, and incentives offered by the government. Now that this is out of the way, let's start.

In summarization, the following are **7 points** to consider before you continue with your journey of solar power systems.

1) Investigate your home's energy efficiency
2) Assess your solar potential and any limitations
3) Assess your options for going solar
4) Estimate your solar electricity needs
5) Obtain bids and site assessments from contractors
6) Understand available financing and incentives
7) Work with your installer and utility to install the system and set up agreements

1. Investigate Your Home's Energy Efficiency

To begin with, investigating your home's energy is an important step to start with. Homeowners thinking of going solar should investigate their energy use. It is equally imperative that you consider potential efficiency upgrades, and low-cost and easy to implement efficiency measures before taking any big steps.

The energy efficiency assessment is divided into two aspects: home energy audit and professional energy audit. I know that you are wondering which one is more effective and better– let me ease your mind, they both are equally important.

Since an assessment can help you determine how much energy is required to power your house, the inefficient and problematic areas, and the fixes that deserve immediate attention. This will help you improve the comfort of your home. Therefore, a home assessment should come before the professional assessment, as well as before adding any renewable energy systems to your household.

Okay, so now that we've established that home assessment is important. You must be wondering how it works. And what do you have to do? Don't worry, I have a list waiting for you.

Now, it is important to understand that this process will not be as thorough as the professional assessment, but it can definitely help you locate some easy problematic areas.

Start with locating air leaks, these leaks can be traced back to drafts that can save up to 10%-20% energy per year. You can also check the baseboard or edge of the flooring, junctures of the walls and ceilings. There can be leakage through windows, plumbing fixtures and doors.

In order to preserve and reduce energy wastage, seal these leaks with appropriate materials. Additionally, during the sealing process back drafting can be dangerous in the ventilation process. It reduces indoor air pollution and minimizes back drafting.

Moreover, check for insulation levels. Insulate your house to reduce any loss of valuable energy. Sealing openings or penetrations such as electrical boxes in the ceiling with flexible caulk can be beneficial. Similarly, you can cover your entire attic floor with the recommended amount of insulation.

In addition to this, inspect your heating and cooling equipment. Replace any filters or furnaces that need to be updated. Furthermore, inspect the light bulbs in your house and consider replacing the inefficient ones with more effective, and energy-saving, brands of LED lights. These are a good way of conserving energy in your house.

Lastly, the appliances and electronics you use in your house also have an effect on your energy cost. It is important that you examine your electronics and estimate their energy consumption.

(Disclaimer! Please wear safety gloves and take necessary precautions before inspecting any electronic devices to protect yourself from any electric shock).

Afterward, you should consider strategies to reduce the use of energy by your appliances. For instance, unplug your items when not in use, purchase efficient products or utilize smart home energy management to control the energy usage of your devices.

Simultaneously, make a list of questions that will help you plan for your house energy consumption. DIY assessments of your energy consumption are a great way of doing home assessments before hiring professionals to accumulate an extensive understanding of the same.

Moving on, professional assessments are extensive and thorough. In order to achieve this, you will have to book a professional energy assessor. You will be required to extract the problems that you identified during the home assessment, and also photocopy bills, so that your assessor is able to review them and understand the issue.

I know I know, finding an assessor can be difficult. Here are some tools that you can use for the process.

- Contact your local weatherization office and ask them to help you identify a local company that performs energy audits.
- Contact your energy utility company and ask them to refer you to a local auditor to conduct a residential energy assessment.
- The Residential Energy Services Network provides a directory of certified professional energy assessors near you.
- Check out the U.S. Department of Energy's Home Energy Score program for assessors.
- Home Performance with Energy Star programs can also help you locate assessors nearby.

In fact, energy auditors will conduct a blower door test that locates air leaks. They will check the attics, basement, ceiling, and kitchen/bathrooms for any leaks, backdrafts, and loopholes.

Why is all of this important?

Well, the number 1 reason is that you are able to identify numerous energy-saving opportunities, which in turn, help you save more money. It reduces carbon footprints from your house, which eventually reduces the emission of greenhouse gasses. This assessment not only helps you save energy but also ensures that you are safe and healthy. You are also able to boost the energy efficiency of your house. In fact, it also increases your home resale value and improves the comfort of your living.

This is a lot to take in, I understand, but this information will only help you be more prepared. I promise I'll make this last bit shorter. I want to equip you with the best ways of conserving your energy and saving your

money. Being able to determine how much your appliance uses can help you understand, and later, reduce your monetary expenditure.

These are the following steps you can use to calculate your annual energy consumption:

- Estimate the number of hours your electronic device runs in a day. It can be a rough estimation but keep a log of it.
- Find the wattage of the product. You can do this by either looking for stamps on the product, or you can estimate it by finding the electrical current draw (in amperes) and multiplying that by the voltage used by the appliance. You can also make use of online sources.
- Find the daily energy consumption using the following formula: (Wattage × Hours Used Per Day) ÷ 1000 = Daily Kilowatt-hour (kWh) consumption
- Find the annual energy consumption using the following formula: Daily kWh consumption × number of days used per year =annual energy consumption
- Find the annual cost to run the appliance using the following formula: Annual energy consumption × utility rate per kWh = annual cost to run appliances.

Furthermore, lighting accounts for 15% of your energy consumption therefore using proper and efficient sources is an important factor. Consider shifting to LED sources to save energy and money. It is obvious, I too can relate to the difficult process of choosing appliances that are good for my house.

2. Assess your solar potential and limitations

What does solar rooftop potential even mean? Well, if you are asking for the entire country, it is the number of rooftops that are suitable for a solar power system. This is dependent on the size, shading, direction, and location of the rooftop. Rooftop potential does not consider the availability or the cost of installation, but rather the upper limit of solar deployment on rooftops.

The story suffers from a twist for an individual rooftop potential. The potential depends on the size, shading, title, location, and construction of the roof. In fact, there are added equipment such as satellite maps and irradiance data used to assist the customers in understanding the potential costs, and benefits, of installing solar panels.

Let me break it down for you– there are two types of potentials, namely, National rooftop potential and Individual rooftop potential.

National Rooftop Potential

As per the analysis of the National Renewable Energy Laboratory (NREL), 2016 it is estimated that over 8 million square meters of rooftops were available for solar panel installation in America, thereby, representing

one terawatt of potential solar capacity. It was, therefore, predicted that, with certain improvements, the national rooftop potential could be greater. Residential and other small rooftops represent about 65% of the national rooftop potential, and 42% of residential rooftops are households with low-to-moderate income. This explains the scope and potential of rooftops in the USA.

Individual Rooftop Potential

In order to estimate the number of solar panels that could be installed on a roof, American company SETO invested in various tools. These tools include:

- **EnergySage:** An awardee incubator

- **PVWATTS:** An online tool that estimates energy production. It is a great online calculating tool. The tool makes use of historical weather data to estimate how much power your solar panels will produce annually.

- **SUN NUMBER**: Gives numerical scores according to the solar suitability of the roof

- **Aurora Solar:** Incubator awardee developed a web base system that would calculate the solar potential of buildings

- **DGEN** (Distribution Generated Market Demand): Stimulates customer adoption

- **FOLSOM Labs:** Created a solar permit generator

- **National Solar Radiation Database**: Serially complete collection of hourly and half-hourly values of meteorological data and the three most common measurements of solar radiation: global horizontal, direct normal, and diffuse horizontal irradiance.

- **PVLIB:** software that allows users to simulate the performance of photovoltaic effect systems.

- **REEDS** (Regional Energy Deployment System): Simulates electricity sector investment decisions.

- **System Advisory Model:** It is a techno-economic software model that enables technical performance simulation and financial analysis of renewable energy projects.

Every home is different; therefore, you need to assess your solar potential and also identify your limitations.

Let me share a success story with you. The Sun Number Score was created through SETO's successful incubator program, which instantly determines a home's suitability for solar by rating it from 1 to 100.

So, how does it work? The technology that is used makes a detailed analysis of your roof thereby determining how much roof area is sustainable for the solar power system. This accounts for the pitch, orientation, size of each roof plane, and the amount of sunlight the roof receives based on surrounding obstructions like trees or taller buildings.

It is important to understand that the score range is easy and intuitive. However, there are factors to consider such as the local cost of electricity, lost cost of solar, local climate, and weather conditions. Moreover, the prominent feature of Zillow's home fact sheet is its accessibility hence it gives room to millions of Americans to explore information about the solar power system. It enables a new level of awareness that enunciates the importance of energy efficiency and the consumption of electricity. They also provide an easy-to-understand assessment of the solar potential for consumers who are not familiar with their house's potential to generate solar energy. Sun Number Scores was able to create awareness for this energy resource to the extent that 84 million people in America use Zillow, and over 110 million buildings in America have been scored on the Sun Number Scores website . It is important to understand the potential of your rooftop and how much power will be generated if you did install solar panels to ensure that you are able to align it with your household electricity needs.

3. Assess your options of going solar

Where to begin from? This entire point will be dedicated to helping you understand the scope, type of grid system suitable for your house, net-metering system, how solar power systems add value to houses, and information about solar leases as well.
So, without further ado, let's jump right into it.

As discussed in the previous chapter and the beginner's guide, selecting a solar power system that suits you best is the primary goal. Consequently, when opting for a grid-tied power system, there are some aspects you should consider.

Renewable energy systems such as solar power systems are more than capable of powering houses and small businesses without any connection to the utility grid. But many people prefer the connection due to certain advantages. One of the major advantages is the availability of power even when the sun's not shining. Thus, any excess energy produced that is not used by the appliances is fed back to the grid. In times of need, the grid supplies the energy back without any additional expenses.

How is the grid-connected to the power system? A simple answer would be that apart from the major components, you will be required to buy some additional equipment that will allow you safely transmit electricity to your appliances. This equipment includes:
- Power conditioning equipment

- Safety equipment
- Meters and instrumentation.

Are there any grid-connection requirements I should have from my power providers? There is a wide variation in the current requirements, especially when it comes to renewable energy systems. However, the main issue that is often detected, relates to the issue of connecting small renewable energy systems to the grid. The regulations usually encompass safety, power quality, contracts, metering, and rates.

What are the safety and power quality regulations? Well, power providers want to ensure that your system includes safety and power quality features. These features include switches and power conditioning equipment so that in an event of a power surge or failure you or the technicians are not electrocuted.

(If you are interested in further understanding the safety and quality issue, some organizations such as the Institute of Electrical and Electronics Engineers, and Underwriters Laboratories have devised certain national guidelines)

Are there any contractual issues related to Grid-connected systems? When you connect your small renewable energy system to the grid, you will be asked to sign an interconnection agreement with your power provider. This agreement will include the following points:

- You can be asked to pay fees and other charges such as permitting fees, engineering payments, metering charges, and stand-by charges.
- You will also be asked to carry liability insurance. In general, most homeowners carry $100,000 of liability through insurance policies.

What are the metering and rate arrangements? So, in a nutshell with a grid-connected power system, if you generate more energy than your net household needs, the excess electricity is used elsewhere. However, under Public Utility Regulatory Policy Act 1978 (PURPA), it is required by power providers to purchase the excess power from the energy owners at a rate equal to what would cost the provider as well. These rates are implemented through various metering systems such as:

- Net purchase and Sale: Installation of 2 uni-directional meters
- Net metering: Installation of a single bi-directional meter

Wait for a second! Net metering? What is that?? I know, it's a tricky concept. Let me elaborate and clear up your confusion.

In general, net metering is an agreement between the power provider and the homeowner that allows the owner to get credit for the solar energy they send into the grid. For instance, your solar panel generated more energy than was required by your appliance, that energy is supplied back to the grid and further transmitted to places where power is required. Thereafter you are compensated for that energy by the utility company, they do so by giving you credits which you can use to draw energy from them.

Additionally, through the concept of the feed-in tariff, your power-providing company installs two meters in your house— 1 to estimate your power usage and the other to estimate the power you generated. These are also considered incentives by the government to shift to renewable energy power sources, thus the utility pays a premium rate as an encouragement to the population. Let's say you bought power at a rate of $0.12/kWh, now you can sell the excess power at double the rate such as $0.25/kWh. Which can be considered a massive turnover.

What about net sales and purchases? This is the opposite in the feed-in tariff system. Even though the power provider installs two meters, they charge electricity at retail rates and buy the excess at a reduced wholesale rate; thus, only paying the avoided cost. Moreover, aggregated net metering, therefore, allows multiple meters to be installed on a property to be offset by a singular solar power system. Moreover, net metering also allows a single customer to offset multiple meters. Yet, virtual net metering plays a different stance, it allows multiple customers to participate in net metering with a shared solar power system.

What role is played by the time-of-use (TOU) rates? It is a simple concept, under the TOU policy, the power provider charges more during peak electricity hours. For example, peak periods can constitute afternoon timings when people are actively making use of the selectivity in schools, offices, and homes. Since the solar power system generates energy during off-peak hours the net metering calculations are affected by the TOU rates. In fact, the rate is lower, whereas if you were to switch on your light during the evening you would be billed at a higher rate. These consequential mandates that even if you generate enough energy to cover all your electricity needs, the utility company will still bill you. How can we stop this? Invest in an energy storage system that allows you to offset TOU.

Additionally, let us talk about restrictions and caps on your net metering policies.

Why do they exist? Easy, to level out the supply and demand of the energy, also to prevent people from taking the policies for granted and make profit moves.

I have enlisted certain restrictions for you to track:

- System size caps of either concrete limits or 125% of consumption.
- No room for outdated or inefficient technologies
- Timeframe implemented for the use of credits
- The difference in policies for different types of properties.
- Aside from solar these policies can be applied to biomass, geothermal and other renewable energy sources.

Moving forward, I will tell you how by installing solar panels you can add value to your property. In a recent study by Lawrence Berkeley National Laboratory, it was concluded that houses with solar panels have an increased value of $14,329 on average. In short, homes with solar power

systems sell for 3.74% more than regular homes. There is an evident boost in the resale value of PV houses (photovoltaic homes). Since an average power system cost around $10,000 to $18,000 in material, homeowners with power systems can easily remake their money when they sell their homes. On top of this, you can expect to save money from bills and take advantage of tax incentives.

In fact, I think you will be delighted when I tell you that in some states of America adding a $15,000 PV system exempts you from paying the property tax on it; however, this would not have been the case if you decided to add a new kitchen to your house. Subsequently, since most buyers are not concerned with the efficiency of the power system, it might make sense to install a small grid-tie system. This would help them make excess energy that they can use, and the house will be enlisted as a high-valued property. However, it would be relevant to mention that houses with solar power systems take longer to sell compared to regular houses.

While some states offer more attractive incentives for buying solar power homes, other states do not offer anything at all. Therefore, it is safe to say that solar homes with no incentives accompanying them can take longer to sell. For instance, in areas with lower electricity costs and no incentives to encourage solar adoption, awareness and purchasing are low. This is because buyers do not understand the complete scope of a PV house, they barely see it as a long-term investment. However, those who understand the scope and importance of a solar power system usually opt for new systems.

Consequently, new PV systems which are made from efficient material, generally have longer warranties and a low probability of replacement. As PV systems age, their value depreciates, I know it is a bummer. So, what can you do to maintain the value of your system? Newer installations can add value to your property.

This brings us to an important aspect of this journey. Should you have leased or owned solar power systems? Well, leasing a solar power system is often seen as a downgrade. Why? Solely because after you agree to a solar lease or PPA (Power Purchasing Agreement) you will not be able to see much of the high sale price returned to you as profit. In fact, let us say you want to sell your home now—the buyer would expect you to pay off your lease or PPA agreement which will offset the additional value of your house. So, in order to reap full benefits, an outright purchase is preferred. I personally would recommend investing in a solar power system instead of leasing it. Let me give you some perspective, a general sale price for homes in America is $431,964, however with an added solar system, this price ranges up to $899,000, doubling the final sale price of the house thereby doubling the investment. Simultaneously, in a report narrated by CNBC 80% of the buyers look for solar panels when hunting for homes. The two main drivers that ensure buyers opt for PV homes are:

1. The need to control overall energy cost

2. The need to save money
3. Great emphasis on green living

It is a contradictory statement but, states which provide ample incentives and encourage people to adopt a renewable energy source increase the rate of selling. Thus, houses with solar panels in such locations are sold 20% faster according to NREL compared to regular houses. This makes solar systems a great investment to include in your house before selling it. This proportionality states that the less time your home is on the market, the more money you can have through storage, transportation cost, and mortgage payment.

While we are at it, let us talk a little bit about whether a shared solar power system would be suitable or a community solar power system.

A community solar power system is defined by the U.S Department of Energy as a solar project or purchasing program, within the locality, through which benefits of a solar power system are equated by multiple clients. These systems depend on where a subscriber is located. Thus, community solar systems allow people who cannot put panels on their rooftops to benefit from the program. In areas where solar power generation is inexpensive, consumers can save money on utility bills.

Subsequently, SETO is a prominent community solar under the national community solar partnership, through which community solar stakeholders work to expand access to affordable solar power in American homes by 2025.

This is an argumentative aspect, should you or should you not lease your solar power system? While I personally do not recommend this, I want you to experience an unbiased pool of knowledge and decide on your own.

The main reason I disregard leasing solar systems is that they are not a viable option in terms of finances. In fact, you will have more money in the long run by exploring finance options like Title 1 loans or traditional loans from your bank. Here are the following reasons why leasing your solar power system can be a bad idea:

- You will not be able to own your system. It is owned by a third-party company and can be repossessed if you miss payments.
- You will not get to claim tax incentives, including the 30% federal solar tax credit. Those belong to the leasing company.
- You will get a much lower return on investment than you would if you chose to finance your system with a loan.

But—

There are downfalls to buying the solar system in the first go as well. Initially, solar installation is expensive. I can understand that not everyone has cash on hand to cover the larger sum of expenses procured by the system. Therefore, if you lease your system you will not have to pay upfront for the installation. Instead, the solar company will bear the installation cost and will own it as well.

Here are some advantages of leasing your solar power system instead of buying it:

1. Long term savings are an inevitable result. You will save money on your energy; however, taking out a solar loan can give you longer term savings than if you lease solar panels. With a leased system you are locked into monthly lease payment for the next 20 or more years therefore you spend more and save less.

2. You will save your money in the moment but, solar leases will not help you save 30% of the federal clean energy tax credit on the installation cost. This is because when you lease the solar panels, you have no ownership thus the installer instead of you gets the tax incentives and rebates. When you buy solar panels, you own them, so you will be able to take advantage of the federal tax credit, solar renewable energy credits (SRECs), plus other utility and state incentives.

3. Houses with solar power systems sell 20 times faster and make 17% more money. With a solar power system installed your house will have added value.

On a lease, monthly payments are not fixed instead they have a price escalator involved whereas, for a loan, fixed monthly payments are required.

The maintenance and monitoring of solar panels are your responsibility when you purchase them; however, if you lease the panel the company takes care of it. Either way, the good news is, solar panels are low maintenance.

Let us talk more about leasing solar panels. I know it is tempting, so I want you to make an informed decision.

I can understand that paying upfront can seem daunting, although with this option you will not have to pay any frontal costs, you won't also be able to save much money if you had bought the solar panels.

However, there are certain situations in which entering a solar lease would make a lot of sense–

Leasing a solar panel would be right for you if:

- You are not eligible for SRECs (discussed later)
- You cannot apply for the federal tax credit
- You do not qualify for a solar loan, and you also do not have the budget to purchase the whole system.

I almost thought of shifting to PPA or leasing my solar system because the idea of low costing is just so attractive. So, I understand that you would also want to consider the option. Let us explore the best solar financing options for your system.

Tip: You can get solar pricing quotes from multiple installers in your vicinity.

I know you would be wondering what a PPA is when I mentioned it earlier. Let me explain the concept briefly. A solar power purchase agreement is a financial contract where the solar developer creates the design, arranges the permit, financing, and installation altogether on your property with little to no cost.

How long is this contract for? A fast answer would be– 10 to 25 years, in fact the developer remains responsible for the operation and maintenance of the system throughout the validity of this agreement. Subsequently, by the end of the final tenure, the customer has three choices, you can either extend the PPA or remove the system to buy the solar energy system from the developer. Thus, you can have your own solar system, for which the installer will charge you a monthly fee depending on the power usage with no money down.

Are there advantages and disadvantages of solar leases and PPAs? Yes, there are certain pros and cons of solar leases and PPAs.
The Advantages of PPAs and Solar Leases are that:
- They allow you to go solar without a large amount of financing burden
- The installation company is usually responsible for the maintenance of the systems and its upkeep such as repairs and replacements (if any needed)

Now that the pros are out of the way let us consider some cons of solar leases or PPAs.
Disadvantages of opting for solar leases.
- If you lease your system, you will not be eligible to claim the 30% federal tax credit offered by your state. Tax credits can play a major role in your ROI and payback timelines.
- PPAs and Solar leases have yearly escalation clauses to protect installers or developers from losing money. These rates can increase 3-4% per year thus by the end of your tenure, you will be paying more than you originally signed for.
- In fact, these rates can increase about twice as fast as the cost of electricity. Even though your payments will start lower than your current electric bill, the gap between the rise and the bills will shrink.

So, what are you truly missing out on? Money. You are missing out on saving big bucks. However, initiatives such as SunShot have been collaborating with communities across the nation to kickstart the local solar market thereby reducing the cost of solar and making it easier and faster to install. They do so by solarizing campaigns which are local community efforts aimed to encourage businesses and households to go solar. It is solely your choice whether you would opt for a leased solar power system or if you would buy the system. However, whichever option you decide ensures that you understand the downsides of it all.

4. Estimate your Solar Electricity Needs

To begin with, let me remind you that I have talked on this matter specifically, in great detail in the Beginner's guide. However, let me give you a quick recap.

How to calculate watts, amperes, and volts

I understand that you are aware of the fact that the bigger the solar system the easier it is to collect sunlight and generate electricity. Subsequently, the power consumption of appliances is usually stated in Watts. In order to calculate the energy your appliances will require; you will have to multiply the power consumption by the hours of use.
To illustrate:
Let us say the power consumption of your appliance is 20 Watts and you make use of these appliances for 4 hours equals

20 x 4 = 80 Watt

In order to convert Amperes to Watts, you can make use of the following formula:

Watts = Amps x Volts

Why is this important? You can make use of this formula when your device does not have Watts labeled on it, such that it should have the input volts and Amps AC mentioned.

Furthermore, in order to calculate your required rate of solar energy you will have to divide your average hourly wattage by the number of daily peak sunlight hours in your area.

Hourly Wattage / Sunlight peak hours

This therefore gives you the amount of energy that your panels are required to produce.

It sounds like an extensive process but, it really is not if you are able to do it the right way.

I have dealt with this specific point comprehensively in the beginner's guide. Check it out for more details.

5. Obtain bids and site assessments from contractors

It is important to obtain site assessments from contractors for solar panel installation. There are certain solar energy companies that offer comprehensive and detailed installation services that are responsive and rapid.

I have made a list of companies that are the best in the industry:
- SunPower: Most Energy-Efficient
- ADT Solar: Best Protection
- Momentum Solar: Most User-Friendly
- Blue Raven Solar: Best Benefits
- Green Home Systems: Best Solar Roofing Options

- Elevation: Best for Whole-Home Integration
- Trinity Solar: Most Experienced
- Sunrun: Best Financing Options
- Tesla: Best Availability
- Palmetto Solar: Best Customer Service

Each company has something to offer therefore in order to choose the one that suits you best, compare them with each other. For example, Sun Power offers nationwide availability and a 25-year all-inclusive warranty; on the contrary, ADT Solar is only available in 21 states. These types of comparisons are a great way to analyze which company you gravitate more towards.

Solar reviews of Solar Companies QR code.

Do I really need to hire a contractor to install my solar power system, or can I DIY it? This is an interesting question, and a good one in fact. Let me break this aspect down to you with a Q&A session.

What does it mean by DIY solar installation?

Let me simplify the concept, when you hire a solar company to install your system; they have control over the location and layout of the system. Do-it-yourself solar installations can give you complete independence when it comes to installing your own systems. However, you will be required to do careful research and become fully involved in the process.

That sounds exhausting, I know right! But it is the cheapest option. You will be designing the system, gaining permits, and assembling the parts of the system by yourself. Fear not, you can find numerous DIY solar resources on the internet which can function as your guide, in fact the whole process is much more manageable than you think.

Then what is contract installation?

It is all in the name. You hire a contractor to do your solar installation for you. However, the key difference is price. You will have to pay them, but the contractor will manage some of the more difficult aspects of the job such as design or the installation altogether. Instead of assembly or seeking permits, you will manage jobs that you are comfortable with, the rest will be left to specialized contractors such as roofers and electricians.

What is a turnkey installation?

Money is important. I understand that the goal is to save as much as possible given that solar systems themselves are not cheap either. Turnkey installation is full service at a premium price point. This option is suitable for someone who has a larger budget at their disposal. These installers manage all the areas of the projects, which include:

- Designing the system
- Sourcing the parts
- Obtaining permits

- Installing to local building codes
- Assisting in filing for incentives

What solar installation is best for me?

I understand that extracting the most value out of your solar system is your top priority right now. If you are on a budget and do not have the time to learn how to install the solar system yourself, answer these series of questions which can help determine which solar installation option suits you best:

Do you have a flexible budget?

1. I do— then do not DIY it. If you have a flexible budget consider a turnkey provider that can provide you with high-quality and professional installation.
2. I do not— DIY it. If you are on a tight budget consider going DIY or using a local contractor to cut down on prices.

Do you have time to commit to a DIY project?

1. Yes? If you do have time to learn the processes, DIY installation sounds like a natural fit for you. However, if you have limited time but want to be involved in some of the designing process then hire a contractor that gives you this much room.
2. No? If you do not have the time or the resources, hire a turnkey contractor that offers you hand-off installations. This might cost you more, but it will be a more convenient option.

Do you want to be in on the installation process?

1. Yes! If you want to have full control over the installation process or are eager to learn how to install a solar system then DIY is the best option for you. Moreover, you can also hire a contractor you will be able to pick designs and help customize your system
2. No! Turnkey is the best option for you. You will have your system entirely installed and processed by experts. You will have full-service installation, and also will be able to access brands that have exclusive distribution channels.

Do you have any experience with home improvement or electric work?

[DISCLAIMER: PLEASE TAKE CAUTION WHILE WORKING WITH ELECTRICAL WIRES]

1. Yes, I do. DIY is the best option for you since you have accomplished home improvement projects. You can also hire a local contractor that can help you install the system.
2. No, I do not. Then I suggest you hire a turnkey contractor with experts working on your system,

Now that the types are out of the way let us talk about the pros and cons of solar installation types. It is good practice that you compare each approach with the other. This helps you make an informed decision.

- DIY Installation

This installation approach is the cheapest. If you are looking to have some hands-on project and learn how to install a solar system let me tell you the pros and cons of a DIY installation option:

Pros:
- You can maximize savings by avoiding labor costs and provider services.
- You will be able to select more brands and components than you would with turnkey.
- You will get hands-on experience to understand the ins and outs of your solar system.

Cons:
- You need to be physically capable and committed to doing the work.
- Some jurisdictions require a certified solar installer, meaning you may not have DIY as an option.
- You will not have a service warranty that you'd get from hiring someone else to do the job.

If you do not have the time to install the system all by yourself, consider hiring a contractor that can do the physical work or manage the technicalities of the process. In fact, this option is cheaper than the full-service providers (turnkey). The pros and cons of hiring a contractor includes:

Pros:
- You can balance savings and convenience.
- Local installers charge less than full-service providers.
- You can choose the brands and components you like.
- You will have a professional contractor for the details, like ensuring the system is code compliant.

Cons:
- It will cost you more than a DIY install.
- It requires more research. You will need to shop for a system and compare contractor bids.
- You will spend a lot of time facilitating communication between all parties involved.

If affordability is not an issue, then the smartest option for you would be to connect with a turnkey provider and arrange a complete package. Let us look at some pros and cons of turnkey providers:

Pros:
- It is quick and convenient, especially if you have limited time or don't want day-to-day involvement.
- They will design your system and install it for you. Easy.
- You can gain access to solar brands that are available exclusively through a distributor.

Cons:
- Full-service installation is the most expensive option.
- Although you may have exclusive access to certain brands, you will be limited in choices. Many turnkey installers have a single panel brand that they sell to customers.

How Much Does Solar Installation Cost?

There are multiple variables to consider when you are seeking out the best solar installation solution. Factor in not only the cost of solar panels but also the added expense for professional installation and other materials.

Learning how to install a solar system may be the cheapest route, but it may not be the most practical. Here are the average costs of DIY, contractor, and turnkey installations I collected that you could refer to when choosing for yourself:

DIY Installation Costs

Let me give you some perspective, suppose if you are buying a 6-killowar power system, on an average, it would cost you around $10,000 to cover the cost. Even if you do not pay labor, you will have to pay additional expenses which will include A/C wiring, breakers, electrical fittings, etc. thereby costing to another $500. Moreover, your permit will range around $200, depending on your local permit rates.

Now, the total cost is $10,700 before federal tax credit, which gives you 30% refunds on your taxes. So, with a 30% off your total cost would be $7,490, thus making this approach the cheapest of the three.

Independent Contractor Costs

On the flip side, you can buy the equipment, and then hire a local contractor to install the system for you. I know, shouldn't I hire an expert? I asked myself the same question— you do not need a solar certified installer, but you do need to hire a professional and experienced contractor.

Let us build on the same perspective, using the same 6kw system you will pay the contractor $1 per watt, making a total of $6000 for the whole installation. The total cost for solar installation through a contractor would be $16,000 and after the 30% tax credit it would be reduced down to $11,200.

Turnkey Costs

This is a complete solar package, which includes design, installation, and purchase of equipment therefore the demand is high. It is a convenient option if you are not on a budget and do not have time for self-installation.

To put this in perspective for you, I will use the same example. Let us say you bought a 6kw system. Since turnkey providers charge 100-200% of the equipment cost for installation your system might range from $10,000-

$20,000 more. Thus, a turnkey provider would charge $3.59 per watt making a total of $21,000 for installation. This would make a total of $14,700 with 30% tax credit.

Lastly, let us discuss the types of panels that will work best for installation. Although we will discuss this aspect in more detail later, I want to give you a brief overview.

There are three types of solar panels namely, polycrystalline, monocrystalline, and thin film. Your choice of solar panels depends on your budget and installation needs that are specific to your property.

Polycrystalline panels cost less and are less efficient, therefore they can help you save money if you have a lot of space. However, if you have limited space and you want to minimize your electricity bills, you should opt for monocrystalline solar panels. Whereas thin-film panels should be your choice if you want to install panels on a large and commercial roof as they are cost-efficient.

Now, moving to the most interesting bit of these seven points. Government incentives and rebates on solar power panels.

6. Understand Available Finances and Governmental Incentives

Let us open with how the government incentivizes solar power installation. While the cost of solar power installation has been reduced significantly, it is still a large investment. Yet, in order to promote the adoption of solar power systems, companies, federal, state, and local governments provide certain incentives. The following are incentive provisions:

- Investment tax credits
- State tax credits
- Cash rebates
- Solar renewable energy credits (SRECs)
- Performance-based initiatives
- Subsidized loans
- Tax exemptions

I know you are a little confused, some of these terms are hard to grasp, or at least they were for me when I was researching this aspect of solar power installation. So, for your convenience, I will expand on each of these incentives.

- Investment tax credits, also known as the federal investment tax credit, are by far the best incentive available in the market. When you make use of ITC you are able to get 30% payback on solar against the taxes you paid.
- State tax credits are a bonus over ITCs, even though they vary in amount; aligned with ITC, the markup makes an enormous difference.

- Cash rebates are a form of buying discount that are given to customers on purchases. Cash rebates are offered by companies as up-front payments for installing a solar panel system.
- An SREC is a standard set in many states by official machineries to indicate that utility companies make a certain percentage of their electricity from solar panels. Therefore, these companies buy excess energy generated from your solar panels at a particular rate which is later paid to you.
- PBIs are a little different from SRECs as these are recorded during the installation of the panel, and the energy produced is not sold in the market. PBI pays you according to your per- kilowatt hour credit for the electricity that you produce.
- You will be able to purchase a solar power system through a subsidized solar loan which would enable a reduced interest rate. These loans are available for a temporary period of time thus they are offered by the state, NGOs or even your utility company. It would be wise to search for these loans prior to your purchase.
- To spice it up a bit! Tax exemptions are a thing. So, even though with the installation of a solar power system the value of your property increases the actual tax rate is unbothered.
- Other than rebates, low interest loans which are below the market rates are also available for renewable energy sources. These loans are available on the market to encourage people to invest in highly efficient solar panels.

However, it is important that I mention; you will not be able to maximize any of these incentives if you lease or PPA your solar systems. In fact, you can use —

Solar Panel Rebates QR Code

And figure out solar incentive programs available in your state.

What is a federal tax credit? And why is it important?

Good question.

Let me break this aspect in parts for you.

1. What is a tax credit? A tax credit is a dollar-to-dollar cash reduction in your income tax that you would otherwise owe to the government. A federal tax credit is often referred to as ITC.
2. What is the federal solar tax? The federal solar energy tax credit is a tax credit that can be claimed on federal income taxes for a percentage of the stated cost of the solar (PV) system.
3. What are the eligibility criteria for this credit?
    - Your system was installed between 2006-2023
    - The system is located at your primary or secondary residency in the USA

- You have bought the system. It should not be leased or under a PPA
- The credit is relevant only to the original installation

4. What expenses are included? The expenses include solar PV panels to power attic fans. Furthermore, it includes contractor labor costs for installation and preparation, the balance of system equipment, energy storage devices that are charged, and sales tax on eligible expenses.

5. How do other incentives affect my federal tax credit?
   - The utility rebate for installing solar is subtracted from your system costs before you calculate your tax credit.
   - SERCs payments will be considered taxable income thereby increasing your net gross income; however, it will not affect the federal tax credit.
   - Unlike utility rebates, state rebates do not affect your federal tax credits.
   - Even though state tax credit does not reduce your federal tax credit, you will have a higher taxable income to report on your federal tax which would otherwise have been since you now have less state income to deduct from.

6. Can I claim the credit, assuming I meet all requirements, if:
   - I am not a homeowner? Yes, you do not necessarily need to own a home to claim tax credit.
   - I installed the system on my vacation home in the USA. Yes, as mentioned earlier the installation can be in a primary or secondary residence within the USA.
   - I am not connected to a grid. Yes, a connection to the grid is not necessary.
   - The panels are on my property just not on my roof? Yes, they can be installed anywhere.
   - I've a home office (my residence is also used for commercial purposes) Yes, but given your situation, claiming the credit can be a complicated process.
   - I have financed my solar system instead of buying it up front. Yes, if you have financed through the seller you are obligated to pay the full cost of the system.
   - I have bought the panels but have not installed them. No, the tax credit is given on panels in service.
   - I participate in an off-site community solar program? The answer is dependent on your circumstance. , this can qualify for the tax credits.

7. Other questions that might be on your mind—
   - If the tax credit exceeds my tax liability, will I get a refund? This is a non-refundable tax.

- Can I use my tax credits against the alternative minimum tax? Yes, It can be used against either the federal income tax or alternative minimum tax.
- I bought a house in 2020 but didn't move in until 2021. Can I claim the tax credit of the already installed PV systems? Yes, you can
- How do I claim the federal solar tax credit? After receiving professional tax advice and ensuring that you are eligible for the credit, you will have to attach and complete IRS Form 5695 of your federal tax return.

Now that the essentials are out of the way, let us focus on what and whys. Investment Credit Tax (ICT) also known as federal solar tax credit allows you to deduct 30% of the cost of installing a solar system from your federal taxes. Let me feed your curiosity about how much you can save on the solar power system through ICTs.

- What is the federal solar investment tax credit? The ITC was originally established by the Energy Policy Act of 2005 and was set to expire at the end of 2007. It is a 30% tax credit for people who are installing solar systems on residential properties.
- How does the solar tax credit work? You are able to receive solar credit if you have a solar panel installed in your house. Even if you do not have enough tax liability you can roll over the remaining credits in future years. However, you need to be eligible for tax credit.
- Are you eligible for the tax credit?
  - System installed between 2006-2034
  - System installed on your primary or secondary residence in the USA
  - For an off-site community solar project, the electricity generated is credited against, and does not exceed, your home's electricity consumption
  - You have owned or financed the solar system. It is not leased or PPA
  - Your solar PV system is new or being used for the first time
- What is covered by the tax credit? Refer to the point above
- When and how can you claim the tax credit? You can claim the credit when you meet the eligibility criteria. You can make this claim when you file your yearly federal tax return

What if I choose to DIY my solar installation? Are there any incentives for that?

Yes, you can take help from the Database of State Incentives for Renewable Energy DSIRE. This is the website QR Code everyone visits to get an updated list of incentives available for people who want to install solar panels themselves. The categorization may be a little confusing but, for instance, states under the category of DIY-friendly give financial aid to individuals such as rebates and buy-downs on local utilities.

On the contrary, states under the category of DIY-unfriendly enable policies that prevent individuals from installing their panels from a DIY approach. Additionally, under the category of non-substantial incentives, there are few or meager statewide incentives that are operative on the entire DIY approach to installing solar systems in your homes.

I am sure you can hear that little voice that stirs at the back of your mind, making you doubt your decision 'is solar energy a good investment?.' Do not worry I heard that one too. It is important to look at the bigger picture, solar energy will cost you less than what your utility provider charges you.

Let me put this in perspective for you through some math. For the sake of this discussion, the utility company bills you for an average of 12 cents per kilowatts hour for your electricity usage.
(A kWh is a measurement of how much electricity you have used. Check your bill find how much electricity you consumed each month)

Moving forward, let us say you used 1,000 kWh in the month of August, that's 1,000 x 0.12 = $120 per month, which would become $1440 per year.

Now let's see how it is done through solar. A solar system would generate 7.8 kW energy which would be listed for $9,791, which would cover 100% of your household energy usage. Subsequently, the federal tax takes 30% off the purchase price thereby reducing the price to $6,853.70 for the equipment. This would help you save $1440 every year that you would have spent paying utilities otherwise. Lastly, the panels have a 25-year warranty which can pay back investments over 4 or 5 times. So, the borderline is, that solar energy is not just good for the environment, in fact, it is also a financially sound option.

If you are interested in calculating your own return on investment (ROI), use these formulas.
[Enter System Cost $, Enter Cost of Electricity, Enter yearly usage, Include 30% Federal Tax Credit]
The manual formula is as followed;

(Total System Cost – Value of Incentives) ÷ Cost of Electricity ÷ Annual Electricity Usage = Payback Period

In the very last of it all, let's talk about how you should finance your solar panel system. You have three options, lease, loan or buy the solar system. When you buy the solar system you are able to own it and reap the recurring benefits in the shape of incentives. When you lease the solar system, after everything is paid you will find that you paid the leasing company more than you intended. Similarly, when you loan the system you pay off the loan with your other existing debts. In a realistic aspect, loaning and leasing the system is not economically viable; however, they are good options regardless of their disadvantages. At the end of the day, you need to decide what suits you best.

7. Work with your installer and utility to install the system and set up agreements.

Let's summarize everything.

- How does solar work? So, in reality PV cells are the most popular way to harness and maximize the sun's power into electricity. This involves installing a panel on your rooftop or in a field where the sun can hit the panel, inciting photons from the light to be absorbed by the cells in the panel. Thereby, creating an electric field across the layers and enabling the flow of electricity.
- Is my property suitable for solar panels? While this has a detailed answer, I will keep it short and simple for you here. Solar panels are designed to work in any climate; however, what should concern you is whether or not your rooftop is suitable for the solar power system. You should be able to detect any corresponding factors such as shade from a tree or age of the rooftop. Additionally, the size, shape and slope of your rooftop should also be considered before making any installations. An ideal roof would be facing south with a 15- and 40-degree slope.
- Where do I start from? Start from the basics. Investigate your electricity needs, look for leakages then move towards understanding the scope and size of your rooftop for any installation.
- Can I DIY it? Yes, you can! It is a great way to install your own solar power system. It is also one of the cheapest ways to install the system other than hiring a local contractor or a turnkey team which would even though get you premium offers, it will not be budget friendly.
- How much power will be generated? It varies from system to system therefore NREL has developed a tool called PVWatts to estimate the energy production and cost of energy of your PV system.
- Will I save money on solar? Yes, you can save from taxes and utility bills.
- Can I get loans? Yes you can. Financing solar power innovation has fueled the formal growth of the solar market. There are two categories based on the ownership of the solar power system namely, 3rd party ownership in which developers or installers own the system and homeowner ownership via a loan.
- Any incentives available? Yes, many. Tax credits, SERCs and rebates offered locally and nationally are some of the incentives offered to solar power customers. Furthermore, installation companies arrange for installation of the system and also provide financing for them.
- Will it impact the value of my home? Yes it will. In a recent study it was reported that solar panel upgrades cause home buyers across the country to pay a premium markup for a home with even a mediocre system. Additionally, there is evidence homes with solar panels sell faster than those without.

- I have heard a lot about solar plus storage. What is that and do I need it? Excess solar energy is stored in batteries. These batteries help when you are experiencing a power shortage, thus your solar system can use the stored energy to generate power.
- Is solar safe? Absolutely! All solar panels meet international inspection and testing standards, and a qualified installer will install them to meet local building, fire, and electrical codes.
- What are the environmental benefits of solar? This way of generating energy minimizes the carbon footprint. It also reduces pollution such as air and water which would in turn mean that we have a cleaner eco-system.
- How can I detect if a company is misrepresenting itself? No one should feel they are being taken advantage of while pursuing clean energy. At the federal level, you can contact the Federal Trade Commission to report fraud, scams, and bad business practices. At the state level, laws vary depending on where you live.

In a nutshell, hiring a company to install a solar power system is one thing, but if you're going the DIY route, you need to make sure of the above, along with the components that you need to gather before you get started.

Installing a solar power system at your home is not an impossible task but is a long game.

In the beginner's guide you can learn more about designing and installing a system, especially the 6-step process of building an off-grid solar power system, but there is one thing that takes the cake from the whole process: the major components of a solar powered system, which are:

- Solar panels
- Batteries
- Charge Controllers
- Inverters
- Monitoring systems
- Racking systems
- Wiring components

And this is where confusion ensues.

Which solar panel should you get? What are the types of batteries you might need? Which controller is better, and when should you use one? These are but a tip of the proverbial iceberg of doubts. But that does not mean you should keep scratching your head. Let's explore each of these components in detail, and see how you can get the best item for your needs...

Chapter 18

Your Harvesting Necessity – Solar Panels

As we know by now, solar energy begins with the sun. Solar panels are used to convert light from the sun, which is composed of particles of energy called "photons", into electricity that can be used to power electrical loads (20).

Solar panels can be used for a wide variety of applications including remote power systems for cabins, telecommunications equipment, remote sensing, and of course for the production of electricity by residential and commercial solar electric systems.

So, now let's explore how solar panels are made and how they function.

Solar cells are made primarily from silicon, a chemical element with conductive properties. Exposure to light changes silicon's electrical characteristics, which generates an electric current. These panels are made up of several individual solar cells which are layers of silicon, phosphorus, and boron. Let's do a Q&A session to further understand the basics of solar panels.

How long do solar panels last?

This is a common question. I'll give you a short and sweet answer; 25 years. Most manufacturers guarantee under their warranty plans that their panels will last you for 25 years with 80% efficiency.

In fact, after the warranty years, the panels don't break; they continue to work under a reduced efficiency. For instance, a panel rated at 300 watts would still work at a rate of 240 watts at the 25-year mark.

Here's a statistic to prove it– according to NREL's study, 75% of panels outperform their warranty lives. However, other parts of the solar power system such as batteries and inverters have a shorter lifespan. For example, lead-acid batteries typically last for 3-7 years whereas Lithium batteries will last you for 10-15 years.

How big are solar panels?

Panels come in two standard sizes: 60-cell or 72-cell.

You must be wondering 'what is this configuration?' I know. It was mind boggling for me as well. So, let me outline the measurements for you. In a 60-cell panel the dimensions measure as 39" by 65", whereas in a 72-cell panel the dimensions are 39" by 77". From a realistic point of view, these measurements can vary; however, the main configurations remain the same.

What are the types of solar panels on the market?

There are two cell technologies that have a monopoly in the market: monocrystalline and polycrystalline solar cells.

In a brief account, mono cells are derived from a single source of silicon, whereas the poly cells have two different types of silicones used. Since the composition of the poly cells is not pure, compared to the single cell the panels are often less efficient. Additionally, there are several other emerging technologies such as thin film and bifacial panels.

How is solar panel efficiency measured?

The efficiency of solar panels plays an important role in the whole installation aspect. Yet, the concept is misunderstood. In reality, these panels have an efficiency rating of 15-25%, it's low if you take it for its face value but that's not the whole picture.

The rating is measured by what is the sun's potential energy and how much is converted into solar power. For example, a 100-watt panel with a 20% efficiency would absorb 20% of the potential 500 watts of constant power from the sun. In fact, the most efficient panels are the ones that fit more solar in less space.

Let's move to the types of solar panels. There are three major types namely, monocrystalline, polycrystalline, and thin film. While each of these panels have their unique advantages and disadvantages, the panel best suited for your installation depends on your property and desired system features. In fact, each of these panels have a different price range depending on factors such as efficiency and material.

What type of solar panel is best?

- Crystalline solar panels have the highest efficiency out of all panels.
- Monocrystalline panels are between 15-20% efficient, making them the most efficient of all crystalline panels
- Polycrystalline panels are between 15-17% efficient and can be the most cost-effective option.
- Thin film solar panels are best for unorthodox roof styles and are the most resilient.

Monocrystalline solar panels: the most expensive

The reason why mono cell panels are the most expensive option is due to their manufacturing process. Manufacturers make use of the Czochralski process which is energy-intensive with a resultant wastage of silicon. Since the manufacturers include the cost of the waste silicon the price tags are usually towards the higher end.

Polycrystalline solar panels: middle of the road

Poly solar panels are usually cheaper compared to their single cell counterparts. This is mainly due to the fact that polycrystalline solar panels are made from two different types of silicon crystals. This is a simpler manufacturing process therefore it costs lower for the users and the creators.

Thin-film solar panels: it depends!

So, for thin film panels there are two outcomes. If you choose the CdTe option it is the cheapest type of solar panels whereas CIGS are more expensive. In fact, installing a thin film solar panel is less industrious because they are lighter and maneuverable which reduces labor cost and eventually the overall cost of installation.

What are solar panels made out of?

These panels are made out of semiconducting material that converts sunlight into electricity. The most common conductor used is silicon.

What are thin-film solar panels made out of?

This is a good question. Thin film panels unlike mono or poly are made from numerous materials. The most common type of film panel is made from cadmium telluride (CdTe). Further, amorphous silicon is also used to manufacture these panels; however, they are not made up of solid wafers. Instead, they're composed of non-crystalline silicon on top of glass, plastic, or metal. Lastly, thin film panels are also made from Copper Indium Gallium Selenide (CIGS) which has 4 elements placed between two conductive layers of either glass, plastic, aluminum or steel and electrodes placed at the front and back of the material. This is the most expensive type of thin film panel.

What do different solar panel types look like?

The difference in material types and production forces the appearance of the panel to be different for each type:

Monocrystalline are the most efficient options. They are panels with black cells, the cells are black because of how light engages with pure silicon.

Polycrystalline is the most cost effective. It appears to have a bluish hue due to the light reflecting off the silicon fragment.

Thin-film panels are much thinner than the other two panels. The frames can be up to 50mm thick and lie close to the surface of the roof.

I understand that it's a confusing process. Let's explore the scope and features of solar panels so that you can decide which one suits you best.

First, we'll discuss the types of solar panels available in the market. There are essentially 4 major types of solar panels namely.

- Monocrystalline solar panels
- Polycrystalline solar panels
- Passivated Emitter and Rear Cell (PERC) panels
- Thin-film solar panels

So, Monocrystalline solar panels which are also known as single-crystal panels are developed from single pure silicon crystal which are cut into several wafers. Since this panel makes use of pure silicon it is the most space-efficient and long lasting amongst the other panels. However, due to the 50% wastage of excess product the panel is usually the most expensive.

On the contrary, Polycrystalline solar panels are made from different silicon crystals instead of a single crystal. The panel is developed with silicon fragments melted and poured into a square mold. In comparison to the monocrystalline panels, polycrystalline solar panels are more affordable since there is hardly any wastage. However, this makes the panels less efficient in terms of space and energy conversion. Moreover, they have a lower heat tolerance, thus they have a lower efficiency in high temperate spaces.

Furthermore, Passivated Emitter and Rear Cell (PERC) panels can be considered as modified versions of a traditional monocrystalline cell. This new and improved version of the cell adds a passivation layer in the rear of the panel that enhances its efficiency in numerous ways. For instance, it reflects light back into the cell, increasing the amount of solar radiation that gets absorbed. It also reduces the natural tendency of electrons to recombine, and it permits greater wavelengths of light to be reflected.

Thin-film solar panels

The thin-film panels are distinguished by exquisite layers that are adequately meager to be adaptable. Each board doesn't need an edge backing, making them lighter and simpler to operate with. Unlike crystalline silicon boards that come in normal sizes of 60, 72, and 96-cell counts, thin film boards can come in various sizes to suit explicit necessities. In any case, they are less productive than ordinary silicon solar panels.

Thin-Film Solar Panel Variations

These films are made up of various materials unlike the crystalline ones. Those materials conclude:

- Cadmium telluride (CdTe)
- Undefined silicon (a-Si)
- Copper indium gallium selenide (CIGS)

Solar Panel Types by Efficiency

Crystalline solar panels obtain the highest efficiency amongst all types of panels.

- Monocrystalline boards have a productivity ratio more than 20%.
- PERC boards acquire a 5% more productivity because of their passivation layer.
- Polycrystalline boards drift somewhere close to 15-17%.

Interestingly, slim film boards are typically 2-3% less proficient than translucent silicone. All things considered:

- CIGS boards have a productivity scope of 13-15%.
- CdTe ranges between 9-11%.
- The most minimal effectiveness is obtained by a-Si at 6-8%

What is the best type of solar panel for your home?

Monocrystalline solar panels are the best solar panel type for residential solar installations. Despite the fact that you will be following through on a somewhat greater expense, you'll get a framework with an unpretentious appearance without forfeiting execution or solidness. Additionally, the high proficiency and power yield evaluations you get with monocrystalline boards can furnish you with better investment funds over the lifetime of your framework.

In the event that you're on a strict financial plan, polycrystalline boards could seem well-versed for you. We don't suggest slim film sunlight powered chargers for private establishments; their presentation and sturdiness don't make the minimal expense worth the effort.

Factors to consider besides solar panel type

The main interesting point, while going sun powered, is the installer. Solar panel framework will be on your rooftop for no less than 25 years, so you want an installer you can trust for two or more years! I suggest neighborhood, legitimate solar panel installers with high client survey scores as they give the most customized client care on sun-oriented projects.

At the point when I began my excursion to go sun induced panel, purchasing sunlight powered chargers that fit my style was very hard. Thus, I made this little purchasing guide that you can use to comprehend what kind of board suits you best. I have broken every one of the viewpoints in questions that you could have-

Coming to the best solar panel available?
What are the best solar panels available?

Remembering the effectiveness, item guarantee, toughness, sticker cost and temperature the following are the most ideal that anyone could hope to find on the lookout.

- **LG:** **Best compared to all.**
- **SunPower:** **Generally Proficient**
- **Panasonic:** **Best Temperature Coefficient**
- **Silfab:** **Best Guarantee**
- **Canadian Sun based:** **Generally Reasonable**
- **Trina Sunlight based:** **Best Worth**
- **Q Cells:** **Shoppers Number one**
- **Mission Sunlight based:** **Best Little Maker**
- **REC Solar:** **Generally Dependable**
- **Windy Nation:** **Best for Reinforcement Power**

These solar panels are characterized are evaluated through various elements. These accumulate:

- **guarantee which ought to go from 10-25 years,**
- **effectiveness which ought to be more than 20%, strength,**
- **sticker cost and temperature coefficient.**

What are the elements that we should look for while buying a solar panel?

It ought to be proficient. This will be one of the vital drivers in setting aside cash from bills and recovering productive edges in your speculations. In fact, any board with 17-20% proficiency is respectable, and an industry standard. Sun power's boards have the most elevated rate all through the business, remaining at 22.7%.

What are the best solar panels available?

Remembering the effectiveness, item guarantee, toughness, sticker cost and temperature the executives, following are the most ideal that anyone could hope to find on the lookout.

- **LG:** **Best compared to all.**
- **SunPower:** **Generally Proficient**
- **Panasonic:** **Best Temperature Coefficient**
- **Silfab:** **Best Guarantee**
- **Canadian Sun based:** **Generally Reasonable**
- **Trina Sunlight based:** **Best Worth**
- **Q Cells:** **Shoppers Number one**
- **Mission Sunlight based:** **Best Little Maker**
- **REC Solar:** **Generally Dependable**
- **Windy Nation:** **Best for Reinforcement Power**

There are, as mentioned, three types of the solar panels, recalling. Monocrystalline, Polycrystalline and Thin-Film. I realize you would maintain that I should let you know which kind of board is the best for you, however I would believe you should choose this for yourself. Allude to this diagram here for more assistance-

Monocrystalline	1. Most expensive 2. Proficiency over 19% 3. Best choice for rooftops.
Polycrystalline	1. Moderately expensive 2. Typical proficiency for 15%-17% 3. Better for abundant places.
Thin - Film	1. Least expensive 2. Proficiency below 15% 3. Best for large and commercial rooftops

Keeping in mind all of these types, there are promising elements that can influence the presentation of the respective panels. The variables which incorporate; direction of the sun powered charger, climate and sun openness, neatness, and shade. In the event that the direction of the sun powered charger isn't precise, with the daylight raising a ruckus around town, the presentation of the board will be brought down. This is something very similar with the openness to the sun and the accessibility of shade, one way or the other the exhibition will be upset. At last, it is an individualistic choice. For certain mortgage holders, going sun-oriented checks out, and for others it's unfruitful. Toward the end, it is for you to choose.

Making it very interesting for you, there can be many elements that can be considered when we are choosing the most perfect panel. The types of panels are loaded with shifting productivity appraisals, guarantees, costs, and other execution specs, making it hard to know precisely which ones are an ideal best for you. Here is a rundown of the factors we use to look at the best solar panels:

1.   Efficiency
2.   Temperature coefficient
3.   Warranty

With everything taken into account, there is definitely not an undaunted rule on the number of sun powered chargers your home will that expect to perform at top proficiency, however the more modest your house is, the less boards you will actually want to introduce — simply ensure they're transformation productivity is premium, to make out really well.

Let's talk about manufactures for a minute.

Below is a list of all the solar power manufacturers that have a monopoly in the market.

LONGi Solar	China	12 years
Tongwei Solar	China	10 years
JA Solar	China	12 years
Aiko Solar	China	10 years
Trina Solar	China	25 years
Jinko Solar	China	10 years
Canadian Solar	Canada	25 years
Zhongli	China	12 years
Suntech	China	12 years
First Solar	USA	30 years

Initially, the idea of solar power systems was given birth in the USA. However, even though the USA created solar panels, there are only 2 leading companies that manufacture panels within the USA– Tesla and Sunrun. On the contrary, China has now become the largest producer of solar panels worldwide. In fact, in 2017 the market of the USA reached a 51% mark; however, in 2019 it declined to a 27% which indicated that new countries started producing and installing solar panels at an increased rate.

Let's move on to understanding how to measure the power of solar panels. For this purpose, you will need a digital multimeter which will measure the voltage and ampere being generated by the panels.

How can you measure the power output of your PV solar panel? In order to calculate the power output, you need to multiply the voltage by the current at the maximum power condition. Use the equation: **$P = V \times I$**

Let's talk about sizing your solar system. It's a daunting process I can understand, so let me help you with the basics. Before you begin to size your system, you would want to determine if there are any constraints on the projects that could limit your design. There are three ways you can approach your project:

- Budget Limitations: Have a target budget.
- Space Limitations: Develop a system that is space efficient.
- Energy offset: Build a system that offsets a certain percentage of your energy usage.

Further, other sizing factors include:

- Orientation of the array
- Level of the sun exposure
- Plans for future expansion
- Performance of the panel and the warranty limit
- Efficiency ratings.

To calculate how many solar panels you need, these are the following points you need to know:

1.   Your average energy requirements, which you can determine by looking at your past utility bills. You can calculate this by multiplying your hourly energy requirement with the peak hours of sunlight, and then divide it with the panel's wattage.
2.   Your current energy use in watts can be determined by searching for your average usage. (Look for KiloWatt Hours used on your bills)
3.   The climate and amount of sunlight in your area has a direct impact on the amount of energy produced in your household.

Now, multiply the hourly usage by 1000 in order to convert the hourly power generation needed to watts. Afterwards, divide the average hourly wattage requirement by the number of daily sunlight hours. This will give you the amount of energy that your panels will need to produce to meet your energy needs.

4.   The efficiency of the solar panels you're considering
5.   The physical size of the solar panels you're considering

I have made a detailed account of the same sizing techniques in the beginner's guide. In the beginner's guide I also discuss the solar panel installation thus one of the major aspects of this is the maintenance of the solar panels.

We know that solar panels are low maintenance, thus, they do not require much attention. However, if you sense that your panel's energy output has started to decrease, you can always monitor the system through an app. By integrating a solar panel monitoring system during your setups, you can track the energy output of your panels regularly. In fact, it is recommended that you clean your panels twice or four times in a year to ensure that there is no debris or dust stuck in them. For this purpose, you will need the following:

- A leaf blower
- A simple, quick rinse with a hose of water
- Or even light rain can wash away panel build-up (rain usually won't clean off flat panels)

For removing a heavy layer of snow:

- Throw a soft football to shake the snow loose (this could end up in a lost football)
- Use a leaf blower
- Use a long pole with a squeegee at the end
- Spray your panels with lukewarm water

Moreover, When it comes to maintenance, the only real difference between ground-mounted solar systems and rooftop solar systems is that ground panels are easier to access, and therefore easier to keep clean. It is true that solar panels can withstand extreme weather, however, it doesn't mean that they are indestructible, just that they have a better standpoint.

If you want to replace or repair your panels, hire a professional. In fact, ensure that during the installation of your panels you should have a warranty as well to protect yourself from losing money if the performance of your panels decreases. It is also advised that you clean your panels every 6 months, especially if you are located towards the highway, or close to a construction site.

I have dealt with the aspect of maintaining and cleaning solar power panels in detail as well in the Beginner's guide. Maintaining and cleaning a panel can be tricky which is why I devised this little guide to help you with the basics. Solar panels are the most crucial part of the entire system therefore they require extra attention. However, as you must have realized, the solar panels need to be mounted. So, let's take a look at the two available options in the next chapter.

Chapter 19

Panel Racking 101

Installation has multiple aspects to it when it comes to solar panels. Determining the correct mount for your panel can make all the difference. There are mainly two roads that can go down: ground mounts and roof mounts. So, what's best for you?

Given the obvious cost benefit that comes with roof mounts, since you've already got the support beams to hold the mounting hardware right, there's also money saved in terms of materials and manpower required because you're not really in need of a structure to hold the panels themselves. They're your best option, provided you don't have an overly crowded roof.

On the off chance your rooftop isn't one that can accommodate solar panels, you've got to take ground mounts. So really all you need to figure out is if you really want to spend the money for the ground piping. At least on the bright side, they're easy to access and maintain.

What are pole mounts? Are they worth it?

If you're wondering about the early Christmas snow blocking your panels. A pole mount is your best bet. They're basically elongated poles that keep your solar array at a higher position than traditional ground mounts. These poles can be adjusted to steeper angles which prevents snow from accumulating and lets it roll off giving your array extra clearance.

Trackers are also considered mounts. Trackers are mounts that automatically follow the sun's position in the sky to maximize the production from your panels.
Does it sound like a great idea? Sure!
Should you buy one? Almost never, no.

The reason is simple: tracking hardware costs more than the solar panels themselves! If you need more production, just add a few more panels to your array—it's far more cost-effective.

The one exception is large commercial or industrial projects. The hardware gets cheaper on a very large scale, and commercial projects

sometimes don't have the land available to reach 100% energy offset. Solar trackers may make sense in this particular scenario, but they certainly aren't right for most customers.

This is true regardless of the type of solar system you're considering: When it is able to receive as much sunlight as possible, every solar array performs at its best.

Systems mounted on the ground can be oriented in any direction. Your system can be positioned so that it faces the sun directly at the right angle. Ground-mounted systems are the most effective because they provide maximum access to the sunlight that powers the array.

If you have enough space in your yard, you won't be restricted in this way if you go ground-mount. After the initial installation, your array can be expanded, and many ground mount racking options make it simple to bolt on new components. Accessibility is yet another significant advantage of ground-mounted solar. Especially during the installation phase, solar systems require a lot of trial and error. Every time you need to fix a problem with your system, you have to climb up on the roof, which is a pain.

On the other hand, installing a ground mount is a lot more difficult and requires more money upfront.

Roof mount may be the best option for you if your primary concern is maximizing your solar panel investment's return. A ground-mount system will take longer to get approved. Additionally, it will occupy more space on your property, which you might prefer to put to better use elsewhere.

Many of these costs are avoided by roof-mounted systems. If your roof is in good condition and doesn't have any structural damage, it should be strong enough to handle the solar array's weight. You won't have to deal with the hassle of building a new foundation to support the panels.

Due to the fact that the system is regarded as a brand-new structure, the municipality or county in which you reside may also have a greater say in the installation process. A building permit must be obtained at the Authority Holding Jurisdiction (AHJ), depending on where you live.

The fact that ground-mounted solar takes up a lot of space on your property is the final disadvantage. A system will be more discrete if you mount it on your roof.

When installing a roof mount, think about the following:

The effect that solar energy might have on the warranty on your roof's age and condition. The shingles on your roof have a 25- to 30-year warranty.

Many people who are thinking about making an investment in solar power have two choices.

Advantages of a ground mount:

1. The system can be easily accessed for maintenance. Carports can be installed in existing parking lots, providing shade, lighting, and protection for parked cars. Ground mounts can be installed to face any

direction and in almost any location, positioning them for optimal energy production.

2. Typically, the cost of installation is higher, restricts land use, occupies large areas, makes it easier for unauthorized visitors to get in, increases the likelihood of accidental damage from rocks or other particles thrown by a mower or other equipment, and more.

3. Installing a fence will likely cost more because it will likely require mowing around multiple posts and under low clearances. The strategy for the land in the long run.

The terrain of your property Solar systems that are installed on the ground or on the roof are viable options. In the end, you have to pick the option that best suits your particular needs. A roof mount is probably going to be the best and cheapest choice if you have a lot of unshaded roof space. A ground mount or carport might be a good choice if you have limited roof space but still want to take advantage of Solar's financial and environmental advantages.

What is racking and mounting for solar panels?

Equipment that holds solar panels in place includes solar panel mounts and racks. To ensure maximum solar energy production, mounting permits the panels to be adjusted for optimal tilt based on latitude, seasons, or even the time of day.

The cost will be determined by the type of racking you select, the quantity of required equipment, and labor costs associated with installation. Heavy-duty equipment known as mounting brackets are typically constructed of stainless steel or aluminum.

Regardless of whether they are intended for the ground or the roof, all solar racking and mounting products must adhere to stringent standards to guarantee their long-term viability and structural integrity in order to withstand severe weather and high winds.

In order for you to have a better understanding of the structure that will hold your solar panels up, we will then take you through the primary components that make up racking equipment.

Which parts of a racking system are most crucial?

There are three main components to solar panel racking equipment. Attachments for the roof, clamps for the modules, and mounting rails are all essential to the structure's support of your solar panels and help you get the most out of them.

Furthermore, sloped rooftop solar panels are frequently used in residential solar installations. For these angled roofs, there are numerous mounting system options, the most common of which are railed, rail- less, and shared rail.

Large, flat rooftops, like those of big-box stores or manufacturing facilities, are frequently used for commercial and industrial solar

applications. Although these roofs may still tilt slightly, it is not nearly as much as on sloped residential roofs. Most ballasted solar mounting systems for flat roofs has few penetrations. Flat roof mounting systems can be installed relatively quickly and benefit from pre-assembly because they are positioned on a large, level surface.

The Spanish roof is the tile roof with solar panels that costs the most to install. This is due to the fact that while the installers are working, they will inevitably step on some tiles and break them.

Although the pieces of wood used to build a roof are frequently brittle, wood shake is a stylish and decorative option. When putting in solar panels, care needs to be taken. Despite this, the solar panel mount installation is actually quite straightforward. In order to secure the panels, the panel installer will locate them beneath a layer of shake roof. Installing solar panels is a breeze on a metal

Moving on, let's discuss how you can ground mount your home.

As mentioned before, ground mounting solar panels are installed on a ground level. However, there are 3 specific things you should know about ground mounting;

1.   Ground mounting can be the best option for you if your household consumption is greater than you expected. While rooftop mounting is preferred by many homeowners, if you want to produce more electricity go for ground mounting.

2.   There is a distinction between the ground mounting systems such that standard ground mounting systems are made from metal framing whereas pole ground mounting systems are driven from multiple solar panels. The pole ground mounting system has a tracking system attached to it as well.

3.   Ground mounted solar panels are beneficial for all homeowners. To summarize, ground mounting solar systems are relatively expensive because they require more labor and equipment for installation. Moreover, they might be a little more efficient compared to the rooftop systems. This does not mean that they are in any way better but logically, the ground receives more sunlight which can help in the generation of more energy. In fact, the cool breeze helps in keeping the temperature of the system cooler compared to that on the roof.

In conclusion, ground mounting systems are a great option for those going solar, much like you or me but at the end of the day it is a subjective decision. Moving further we will discuss the most essential part of the solar power system– batteries. Let's go.

Chapter 20

Best of the Batteries

Batteries are an essential component of the solar power system. The main question is, does your system need a battery extension or not?
Off-grid systems require batteries, whereas grid-tied systems can use them if they so choose. There must be a way to store the power generated by the panels in every solar energy system. You can basically use the utility grid as a huge battery by feeding that energy into grid-tie systems.

If you sign a net metering agreement, the utility will credit you for any contributions you make, and you will be able to use those credits to get power whenever you need it. Grid-tie systems operate without the need for batteries because the grid serves as an energy storage system.

However, off-grid systems are different. You will need batteries to store your own power if you do not have access to the grid. Due to the inclusion of batteries, off-grid systems are significantly more expensive, but they can still be a cost-effective alternative to running power lines to a remote property.

How do grid-tie systems function with batteries?

Batteries aren't necessary for grid-tie systems but adding them has its advantages. In the event that the grid goes down, backup power is the main benefit.

Grid-tie systems lack power outage protection by default. The system must be set up to shut down when grid power goes out because it is connected to the grid. While working on the grid, utility workers should not come into contact with live wires because of this safety precaution.

In fact, your system can keep the lights on during a power outage by adding energy storage, which stores a small amount of backup power in a local battery bank. Batteries offer additional advantages. They can, for instance, store power temporarily and then resell it to the utility at higher time-of-use rates, ensuring that you sell power at peak rates.

You might wonder if there are any different kinds of batteries on the market. The kind of battery you want and what you want to get the most out of your battery are two things to keep in mind.

In order to assist you in selecting the appropriate battery backup for your solar panel system, I have broken down the most widely used energy storage technologies. As a result, there are four primary types of solar batteries:

Lead Acid: In the solar battery industry, lead acid batteries are the tried-and-true technology. Since the 1800s, deep-cycle batteries have been utilized as energy storage devices. Additionally, their dependability has enabled them to remain.

Ionized lithium batteries: The newest addition to the field of energy storage is lithium-ion batteries. Manufacturers of electric vehicles discovered lithium ion's potential as an energy storage solution as the popularity of electric vehicles began to rise.

Batteries based on nickel: The use of nickel cadmium (Ni-Cd) batteries is less common than that of lead acid or lithium-ion batteries. Ni-Cd batteries first appeared in the late 1800s, but in the 1980s, they were given a makeover that significantly increased the amount of energy they could store. They are favored by the aviation industry.

Battery Flow: In the field of energy storage, a recently developed technology is flow batteries. They circulate between two distinct battery chambers, or tanks, and contain an electrolyte liquid based on water.

The next step would be to decide which kind of battery is best for you. In most cases, a lithium-ion battery is the best one for a home solar installation.

Why is that so?

Well, they can store more energy in a smaller space, release most of the energy they have stored, and have high efficiency. A lot of solar companies will also be able to install a lithium-ion solar battery safely and accurately because these are the most common types.

However, lead-acid batteries might be your best option if you're on a tight budget. They are inexpensive and have been used for decades. Even though you could pair a flow battery or a Ni-Cd battery with your solar system, lithium ion and lead acid batteries are the most popular. Interestingly, batteries are used differently. Batteries store electricity produced by direct current (DC) solar panels. However, our homes and businesses are powered by alternating current (AC) electricity. This implies that the electricity generated by your solar panels or battery will need to be flipped from DC to AC in order for you to use it .

I am aware that you must have a million questions, I know I did when I decided to go solar, it's pretty natural. So, in terms of storage capacities, this is an intriguing aspect of the solar power systems. However, I always respond that a high-quality home battery can be a good choice for any homeowner looking to get the most out of their PV system, and this is one of the most frequently asked questions.

In fact, there are three good reasons not to use a solar battery that works for everyone:

1. The technology used by the battery is rarely mentioned. The majority of one-size-fits-all batteries store energy using lead-acid technology. This is not the most advanced technology available.

2. Despite their size and bulk, these batteries frequently lack power storage capacity. The power capacity is rarely justified by the cost.

3. Most of the time, these standard solar batteries are either too big or too small. The small batteries cannot meet the demand for power. However, especially during the winter, the large batteries are not always fully charged.

Additionally, the rating of a battery is expressed in amp-hours, or amps. Typically, the battery's fully developed capacity is represented by the indicated power rating. This indicates that the battery may require tens to hundreds of charging cycles before it can reach the stated maximum capacity. To put it another way, testing your battery after only a few charges can be misleading.

Why is a solar panel battery bank so important? Before discussing the best solar batteries, let's discuss the significance of energy storage.

How does solar power operate?

You will have a collection of solar panels installed on your roof if you decide to go solar. If you don't already know, solar panels take energy from the sun and turn it into electricity. An inverter converts this direct current (DC) electricity into alternating current (AC), which is the kind of electricity we use in our homes.

Any excess energy generated by your solar energy system is fed back into the grid because most home solar panel systems are connected to local power grid systems. You may be eligible to receive credits for this excess energy if your utility company has a net metering program. On the other hand, you will use energy from the grid if your solar system does not produce enough energy to power your home at any given time.

What role do batteries play then? A solar energy storage system known as a "solar battery bank" will store the energy generated by your system rather than returning it to the grid, allowing you to use it later. Then, you can use the energy reserves in your solar battery bank when your unit isn't producing any energy, like after dark or on cloudy days.

Battery options and solar panels are becoming essential for people living in outage-prone regions like the Southeast and West Coast as more and more extreme weather exposes our infrastructure's weaknesses.

How significant is your electrical load?

Your property's electrical load may have two distinct effects on your monthly utility bills: First, if you are on a demand charge rate, the

maximum amount of power you use from the grid in a single hour each month is used to calculate your monthly bill. As a result, figuring out how much electricity each appliance uses can help you figure out how much your demand charge will be at the end of the month.

In addition, knowing how much power each appliance needs can help you cut down on your demand charge by letting you know which appliances should not be turned on simultaneously. You can reduce your maximum monthly power requirement and save money on your demand-based electric bill by carefully planning.

Second, and more crucially for the majority of homeowners in the country, the amount of energy required to run an appliance is directly proportional to the amount of energy consumed, which ultimately affects your electricity bill. You can also save money on your electricity bill by learning which power-hungry appliances play a significant role in your monthly electricity consumption.

Lead Acid Sizing 10kWh x 2 (for 50% depth of discharge) x 1.2 (inefficiency factor) = 24kWh

Lithium Sizing 10kWh x 1.2 (for 80% depth of discharge) x 1.05 (inefficiency factor) = 12.6kWh

For better comprehension, let's compare the batteries.

Lead-acid

Tried and tested, lead-acid batteries are the standard for electrical energy storage. These were the only practical batteries that could be used to store electricity for home or business use up until five years ago.

Advantages of lead-acid batteries

1. The primary advantage of lead-acid batteries is their affordability. Because they are less expensive to buy than a power mains grid extension, they are frequently installed in rural and remote areas.
2. Lead-acid batteries are deep-cycle batteries, meaning that they can output steadily over a long period. Their rate of discharge is constant. There are sealed and flooded versions of these batteries. They are both based on the same idea.

Cons of lead-acid batteries

1. At first glance, lead-acid batteries are uninteresting because they are heavy, bulky, and unappealing.
2. They must be installed in a climate-controlled shed because they take up a lot of space and the temperature at which they work is below room temperature.

Lithium-ion

Lithium-ion batteries are gaining popularity as the preferred power storage option for manufacturers of electric vehicles. Although there is still a long way to go, the prospects for lithium-ion as a medium for storing energy are encouraging. Lithium-ion batteries come in two varieties on the market.

The first type, known as NMC (nickel-manganese-cobalt), is the one that electric vehicle manufacturers use the most.

The second battery is of the LiFePO 4 (lithium iron phosphate) variety.

Pros of lithium-ion batteries

1.   Lithium-ion batteries require little to no upkeep. Their battery energy density is higher. This indicates that a lead-acid battery of the same physical size can store less energy than a lithium-ion battery.

2.   They have longer lifespans and a deeper discharge depth due to their longer life cycles. The Lithium-ion battery has a lifespan of up to 15 years and can run between 4,000 and 6,000 cycles at a depth of 80%.

Cons of lithium-ion batteries

1.   The most significant drawback of lithium-ion batteries is their high cost. They are twice as expensive as lead-acid batteries with the same capacity for storing energy.

2.   In contrast to lead-acid batteries, these batteries are also extremely fragile and require a stabilizing circuit for safe operation.

The flow battery

They are also known as redox flow and are a newcomer to the solar battery market. In order to store electrical charge, these batteries make use of vanadium and a solution of zinc, bromine, and water. Currently, only a few companies produce this battery.

Pros of flow batteries

1.   Flow batteries are extremely scalable. This indicates that the battery's outputs and capacity can be altered in proportion to its size. In contrast to the other batteries on this list, deep discharge has no effect on the battery's performance or lifespan.

2.   They have a very low rate of self-discharge and a lengthy life cycle. The fact that flow batteries do not heat up when used is also noteworthy.

Cons of flow batteries

1.   The cost of the fluids used to make them is too high. Despite the fact that the technology they rely on has been around for decades, few commercially available manufacturers make these batteries.

2.   The chemistry of flow batteries makes them heavy. Additionally toxic and highly corrosive, the battery's zinc and bromine components.

Sodium-nickel-chloride

The lithium-ion battery faces stiff competition from the sodium-nickel-chloride battery. The chemistry of this energy storage is one of a kind, making it completely recyclable.

Advantages of sodium-nickel-chloride batteries

1.   The sodium-nickel-chloride battery is dependable and secure. Even at extreme temperatures of -4°F to 140°F, it can function effectively.

Because they contain no harmful or toxic chemicals, the batteries can be recycled in their entirety.

Cons of sodium-nickel chloride batteries:
1. They only have a depth of discharge of 80% and a limited lifespan of about 3,000 cycles. As a result, it can't use more than 20% of the power it stores.
2. Installation of these batteries is also quite expensive, especially for large projects and residential solar systems.

What factors impact solar battery system sizing?

No matter what you would want to get out of your solar storage system, there are some universal factors that will always have an impact on how many batteries you should purchase for your system. These factors majorly include the electricity loads, size, and ability of your PV panels and what do you expect out of a storage system.

Size and production of your solar panel system

In order to charge up a battery with electricity, you will either need to take from the grid or charge the battery from the solar electricity. Even though, if you are looking to save money or build up the resilience of your house, charging your battery with solar energy is a great option.

Various factors impact upon how much a house a battery can stack potential power for, when we deliberate about the amount of a house that can be driven by the latter, the two fundamental variables to consider are: Amount of power that is needed and what amount of power that your respective battery generate, with power estimated in kilowatts (kW) or amps (A).

1. The respective circuits and electric accessories you need to save.

Power appraisals are provided by the batteries in kW and current evaluations in amps, so the lucky chance is if you can contemplate the electric draw or current prerequisites
of various appliances. By detecting every apparatus, you can compute the power necessities for the support of your home.

2. Instantaneous and Continuous power rating of your battery.

The two key measurements to be checked out are the instantaneous power and continuous power. Instantaneous power decides whether you can give an additional flood of electric power to the respective appliances that need it. Continuous power addresses how much power (in kilowatts) that your battery can give consistently.

Elements determining the run time of how long a house can be powered by a battery.

The functional capacity of storage of the battery and the respective appliances you are utilizing, and their time span are the essential elements

to consider when you are deciding about how long you can operate your house with a battery.

Step1: The amp-hour calculation:

1. Inverter size

For the decision of the size of the inverter, we need to determine the pinnacle load or the greatest wattage of any house. This is invested on the basis of including the wattage of the appliances and gadgets that could be run simultaneously. Incorporate all that from microwaves and lights to PCs and clocks. The aggregate will let you know which inverter size you want.

Example: A room has two 60-watt light bulbs and a 300-watt desktop computer. The inverter size is 60 x 2 + 300 = 420 watts

2. Daily energy use

Next, find the energy used in a day. Figure out how long each electronic device will be run in hours during a day. Multiply the wattage of each device by its run-time to get the energy in watt-hours per day. Add up all the watt-hour values to get a total for your home. This estimate is likely too low as there will be efficiency losses.

3. Autonomy Days:

Afterwards, conclude the number of days' worth energy you need to store in your battery bank. For the most part this is somewhere in the range of two to five days.

4. Capacity of the battery bank:

At last, we can ascertain the lowest battery AH limit. Pick the watt-hours out of every day and duplicate them by the number you chose in 3. This ought to address a half profundity of release on your batteries. Subsequently increase by 2 and convert the kwh result in amp hours (AH). This is finished by separating by the voltage of the battery.

Step2: The Batteries shouldn't be overcharged!

Once the battery bank and the array of the solar panel are measured, figuring out which charge regulator to utilize is relatively straightforward. We should simply track down the power through the regulator by utilizing power = voltage x current.

Step3: Battery Wiring

Prior to purchasing your batteries, you really have to sort out the number you actually would need. Wiring will assume a significant part in deciding this number. The objective is to find a design that produces target AH and voltage. Mentioned are the two strategies for wiring parts in a circuit: equal and series. Simply recall:

Series → voltage adds, current does not

Parallel → current adds, voltage does not

The intention is not to confuse you, however, are you familiar with a battery enclosure? If not, relax, I created a rundown of significant inquiries

that you can use to get a superior comprehension of what a nook is, and why you really want one.

• What is meant by the Battery Enclosure?

A container intended to shield batteries from likely climate and battery disasters is a battery enclosure. They can be intended for indoor or outside use and may incorporate space for gadgets. Explicit plans consider post, wall, or ground mounted frameworks.

• Why Do I Need One?

The battery enclosures are the fundamental parts of off-work solar system groups for various reasons including actual assurance from outside components including individuals and weather conditions, keeping up with reliable temperatures, and meeting the necessities of the Public Electrical Makers Affiliation (NEMA) .

• **The right type for you?**

The sort of battery enclosure configuration is different given the application and prerequisites of the venture. The elements and capabilities vary contingent upon the area and necessities of the framework. In general context, all battery enclosures ought to be vented.

• **SOP (Side of Pole), Indoor and Outdoor**

1. **Indoor:** Indoor enclosures aren't necessarily confined to complex designs. Majorly, they primarily only need to save things from falling onto the battery, so typically a Nema 1 rating is fine.

2. **Outdoor:** Outdoor enclosures should be rated Nema 3R to save the intrusion of the water from falling into the enclosure.

3. **SOP:** More modest battery enclosures can be mounted on a post or a wall. Bigger ground enclosures fenced in areas typically have no cutoff points.

Furthermore, are you wondering what a battery bank is? No worries, I have got you!

A battery bank ought to be measured (as a base) to a limit of 5 days of burden. Energy use in most home power frameworks increments over the long run, so consider measuring bigger than that.

There are various techniques you can use to protect your battery. For example, in flooded battery establishments, erosion of terminals and links is a monstrous disturbance that causes opposition and expected dangers. When erosion gets hold, it is difficult to stop.

The good news is this is easy to prevent! So, you can apply a non-hardening sealant to the metal areas of the terminals before you assemble the parts. If you apply a sealant after assembly it will not be able to reach every junction thereby inviting corrosion to occur instantaneously. Afterwards, completely coat the battery terminals, wire lugs and the nuts and bolts of the system individually.

How can you clean your batteries?

Since battery terminals need to be cleaned regularly, try using a mixture of baking soda and distilled water with a terminal cleaner brush. Furthermore, rinse the terminals with normal water, ensure all the connections attached are tight and coated with a commercial sealant or high temperature grease. **Important: Open the negative clamp first.**

Let me create a distinction for you between FLA and VRLA batteries.

Solar batteries should be maintained, but there are also some differing requirements depending on what type of batteries you have, whether they are a gel, AGM, or flooded battery. Let's point out some of these differences.

FLA BATTERIES (FLOODED)

The most significant difference between FLA and VRLA batteries is that they need to be refilled. Let's explore the specific guidelines of maintaining flooded lead acid batteries.

- In order to charge the FLA batteries properly, you need two things
  1. Appropriate charger
  2. Charge program
- You can refill FLA batteries using distill water

Disclaimer; Do not touch the electrolyte. Also, do not use seawater to refill these batteries.

- In order to orient FLA batteries, make sure you never store them on their side. Instead, they need to be stored in a very well-ventilated area.

VRLA (GEL AND AGM)

One of the major advantages of using VRLA batteries unlike FLA batteries is that you will not be required to put in extra effort in terms of refilling. In fact, you cannot measure the charge with a hydrometer. Let's see the specific guidelines that are associated with maintaining a VRLA battery.

- Since the charging voltage of AGM batteries is precise therefore it must be maintained if you want it to have a decent life span. If your battery has a high voltage and it heats up, release hydrogen gas then it will be permanently damaged.
- A VRLA battery does not need refilling as much as a FLA battery. They are not designed to go through the cycle of maintenance.
- When you orient your VRLA batteries, it gives to more flexibility in terms of storage which makes these batteries extremely versatile.

In a nutshell, solar power batteries are tricky to manage; however, if you have ample information and the right amount of guidance you can figure it out. Now that was a lot.

But now that we're talking about batteries, it's important to make sure that we also look at charge controllers...

Chapter 21

Taking Charge with Controllers

A solar charge controller is an essential component of a solar power system that uses batteries. It is used for charging batteries effectively and safely. What exactly is a charge controller? I know it's a perplexing concept, to some it might even sound daunting. Your apprehensions are valid, but a charge controller is a basic regulator of voltage.

So, what is a solar charger controller? Like I mentioned earlier it is a voltage regulator which keeps the batteries from overcharging. It effectively regulates the voltage and current that is supplied from the solar panel to the battery. In fact, most *12-volt* panels are able to put out an estimated voltage of either 16 or 20 volts. The numbers may look miniscule to you but any voltage over *12 volts* can severely damage your batteries therefore regulating this voltage is necessary. Most batteries usually need 14 to 14.5 volts to get completely charged

It also stops the reverse flow of power, which can be draining and damaging to the battery bank. You must be wondering where exactly these controllers are used? Usually, they are used where batteries are involved. This might be in:

- An off-grid system
- A grid-tied battery backup system

As a matter of fact, controllers can tell you how much power your solar panel has generated, how much you have used and how much power is stored in your batteries.

This begs the question; will you always need a controller? Not really, but usually. The concept is to release any built-up charge that may damage your battery, reduce its efficiency, or cause any trouble in your power flow. Generally, there is no need for a charge controller with small charge panels such as 1-5 watts panels. The rule is that if your panel puts out about 2 watts or less for each 50-battery amp-hours, you do not need a controller.

I can sense an obvious question here; 'Why aren't panels just made to put out 12 volts?' I understand this frustration. With the advancement of technology, we want to be equipped with the latest tech resources all compiled under one unit. There is nothing so wrong about wondering why this hasn't been the case yet. It's simple logic, if our batteries were to let's

say put out 12 volts altogether, they would be required to function in a completely perfect environment (cool, and full sun), which is relatively harder to maintain. Thus, the panel provides some extra voltage to cope during cloudy or humid weather changes. It is due to this reason, a 12-volt battery produces 16-20 volts, which is put out by the controller to whatever your battery needs at that time.

Obviously, charger controllers come in all shapes and sizes. There are certain types of controllers that you need to be aware about. They are as follows:

1. **Simple 1 or 2 stage controls:** These rely on relays or shunt transistors to discharge any excess voltage that might circuit through the battery. They usually disconnect the solar panel from the main power supply when a certain voltage is procured. The main reason why people gravitate towards this old technology is due to its reliability.

2. **3-stage and/or PWM:** These pretty much set the standard in the industry, but you will probably see some of the older stunt controllers, specifically in cheaper systems that are offered by discounters and mass marketers.

3. **Maximum power point tracking (MPPT):** Do you want to save a considerable amount of money on larger systems? Well, MPPTs are your best friend. These are the showstoppers in the category of controllers; despite their high price range they offer efficiency in the 94% to 98% range. They also provide 30% more power to the battery.

This strings the question– how can we neutralize a battery bank? Meaning, how can we bring all the cells in the bank to the same charge? Equalize.

If you have some cells in the string lower than others, equalizing the battery will bring them to their full capacity. Simultaneously, in flooded batteries it serves an important function. Through equalizing the liquid in the batteries are stirred by causing gas bubbles. In many off-grid systems, a battery can be equalized by using a generator and charger together.

Moreover, some controllers have an element called LOAD or LVD output. This is essentially used for smaller loads such as lights and phones. The main advantage of this LVD output is that these terminals have lower voltage disconnect. A LVD output is connected to a load terminal and thus keeps the battery from running down.

Disclaimer:
Do not use the LOAD output to run any but very small inverters. Inverters can have very high surge currents and may blow the controller.

So which controller is right for you? If you have a rooftop or ground mounted solar system with battery backup, you do not need a controller. This is because your excess energy will be re-routed to the electric grid.

However, if you have a small off-grid energy system it is advisable to have a PWM controller. This is especially for small batteries which carry 5-10 watts within the solar panels.

Yet, just to be sure; I decided to make a list of questions you must ask yourself before deciding which controller is the best for you, PWM or MPPT.

1.   What type of panels do you have?

Generally, off-grid panels are 36-cell panels developed to charge a 12V battery. These systems work well with PWM controllers. However, a 60-72 cell panel is typically used for an off-grid system with higher voltage which would require an MPPT controller.

2.   How big is your system?

Even though a PWM controller works for a system of any size, it is important for the voltage between the solar panel and home battery to match. Although the voltage does not typically match the solar system, adding a PWM is an ideal step. However, MPPT controllers are less efficient unless the array installed in your house is of 170 W.

3.   What temperatures can you expect?

PWM controllers are ideal for a warm temperature while MPPT works better in a cold temperature. As the temperature drops and the voltage increases, an MPPT control can effectively catch excess voltage. If the temperature does not get very low, MPPT controllers are not necessary.

4.   What is your budget for a controller?

In general, PWM controllers are less expensive thus they are considered to be cost effective. PWM controllers are more versatile, easily installed but less efficient. However, MPPT controllers are more expensive, this is due to their high charging efficiency, such that an MPPT controller can reach up to 20% functioning efficiency which is in turn due to the 4-stage charging method used to keep your battery life at a healthier standard.

So, it's either PWM or MPPT right? What's next!? I think at this point you would be hit by a string of confusion due to the excessive information. That's okay, let me clear some facts for you.

MPPT Controllers–

As you know from the definition of an MPPT mentioned above, it is a solar power charge controller. It is a DC-to-DC converter that optimizes the match between a PV panel and battery bank. To simply put, MPPTs convert higher voltage DC output transferred from the solar panel down to a lower voltage needed to charge batteries associated with a PV system.

Since most solar panels are used to put out nominal 12 volts, they usually make 16-18 volts; however, a nominal battery is pretty close to 10.5-12.7 volt, depending on the charge associated with it. This is quite different from what normal solar panels are designed to put out. Enter– MPPTs.

If you take the word MPPT at its face value, the term 'tracking' may confuse you. A Maximum Power Point Tracking is digital tracking, where the charge controller looks at the output of the panels and creates a comparison between the voltages of the batteries. Initially it retrieves the best power rate offered by the panel that it can put out to charge the battery. Later it takes this rate and converts it to the best possible voltage in order to get the maximum AMPs into the battery bank.

Lastly, there are certain conditions that allow MPPTs to work in an effective format. These conditions are as follows:

- Cold weather: While solar panels work effectively under cold temperature, without the installation of an MPPT you might lose most of your energy.
- Low battery charge: The lower the state of charge of the battery, the more current is supplied by the MPPT.
- Long wire runs: If your panels are 100 feet away and you have a 12-volt battery installed you are losing a considerable amount of power unless you use a very large wire.

PWM Controllers—

So, now that MPPTs are out of the way, let's dive into the specifics of a Pulse Width Modulation Charge Controller. Put simply, it is a transition between the solar panels and the batteries. It actively controls the current flowing from the solar panel to the batteries thereby preventing the batteries from overcharging.

So, what is the 3-stage battery charging technique?

Bulk Charge — Absorb Charge — Float Charge

Firstly, bulk charge will occur, during which the PV device will charge the battery from a higher voltage and current especially when the voltage is down. The second step after the initial charging stage would be waiting promptly. The battery will wait for the voltage to decrease and come back to the balanced charging state. Lastly, during the floating stage a slight current is supplied to the battery. This current allows the battery to stay at a low current thus at a self - discharging rate where it can sustain charge capacity.

MPPT v PWM

Which one is better? **PWM** or **MPPT?** It's a straightforward question right? Let's put the two to the test and see which one suits you best. In fact, *Jim Burton* designed a test to determine which one is better.

He used a partially charged lithium battery as the main load. In order to protect himself from falling into the trap of two batteries that look identical, he carried out a test on both controllers using a 2 x 100 watts panel and the same battery for 2 hours each in controlled and same solar conditions. Initially the panels were connected in parallel for PWM test and series for the MPPT test. Most importantly, the panels were tilted at the same angle which was perpendicular to the sun on a sunny day. He

connected the battery to the PWM controller and solar panels, allowing them to charge the battery for 1-2 hours. The same was repeated for the MPPT charge controller; however, it was ensured that the sky was clear as MPPT controllers work best under cooler conditions.

Test Results of the MPPT v PWM test

The test results showed that the MPPT controller gives a gain of 20-25% in various conditions. This means that in the majority of conditions the MPPT charge controllers are 30% more efficient than PWM controllers. However, an MPPT controller matches its internal resistance to the solar panel characteristic resistance when it draws power from MPPT. Thus, it is important to take into account the resistance time in your design otherwise a large proportion of your energy generated from the sun will be wasted.

Table of Comparison between PWM and MPPT Charge Controller

	PWM Charge Controller	MPPT Charge Controller
Array Voltage	Solar panel array and the battery voltages should match.	Solar panel voltage can be higher than the battery.
Battery Voltage	Performs well in warm weather/temperature and when the battery is fully charged.	Operates the best in cold temperatures and when the battery is low.
System Size	Typically recommended for use in smaller systems where MPPT benefits are minimal	Recommended for 150W – 200W or higher to take advantage of MPPT benefits
Off-Grid or Grid-Tie	Must use off-grid PV modules typically with Vmp ≈ 17 to 18 Volts for every 12V nominal battery voltage	Enables the use of lower cost/grid-tie PV Modules helping bring down the overall PV system cost
Array Sizing Method	PV array size in Amps (based on current produced when PV array is operating at battery voltage)	PV array size in Watts (based on the Controller Max. Charging Current x Battery Voltage)

Now that you are aware of **MPPT** and **PWM**, let's discuss the possible options that are available in the market.

Before we move any further and explore our options, I want you to consider the factors that might have an impact on your purchase. If your system is situated in a remote setting, I would suggest opting for a reliable and high performing controller. Therefore, lower cost solar controllers will not be the most reliable for you as they will not meet your charging

requirements. So, the main components that have a vivid impact on your PV systems are:

1. High reliability   2. Longer Life   3. Greater Efficiency

Now, I have made a list of important companies that offer the best charge controllers. It is important that you compare whichever brand suits your capacity, total household power usage and budget.

No#	Brand Name	Model	Current (A)	Max Voc	Battery Voltage	Price Range
1	Victron MPPT	SmartSolar	35A	150V	12V 24V 48V	$350 to $480
2	EPever	Triron Series	40A	150V	12V 24V	$150 to $250
3	Morningstar MPPT	Prostar	40A	120V	12V 24V	$460 to $540
4	EPever	XTRA Series	40A	150V	12V 24V 36V 48V	$130 to $190
5	Renogy	Rover	40A	100V	12v 24V	$150 to $250
6	EOever	BN Series	40A	150V	12V 24V	$170 to $250

How are charge controllers sized? Well, they can be sized depending on the current of the solar array and the voltage of the PV system.

For MPPT controllers, you should be looking for an amp reading that is usually located on the controller's manual or the appliance itself. Furthermore, you should also look for the voltage reading such as the input voltage mentioned, mind you it will always be higher. Finally, look for the ROV value and minimum solar voltage.

On the contrary, for a PWM controller you will need to look for the nominal voltage. This will inform you about the voltage of the battery bank and whether it is compatible with the controller or not. Lastly, check for the type of battery and the terminals for any additional measures.

Well, I told you this would be a short chapter. The feature of charge controllers has a lot of additional information that you do not require. Therefore, I wanted to ensure that you do not spend too much time pondering over unnecessary details, because I know I did when I started my research. Moving forward, we will be focusing on one of the most important aspects of solar power systems and that is– Invertors. Let's go..

Chapter 22
Inverters and Power Optimizers

So, optimizers, and inverters are important components of your PV system. What is the hype all about? Let me break down inverters for you and hopefully, by the end of this chapter, you will understand why inverters are crucial for your systems.

The main function of an inverter is that it converts DC (direct current) into AC (alternating current). This is because solar panels produce energy in the DC format; however, the appliances installed in your house run on AC. So, the inverter simply turns the energy your PV system generated into the one that you can use to power your house.

Now, micro-inverters. What are those? Well, since there are no centralized inverters therefore each panel of the system is connected to its very own micro-inverter. As the name implies, it's a small, personal inverter instead of a big one which are also known as optimizers.

I know you might wonder why you should even opt for a micro-inverter. It's a great way to start and then later you can build your system down the road. In fact, there is no relative difference as they provide the same monitoring capability as an optimizer.

So, now you know what micro-inverters are right? Moving on to string inverters. Unlike micro-inverters, they are inexpensive and simple to use. The panels are wired in strings, either in series or parallel while the last panel is connected to the inverter for any input.

Even though we will explore the idea of stringed panels in the upcoming chapters, let me give you a brief overview as to what you are looking at.

In a series string panel, each panel is connected to the next whereas in the panel wired parallel they are connected to each other in the opposite (north-south) direction which means each panel in the string is connected to the same circuit thus the performance offered is the same.

Let's move to power optimizers. They are connected to your solar panels, which allows the system to control the output of each panel separately. In fact, if a single panel does not produce enough energy or under-performs, the optimizer ensures that other panels are not affected by

this. In fact, when the PV system is exposed to the sunlight, and the electrons move around the cell while producing DC current the energy generated is used by your home.

In other words, your inverter which converts DC power into AC power, changes the voltage and keeps the current the same is called a power adapter. Moreover, since the power output received by the solar panels is not consistent as it is interlinked with the weather. Therefore, on account of these fluctuations, every inverter includes MPPT solar charge controllers that are able to optimize the generation of solar energy.
All solar inverters are:

- Robust to operate in all kinds of climates
- Reliable for continuous operation (Always-On mode)
- Powerful enough to absorb your solar production and cover your power needs
- Efficient to convert DC to AC (above 90%)
- Versatile

So, what are hybrid inverters for solar panels? Also known as off-grid inverters they are designed to generate AC power at any time of the day, specifically in the absence of grid electricity. This begs the question; what type of inverter would be suitable for your PV system? The simple answer to this is, you can install as many inverters as your solar panels. However, a micro-inverter is recommended for domestic production only due to its durability and efficiency.

Should you use a string inverter?

While they are a good addition in terms of convenience and installation; however, the system suffers from low efficiency when local shading occurs. Even though on most occasions solar panels are connected in series to the inverter, the effect of 1 panel being shaded is felt by the rest . Therefore, it is often advised to have hybrid inverters installed that include a battery charger and smart energy management systems. Hybrid inverters are very versatile and therefore can be installed even when you have access to grid electricity.

Moving on, what size of inverter do you need in a grid-tied configuration? We know that you are not afraid of power shortage when connected to the utility grid, in which case the size of your inverter is related to your array's peak power ratio. So, what can be done? I recommend oversizing your inverter's capacity by 30% compared to your panel's peak power. What about off-grid configuration? Well, since there is no grid backup in case you suffer from a power outage, I would recommend that you oversize your inverter 40-50% compared to the peak power of your panels because some appliances are active loads and consume a higher rate.

With that being said, what are the features you should look for when buying an inverter? Here are some things you should always look for when shopping for inverters:

1. **Warranties:** Solar inverters come with warranties ranging from anywhere between 5-10 years thus, anything below this range is not acceptable.
2. **Operating Temperatures:** Inverters operate best when they are running cool. It is obvious that weather conditions will not always be ideal therefore the higher the operating temperature, the better it is .
3. **Efficiency:** The two main aspects in this regard are the peak efficiency and the weighted efficiency.

Moving on, let me clear the confusion about optimizers.

How do optimizers even work?

So, the process is simple, power optimizers have MPPTs installed in every panel of the array. They turn individual panels into smart modules by keeping a track of their peak out and regulate the voltage before sending the power to the main inverter. The result is that every panel's performance is optimized regardless of the orientation of the sun, availability of shade or whether or not a panel is damaged.

Let's surf through some of the major advantages and disadvantages of DC optimizers:

Advantages of DC optimizers :

1. It has a higher rate of efficiency in shaded conditions which means that it allows you to generate more electricity when your panels are either shaded or facing multiple angles.
2. Individual-level panel monitoring is where the optimizer is able to connect and feed solar energy production data such as output voltage and peak efficiency from each of the PV modules to the cloud. This would essentially report the financial and performance data to your app.
3. We know that the panels and batteries both operate with DC electricity therefore it is only fair to fuel it with DC energy output from your panel directly to your storage.
4. Since voltage tracking and maintenance requires individuality, it makes sense to install an inverter smaller in size.

Disadvantages of DC optimizers

- Limited inverter selection means that you cannot mix and match inverter brands to pair with power optimizers.
- Installing an optimizer can be slightly more expensive than the normal string inverters installed in solar panel systems. For instance, the average estimated price rise from a traditional equipment to an optimizer will be $300.
- There is an active difference between the warranty lengths of optimizers and panels. For instance, an average warranty length for an

optimizer is 8-12 years whereas for a panel it is 25 years. This means that you may have to replace your inverter before your panels.

DC optimizers vs. microinverters

	DC power optimizers	Microinverters
Cost	Moderate	High
Ease of system expansion	Moderate	High
Lightning Risk	Low	Moderate
Panel-Level Monitoring	Yes	Yes
Performance with multiple roof angles	Excellent	Excellent
Performance in the shade	Excellent	Excellent

I know what's on your mind. You must be thinking, are power optimizers safe to use? Yes. In fact, they include a safety voltage function that automatically reduces the output of each power optimizer to 1 Volt DC in the following cases:

- During faulty conditions
- Disconnection between modules and the optimizer
- When the solar inverter's switch is turned off
- When the Safety Switch is turned off
- When the solar inverter's AC breaker is turned off

In a nutshell, inverters are the main component in a solar power system. Moving on, the next on our list are monitors that track how your solar power system is performing,
and can be great for you to include in your design to keep an eye on things.

Chapter 23

Utilizing Monitoring Systems

If you have installed something, you will have to monitor it right? Especially when it is something like a power generator.

So, a solar power monitoring system allows you to track your solar panel outputs. They are usually installed at the same time as your solar panels.

How do these monitoring systems function? The hardware is attached to a solar array, internet connection and software. The monitor reads the influx of data through a solar array's inverter. The main purpose is to help customers determine when the panels achieved peak performance, thus this in turn helps the consumers maximize their use.

It is also used to detect errors or defects in the software. In fact, it is also used to monitor the current system and accumulate data to compare panel output overtime which can be also used to calculate financial expenditure.

Moving on, let me give 7 reasons as to why you should opt for a solar monitoring system.

Reason 1: By installing a good monitoring system you are able to get alerted when the system trips off. You are alerted as soon as the solar system experiences a defect. With a good monitoring system, you will get an email or message within days of the system going off, which will give you time to check what happened or contact your installer ASAP.

Reason 2: You will get alerts when the performance of your system will drop. Even though solar systems come with a warranty of 25 years often their performance drops which is where a monitor can indicate such a happening and help you take proper measures.

Reason 3: You will be alerted about the drop in your solar inverter's performance. Since we know that the efficiency of your solar inverter is correlated to your power output if the performance drops then so does your savings. So, a monitoring system will alert you about this as well.

Reason 4: Since our homes turn into power stations, any electrical fault would be detrimental to us. And I believe that our homes should have a high degree of protection. A monitoring system does just that, it detects faults before they go out of control.

Reason 5: A good solar monitoring system can give you the reason in two minutes, so you can take the right action to get your bills back down.
Reason 6: A good solar monitoring system can continuously track your usage, compare it with current offers and alert you when a retailer offers a new tariff that will save you money.
Reason 7: Energy efficiency is improved after you install a monitoring system you are able to monitor any excessive power consumption.

With that being said, Are there any relevant solutions that can offer you help? Yes, there are certain solutions that can help you monitor your system. In fact, the purpose of a grid-tied solar power system is to generate energy using the sun and store it in the utility grid. This, however, allows you to access the stored energy whenever it becomes necessary. The upfront cost is usually low since there is no punctual need to purchase batteries to store generated power. So, the grid-tied system helps you support your entire solar power system to operate efficiently, transmitting data to monitor and regulate the PV panel output.

I have compiled a list of the *best grid-tie solar panel* monitoring systems. I hope they are useful for you:

Name	Features	Model	Price
Enphase	The IQ Envoy has consumption-metering capability, offers flexible networking with integrated Wi-Fi, and even offers 3G and 4G cellular connection options.	Enphase IQ Envoy ENV-IQ-AM1-240M	$627.35
SMA	With no additional add-ons, you can monitor real-time system performance using the SMA Sunny Portal on any web-enabled device.	SMA Sunny Boy 5.0-US-41 Inverter w/ Integrated DC Disconnect, Triple MPPT, 208/240 VAC	$1695.00
Solar Edge	Integrates solar panel monitoring within the inverters through ethernet connections. They let you monitor the system's performance wirelessly or cellularly.	SolarEdge SetApp Enabled SE9K Grid tied Inverter - 3 Phase 208V	$2,855.00

Moreover, for an off-grid system it is important to optimize the battery life so that your system can run smoothly and effectively. In fact, an off-grid system monitors the state of charge associated with the battery so that you know when it's time to charge.

The following off-grid systems are the best monitoring systems who offer wireless and/or ethernet capabilities that make real-time monitoring easier.

- **Magnum:** It offers both wireless and ethernet options for monitoring as add-ons through their line of MagWeb products. Their devices allow real-time monitoring of your inverter as well as the device connected to it. However, the only limitation of the MagWeb system is that you are unable to modify the system settings remotely.
The price range is around **$435.00-500.00.**

- **Midnite:** It has a free application that allows you to monitor any of the Midnite's classic line of products through an ethernet connection. However, again the limitation of the MyMidnites's system is that you are unable to modify the system settings remotely.
The price range started from **$825.00.**

- **Morningstar:** It enables communication between the PC and an applicable morningstar charge controller or inverter. This means that you can remotely control the system settings of morningstar products. In fact, you will be able to monitor system performance even without the ability to change system settings remotely.
The price range starts from **$710.00.**

- **Outback:** It includes an optic RE monitor through the ethernet connection which allows you to remotely change system settings. You can also quickly access the system performance data from any web-enabled device if you are using the optic RE platform.
The price range starts from **$577.00.**

- **Schneider:** It provides the feature of live monitoring as well as local system configuration. Since they offer both wireless and ethernet connectivity, the Conext gateway can be advantageous for cloud-based data storage.
The price range starts from **$555.00.**

Overall, the variations in these systems exhibit that no one-size-fits all solution exists for solar monitoring. The best technology depends on the features that matter the most to you.

In a nutshell, monitoring your solar power system is an essential part of the whole maintenance aspect. There are several systems and brands that you can include in your whole system to ensure that you are able to monitor your system properly. Every part of the solar system is connected to one another.

Finally, let's take a closer look at the connective tissue that combines all these components together...

Chapter 24

Wired for Greatness

If you are thinking of going solar, it's important that you have a baseline understanding of what your solar panel electrical requirements look like so that you are equipped to make an informed decision.

There are some terminologies that you need to be aware of, such as:

- **Kilowatt-Hour**

What is Kilowatt-Hour?

It is an important electrical term to understand with regards to solar powers or any electrical mechanism to be honest. In simple words, kWh is a unit of measurement that determines how much energy you have used over a certain period of time.

For example, let's say you have an appliance that is rated at 1200 watts (1 kWh = 1000 watts) therefore, after operating for an hour it would use 1.2 kWh of energy over the duration of that time.

- **Voltage Drop**

What does Voltage Drop mean?

As the name suggests, when current moves through a circuit, a small amount of voltage is lost due to resistance in the wires. This is referred to as voltage drop. However, this drop can lead to a slight loss of production from your solar system, which can become more pronounced with a longer wiring run.

How can you reduce this loss? Well, there are 4 main approaches that you can use.

1. Reduce the length of the wiring run associated by the system.
2. Consider the placement of your inverter carefully.
3. Bigger wire=Lesser resistance thus use a larger wire.
4. Develop your system to have higher voltage so that you can overcome resistance.

So, for a grid-tied solar system, the size of your electrical service panel can place inherent limitations on the size of your solar power system. Be cautious of that and ensure that you are well aware of the sizing restrictions (for any clarification on sizing refer to chapter 4) as they help you unload the combined energy from the utility grid and solar power

system that could potentially overload the electric panel when you are backfeeding. (We will discuss how to size wiring for your solar power panel later in this chapter, so stay tuned for that)
- **Electrical current**

Electric current is represented by "I" in the power equation and is defined as the rate at which charges flow in a circuit. It is measured in amperes.
- **Electric Power**

Electric power is the measurement of the rate at which energy is transferred throughout the PV system. It is measured in Watts (W). In fact, an important function of the inverter, other than converting DC power into AC power, which is used by home appliances, it also maximizes the power output of the array by varying the current and voltage in it.

Moving on, what is the *120% rule?*

The 120% rule states that you cannot have more than 120% of your rated service that is in amps running through the busbars of the main breaker. So, when sizing your system in accordance with your electric panel make sure you remember the 120%.

Let me give you some perspective, for instance; you have a standard service rate of 300 amps ok? And your main electrical breaker is also rated at 300 amps. How can you determine how large of a solar breaker should you get for your grid-tie system?

It's simple, we know you cannot exceed the 120% limit of the rated service (340 amps) right? So, in that case your largest breaker should be rated at 40 amps, thus, with this, your system will be able to handle up to 7600 watts of backfeed solar.

How can you understand the entire wiring system? Because I know it is difficult and sounds even more complicated. By now you would be wondering what a diagram of the entire wiring system would look like. I did too, and when I found it, I was fascinated.

An electrical diagram is an invaluable source that you can use during the permitting and installation process. Therefore, a diagram will be required when you are applying for your permit and even for the final inspection of your PV system. So, you need an electrical wiring diagram because:

1. It enables a quicker permitting process. Since permitting can be the most time-consuming process, you can speed it up by submitting a ready-to-go diagram to get started early.
2. An accurate electrical diagram reduces the chances of re-submissions.
3. It has a fast turnaround, such that revisions in the diagram are catered within a few business days.
4. There are fewer errors during the installation since either you or the professionals have a baseline to work with.

Thus, an accurate wiring diagram leads to fewer errors, overall smooth installation, and less downtime.

So, now that the terminologies are out of the way; let's start with the basic principles of solar panel wiring. In order to conceal a high functioning solar panel system, it is imperative for you to wire the panels together, allowing the current to flow through the circuit and also wire the panels to the inverter so that the DC power produced by the panels is converted into AC power that is used by your home appliances. This whole process is termed as 'stringing' and each series of panels connected together is referred to as a 'string.'

There are different types of stringing processes, but the main ones are series and parallel stringing.

Series v Parallel Stringing

So, what is the difference between series and parallel stringing?

Well, when you string panels in series, each panel is connected to the other in a line. Thus, each additional panel adds to the total voltage of the string; however, the current remains the same. Contrary to the process, one of the biggest disadvantages of the same is that a shaded panel can reduce the current through the entire string. This is because the current remains the same throughout the string, thus the current is reduced to the lowest level in the panel.

Simultaneously, the optimal area for solar panels in series is for unshaded conditions. Therefore, if a shade is present over your series array, even a single panel, it will decrease the entire performance of the system. Since we know that each panel, in the entire series connection, is critical, panels planted in series are best suited for systems with lower amperage.

On the contrary, if you are hoping to string your solar panel in a parallel position, it's complicated. So, how does it work? Well, unlike series, the positive terminals of all the panels on the string are connected to one wire and the negative are connected to another wire. Interestingly, unlike in series the current increases in a parallel string; however, the voltage remains the same. Therefore, the main benefit of stringing in parallel is that one panel is heavily shaded while the rest can operate at a normal current.

Subsequently, in a parallel system since the panels operate independently from one another therefore it is considered best for a mixed-light condition. Such that even if a shade covers 1 or more panels of the array, the panel will continue to generate power.

At this point, you must be wondering what if you can or cannot mix solar panels? It is possible to mix solar panels from different manufacturers with different electrical ratings. So, this is the distinction between series and parallel wiring of solar panels. While there is a lot to unpack under this heading, I will be dealing with certain important aspects only.
Let's expand on this for a brief minute.

So, we already know what a solar panel wire means in terms of being stringed either in a parallel or series format. But the main question is how do the panels compare in terms of series and parallel setting?

Remember MPPTs and PWMs from the previous chapter? Well, charge controller(s) are a determining factor when it comes to solar panel wiring such that MPPT is used for wiring solar panels in a series whereas PWMs are used to wire panels in parallel.

Let's take an example of fairy lights to create a better outline of how series wiring works, in comparison to parallel wiring. In a series capacity, if a bulb broke, came out of the socket, or burned out, the entire string would not work. However, in a parallel wiring, when a similar issue occurs the string of lights stay lit even if one is not working.

So, to summarize the whole concept, if there is a problem in the connection of one panel aligned in a series format, the entire circuit is bound to fail. In contrast to the series wiring, one defective panel does not have an impact on the product of the rest in a parallel wiring. In fact, nowadays how solar panels are wired is greatly dependent on the type of inverter being used.

What's the point of string inverters? Well, they have a rated window of voltage that is required for their functionality. In fact, it also requires a rated current that needs to function. They also have MPPTs installed in them so that they can vary current and voltage to produce the maximum amount of power for the household.

Which one of the wiring is better? Well, in practice, parallel wiring is a better option compared to series wires as electrical applications require a continuous flow of power. However, parallel wiring is not always the suitable choice for the overall power input since you would need to meet certain current and voltage requirements in order to keep your inverter functioning properly. So, what should you do? Well, to create a balance between the voltage and current, you need to ask your solar designer to design your array with a hybrid wiring system.

Let's take a step towards micro-inverters and optimizers and their role in how solar panels are wired. You can make use of micro-inverters or optimizers in order to avoid inverter-size limitations that string inverters face. Your system can be expanded by connecting micro-inverters with each panel.

Tip: You don't necessarily need to buy new string inverters, use the ones that have maxed out. However, make sure that the additional panels are wired on the AC side of the inverters that are stringed.

Quick question, how will you connect your panels to the grid? Simple, in accordance with a series circuit, singular wires will be used to connect the panels to the grid, whereas, for parallel wired systems, there will be multiple wires involved.
Which one is the best for you?

Well, there is no real answer to this, in fact the choice is subjective. This decision is based on the application of the wiring system and the needs of your solar power system.

In a slightly different context, how can you connect batteries in either parallel or series?

Well, wiring batteries in parallel evidently increases the amp-hour capacity but keeps the voltage of the system at the same level. On the contrary, if you connect the batteries in a series, it will increase the voltage, but the amp-hour capacity will remain the same. Meanwhile, if batteries are connected in a hybrid arrangement it will increase the both amp-hour capacity and the battery bank voltage.

Let's consider how batteries are connected in off-grid and grid-tied systems. For either one connecting batteries together to produce a larger battery array of a required operating voltage or 24-hour current demand plays an important part in your solar system.

Specially for off-grid systems the power is used in homes and business etc., are typically wired to give out 24–48-volt DC. Moreover, the low-voltage DC electricity can also be converted to AC electricity by an inverter which is able to increase 120V to 240V.

Moreover, when more than 1 deep cycle battery is connected together the resulting battery bank either has a different voltage or a different amp-hour capacity in comparison to a single battery.

We know that batteries are connected in series or parallel combinations, or both to increase the voltage or current capacity of the battery bank. Thus, connecting batteries together allows for more battery storage. In fact, in a series battery bank the positive terminal of 1 battery is connected to the negative terminal. Thus, connecting batteries together in a series can give a higher voltage.

Battery banks made from deep cycle batteries that are connected in parallel have the same voltage as the individual batteries, but the current capacity is multiplied by the number of batteries. In a parallel connected battery bank the positive terminal of one battery is connected to the positive terminal of the next with the negative terminal connected to the negative terminal. Connecting batteries together in parallel branches means a higher current for the same terminal voltage.

Moreover, before you start stringing, there are certain aspects that you need to know before determining how you will string your solar panel.

In terms of inverter information, you will need to understand the following specification, which can be found in the manufacture date sheet of the product you will be using:
- Maximum DC input voltage: the maximum voltage that your inverter can receive
- The voltage level necessary for the inverter to operate

- The maximum input current which determines how much energy the inverter can handle before breaking.
- How many MPPTs (refer to chapter 7 for further details) does the inverter have?

Additionally, after acquiring the above information about your selected inverter, you'll also need the following data on your selected panels:

- The maximum voltage your panel can produce in its no-load condition.
- Short circuit current which is the current running through the cell when the voltage is zero.

You might be wondering; are there any basic rules of stringing? Well, I have collected 3 basic rules of stringing that I'm sharing with you that I think might help you when going solar. They are as follows:

1. Ensure that the minimum and maximum voltage of the string is within the range of the inverter.

Tip: Do not use STC (Standard Test Condition) values alone to determine the voltage range, instead take into account how the voltage of the entire system changes depending on the temperatures it may experience in the area it's installed in.

2. Ensure that strings have similar conditions. If your strings are different in terms of conditions, try to connect them to different MPPT ports.
3. Gravitate towards advanced considerations to optimize your design

When it comes to optimizing your design, sizing the wire you will use to string panels is a crucial component. Thus, when wiring the PV system together, there are essentially two sections you need to consider, specifically when calculating the size of solar panel wires.

1. Solar panels – charge controllers
2. Charge controllers — battery.

Simultaneously, the two factors that determine solar panel wire sizes are:

1. Wire style (series or parallel)
2. Array's total wattage

Let me break the sections down for you–

Section1

Calculation of wire size of panels to charge controller. The wire size you need to connect your solar panels to the charge controller is determined by total amps produced by the array. You can refer to the chart below for some guidance:

Panels Connected in Series

Solar Array Size (Total Watts)	Wire Size (AWG)	Where to Buy
0-200W	12	Amazon
200-800	10	Amazon

Panels Connected In Parallel

0-200W	12	Amazon
200-440W	10	Amazon
440-550W	8	Amazon
550-800W*	6	Amazon

Moving on, in order to calculate the wire size from charge controller to batteries you need to consider the amp-rating of the controller. This is dependent on your total solar array wattage. The order should be:

1. Decide your solar array size
2. Calculate charge controller amp-rating
3. Determine section 2 wire size

Below I am mentioning the charge controller sizing chart for you to better understand and take help from it.

Solar Array Size (Total Watts)	Charge Controller (Amp Rating)	Buy Charge Controller
0-200W	15A	Amazon
200-260W	20A	Amazon
260-400W	30A	Amazon
400-520W	40A	Amazon
520-650W	50A	Amazon
650-800W	60A	Amazon

Now that you are aware of the amp-rating of your charge controller, you need to determine the correct solar wire size for the connection. Refer to the chart below:

Section 2

Charge Controller (Amp Rating)	Wire Size (AWG)	Buy Wire
15A	12AWG*	Amazon
20A	12AWG*	Amazon
30A	10AWG	Amazon
40A	8 AWG	Amazon
50A	6 AWG	Amazon
60A	4 AWG	Amazon

I'm sure you must have heard about the marine-grade wires.

What does marine-grade mean? It actually refers to the wire's ability to hold up against the natural elements such as rain, winds, and saltwater corrosion. If a marine-grade is able to survive a rough storm, it's good enough for the roof of your van. However, the main thing you should consider is how safe the wires are.

So, we have established till now that choosing the right size of wire in your PV system plays a crucial role in terms of performance and safety. If the wires you use are undersized, there will be a significant voltage drop due

to excessive loss of power. Simultaneously, if the wires are undersized, there is an active risk that they may catch fire.

Advice: Use copper wires. They are sized using the gauge scale (AWG) thus the lower the gauge number the less resistance and higher current it can handle safely.

I know, the word 'gauge' sounds mathematical. There are certain things you need to know when you are estimating what wire gauge you need for your system. There are 3 main terms you need to become aware of. These terms are important, as they can help you pick out the right solar panel wire, take a look at each one of them:

1. **System voltage:** It's the electric potential difference, which means that it is the difference between two electric ends.
2. **Voltage drop index:** It is able to state how much an undersized wire will reduce the voltage thus, how much power will be lost.
3. **Maximum current:** It is the current that flows between the electrical circuit. It tells you the rate of flow and is measured in amps.

The Formula   Amps = Watt / Volt.

We will use this formula to find out the amperage, wattage, or voltage. This formula holds significance because you should know the amps to determine the size of the wire for your solar panel.

Let me give you some perspective, considering that your PV system is 12V.

What type of cable should you use?

Well, unfortunately, knowing the voltage of your solar power system is not enough for this case. However, in a more general view, the solar systems perform well with wires between 8-14 gauges depending on the wattage and amperage. Furthermore, a 14-gauge solar wire can only handle 15 amps at most, however, many solar panels need a higher amp so it may be better if you go for a 10-12 AWG wire.

Nevertheless, 14-gauge wires are not acceptable when there is a battery bank involved, that would need a 3/0 AWG cable. Similarly, if you don't have a charge controller or a solar battery system then you do not need a 14-gauge wire as there will be less loss of power.

Ah! Wire length is still a missing piece in the whole process. How can you know which length to use? Well, your PV array amps can tell you how long the cable should be.

And how is that?

For example, your solar panel is expected to use 10 amps. In that case your cable length should be around 4.5 feet with a 14-gauge cable. However, 4.5 feet does not have the capacity to host most cables, therefore you will have to select either a 10- or 12-gauge wire.

Comparatively, a 12-gauge wire can also be 7 feet long if the panel has a 10 amperage. This means that when you choose the right cable for yourself, you need to think about the diameter and length of the cord and

decide if it is the right one for you. Nonetheless, it becomes relatively easier once you know the amp, after that you are easily able to find the cable size required for your solar panels.

Now that you understand how to size the right wire for your solar power panel, your next step would be wire management. This is a crucial step which is often overlooked, however, considering the management of wires can help the installation of your solar panels easier in the long run. Here are a few tips you can refer to when managing wires:

- Plan the wiring run in advance so that wires don't interfere with the access to the array
- Make use of wire clips to secure the factory wire leads so that they don't move when there is wind.
- Use the spring clamp to push down the metal bar and open the terminal so that the wire can sit. Once the wire is firmly seated, remove the clamp.

Subsequently, the actual path of your wiring will differ based on the system you will be installing. I have extracted a list of how wiring is connected for each system type:

- Grid-tied Wiring Path
  - → PV strings to junction box
  - → Junction box to inverter
  - → AC out to main or sub panel
- Grid-tied Wiring Path (Enphase Micro-Inverters)
  - → PV panel to Microinverter
  - → Micro Inverter to trunk cable
  - → Trunk cable to junction box
  - → Junction box to main panel
- Off-Grid Wiring Path
  - → PV strings to combiner box
  - → Combiner box to charge controller
  - → Charge controller to battery storage bank
  - → Battery storage bank to inverter
  - → Inverter to Load panel

Wait, so, what are micro inverters? We did discuss inverters and optimizers in the chapter above, but not micro inverters right?

Well, their job is the same as an inverter however they are tucked away behind the panels. In fact, they are a great add on if you need to comply with rapid power shutdowns. So, if your system uses them or even optimizers, you should make an array map that is able to help you identify where the inverters are located in the array.

How can you manage an off-grid DC wiring system?

- The system used by off-grid has more wire termination. It also works with a higher amperage. It is important that you check all the AC, DC, and communication connections to be sure everything is properly connected and torqued.
- You can mark connections by a paint pen after you have tightened the wires to know which connections have been torqued.
- If you bring combined DC power from a solar panel array to a power center, take care to terminate your solar positive wire at the SOLAR INPUT (+) busbar, not the DC BATT (+) busbar.
- After wiring, check terminals or busbars with a meter and determine they are operating at a safe voltage before proceeding with the rest of your build.

Moving forward, we will be understanding how to plan your electrical route. Before you make any plan, take into consideration which type of system you are installing in your house or property.

Disclaimer: Please wear gloves, eye protection and closed toe boots when installing wires of your panels.

- PV Sub-Panels
  → This system has multiple inverters therefore they can use AC sub-panel combined with AC circuits into a single set of conductors.
  → It also has dedicated solar sub-panels that must not contain any load breakers.
- Roof Mount Electrical Route
  → Even if you want to hide your wiring, make sure it is accessible enough so that you can connect it to the array, breaker box, panel, meter, and other parts.
  → Use cable clips to secure the wiring.
  → Do not allow exposed wiring to contact the roof.
  → Also, run the wiring from the source to the junction box, then pass it to your conduit run. Furthermore, if possible you can use conduit penetration flashings to transition into the conduit.
- Ground Mount Electrical Route
  → Use cable clips for safety of exposed wires under the array. They should be secured so that they do not interfere with maintenance.
  → Communicate with the local authority before starting any type of digging to avoid breaking any underground pipelines.
  → Use your wiring diagram to help you dig a certain size of trench and type of wiring and conduit required.
  → Make sure you do not drive any heavy machinery over buried gas lines or septic systems.

Afterwards, your inverter installation can also look different depending on the type of system you have installed. Grid-tied systems are wall-mounted indoors, outdoors or rigged on the back of a ground. Whereas off-grid inverters are wall-mounted indoors.

- Wall-Mounted Inverters (Grid-Tie & Off-Grid)
  - → Any inverter with an integrated disconnected switch must be mounted less than 2 meters off the ground which is 6.5 feet. The exception can be made if the system has another switch that meets the AC disconnect requirements of NEC (National Electric Code).
  - → Follow the manufacturing guidelines for installation clearances.
  - → If installed in a garage make sure the ignition sources are 18 inches off the ground. However, if installed outside, ensure that the inverter is out of direct sunlight and clear any sprinkling systems.
- Inverters Mounted on Ground Mount Substructure (Grid-Tie Only)
  - → Keep inverter out of direct sunlight
  - → Mount the inverter higher than 36 inches off the ground to avoid any mud during rainfall.
  - → Use thread lock tight on the hardware that secures the inverter bracket to the support structure.

So, are there any grounding systems? If yes, how can you ground your system?

Well, grounding is an essential step when it comes to electrical components of solar systems. This reduces the risk of shocks, power surges and buildup of static electricity that is dangerous. In fact, grounding provides a safe pathway for faulty current. So, metal parts of an electrical system must be connected (bonded) to the ground, and conductive materials (EMT, metal boxes, etc.) must be grounded together. This ensures that each piece of the component in the system shares the same level of resistance to the ground.

Let's talk about EGC, GEC & Integrated grounding.

EGC and GEC Grounding:

- EGC grounding is short for Equipment Grounding Conductor which is either green or bare copper wire that connects the hardware, metal enclosures and EMT conduits together.
- GEC, which is Grounding Electrode Conductor, is a wire connecting the ground rod to the electrical distribution service. In the case of an AC power system, the neutral conductor has a single bonding point.
- Neutral to ground bonds can be found in generators, breaker distribution panels, power centers, and other equipment. Your system should only have a single neutral-to-ground bond.
- A DC negative to ground bond is necessary for any system. It is included with any system that features "ground fault protection."

Integrated Grounding

- IronRidge's UFO (Universal Fastening Object) and bonded fasteners make it so that an entire solar array can be grounded with a single grounding lug.
- Other mounts, like pole mounts, will not have integrated grounding solutions.

The next important component is the backfeed breaker which is only available for grid-tied systems. The grid-tie system requires a backfeed system because it's added to the main breaker panel thus it enables your system to fuel the power generated into the utility grid. In fact, the backfeed is installed at the opposite side of the breaker panel from the grid input breaker therefore you may need to re-arrange circuits.

Since you know how wiring and stringing can affect your current, voltage and overall performance of your array, it is important that you are aware of certain features of the wiring system:

1. Solar Cables: The main purpose of the same is to provide resistance from the UV lights, extreme temperatures, and bad weather conditions. Yet, the two common conductors used, as the material, are copper and aluminum, which are also mentioned in local and national electrical codes. The cables are required to be solid or stranded, either way flexible.

2. A junction box is an important feature of solar modules. It is attached to the rear of the solar panel. The junction consists of a bypass diode which keeps the power in the panel in a unidirectional format. In a shaded panel, the strings consume power by reversing the flow of energy. Hence, the diodes inside the box prevents this from happening. Cables such as MC4 and MC5 are used to connect to other solar panels of the array. It is advisable that you check the IP rating off the junction boxes. These boxes are supposed to be water-resistant otherwise it can short circuit and damage the entire series of string of the panel.

3. Earthing an electrical system enables you to protect yourself and your appliances from any excess electrical influx. Thus, solar panels are mostly earthed, not grounded, and they are usually installed near a lightning conductor system. This helps the system protect itself from surges and shocks of power.

What's next?

Circuit breakers.

Well, DC circuit breakers are an essential component of any electrical system. What does it do? It acts as a barrier between the DC (direct current) and AC (alternating current) thus they are essential for the electrical protection. However, not only are they installed as protective devices in PV solar systems, but they are also crucial for electrical vehicles, lamps, or LED lights, as they require DC breakers to function properly.

As a matter of fact, if you have a heavy-duty battery, heavy machinery or PV system installation, DC current is able to provide these sources with the required input to function. On the other hand, AC current is used during high-power motor drivers, and even transmission of power over long distances.

We know that PV systems host powerful mechanisms of generating renewable energy. Since they contain 1 or more solar panels it is essential that a DC breaker is installed in it.

And how is that possible? Well, a wire joins the DC breaker to the panel which should be shaded and provided with ample current to operate effectively. Thus, during the maintenance and installation of a PV system it is important to have a separate AC side from the panel, which is why it is advised to people shifting to solar to adopt a DC isolator. A separate fuse box is also required with both AC and DC breakers.

What is a Circuit Breaker? and why is a fuse necessary?

Let's talk about the fuse first. So, what exactly is a fuse?
It is an over the current protection device which sacrifices itself, when the current supersedes its maximum potential, to protect assets.

Subsequently, a circuit breaker does not give its life, instead it has a long life that is extended over numerous functions.

There are 3 parts of the circuit breaker. A sensing system, which is able to detect situations of overload (there are 3 types of sensing systems namely, magnetic, thermal, and electronic), a relay that signals information to switch arrangement and a combination of contact actuators and contacts.

Moving on, *how can you fuse your solar power system?*

As we know, fuses and breakers are used to protect the wiring of the system from catching fire, in the case of an immediate power surge. They are also used to protect the household assets in the face of a short circuit. What is the scope of fuse in solar panels?

Well, usually, a solar panel, that is commercially made, can handle 30 amps of current flow. Therefore, if you connect a solar panel in series, there will be no increase in the current, so why would you want to install a fuse in your system?
Right? I know. So, we don't.

But we need to take a completely different approach when it comes to parallel connections because, in them, the current is additive.

So, what about charge controllers? Will they be of any help? PWMs won't be of any help; however, MPPT controllers can lower the voltage and the current flowing between the charger and the battery bank, so they are helpful.

Important: The wiring and fusing of DC/AC inverter is imperative, specially where there is a possibility that current might flow.

All of these components are connected. But how?

There is equipment called 'solar panel connectors' which play an important role in the installation of the PV systems. They are able to speed up the installation process and ensure that cables are connected to the modules, and solar arrays are coherent as well as continuous.

The most popular connectors are:

- MC3: This connector was once very popular until it was replaced by its more efficient version (MC4). It was one of the earliest connectors that were simple and good. They were manufactured by the Multi-contact, attaining a 3mm single contact plug for the male connect and socket shell, which was created for the female connector. In fact, this connector has both the female and male terminals working + and - leads.
- MC4: Also designed by the Multi-Contact, this connector has a single- contact plug that fits with the socket shell perfectly. They have an excellent performance ratio. In fact, they were established, as the standard connector, to build a connection between PV modules and other solar power system equipment, specifically to secure them. However, the connector can withstand up to 22-30mms depending on their wire.
- Helios H4: It attains a design that is compatible with the MC4 which makes it easier for residents to install Helios with MC4 and not worry about their compatibility.
- Speaking of compatibility, it is advised that connectors should not be mixed because they do not meet the standard requirements; however, it is not an issue if connectors are mixed because most of them have an affinity for MC4.
- SolarLok: This is used to connect one module to another in series of parallel depending on the configuration of the solar panel or array.
- Radox: They have a lamella design with copper-beryllium as the main material used in it, which ensures the right passageway of current through the wires. But they are not common in the US.

What is a busbar?

They are referred to as metalized strips printed on the rear and front of the silicon solar cells. Their main purpose is to conduct the DC current generated from the solar cell, from the incoming photons. These bars have a larger thickness and width which allows them to maintain low resistance per unit length, than the tabbing wire.

In fact, the most common type of busbar used in solar cell designs are 2-3 full line bars printed on the cells. You will not come across PV systems using 3 busbars. However, sometimes you will see that 5 busbars are also

used as they are currently trendy in the solar system market. The reason why the number of bars has increased is because it reduces the loss of power due to internal resistance. They do so by decreasing the distance.

However, optimizing the performance of solar cells is improvised by tab wires. Some tab wires have a better chance as they take up less space. Some companies make use of colored tabs for aesthetic reasons as well.

A battery monitor shunt measures amps only, on the negative side of the circuit. The battery monitor shunt needs to capture all currents going in and out of the battery negative. A simple way to accomplish this is for all the negative connections to be wired on a DC negative distribution bus and have the cable between the negative bus and the negative of the battery be intercepted by a shunt. Basically, splitting the cable in two and having the battery shunt inserted in the middle.

In a nutshell, wiring is a crucial and essential part of the whole PV system. Thus, this concludes a detailed and advanced guide to the major components of a solar power system. But what if you want to buy a combined package? Which ones are good for you?

Chapter 25

Best Off-grid Solar Power Packages

So, if you have come this far I know that you are looking for a conclusive answer.

What are the best solar power systems?

For—

RVs and Boats	Windy Nation 400W Kit $769.98-$1,899.99	The pros of WindyNation are. 1. Ideal for boats and RVs because it has a small system footprint. 2. The inverter capacity (1500W) is high for the system of this size. 3. This system can be expanded by adding panels and batteries	Cons of WindyNation; 1. Not ideal for running sensitive electronics. 2. It uses polycrystalline solar panels which are low in efficiency. They are also very unattractive compared to its sleek siblings.
Cabins and Sheds	altE 1.83kW 'Tiny House' Base Kit #3 Starting at $5,329.27	Pros of 'Tiny House' base kit. 1. It has a reputation for good sales and support. 2. They have a monocrystalline Seraphim solar panels which are efficient and attractive. 3. It has an inverter that has a pure sine wave system which means it can power almost all appliances. 4. It gives mounting options such as metal, shingle, and pole	Cons of 'Tiny House' base kit; 1. Low warranty of 2 years which is not good enough as brands offer 5 years of inverter warranty. 2. 5-year warranty offered on lithium batteries even though companies such as Tesla offer 10 years of warranty on the same type of batteries.

However, before you buy any of these systems keep in mind that there are a variety of options that can be added or subtracted from your off-grid system. Make sure you hire, or speak to, a professional who can advise you on your design and requirements.

Moving towards the best off-grid solar power systems, I have made a list which you can refer to, when deciding which system to purchase.

Renogy 100W Off-grid Solar Premium Kit	Pros of Renogy; 1. Has 4 stage battery charging 2. Has bluetooth mode installed 3. High quality 4. Sleek and durable panels	Cons of Renogy; 1. Does not have any installation instructions.
ECO-Worthy 1200 Volt Solar Panel	Pros of ECO 1200 volt; 1. Easy setup 2. Can produce daily 4kWh 3. Comes with a 1-year warranty 4. Has a combiner box installed	Cons of ECO 1200 volt; 1. Batteries are difficult to change.
ECO-Worthy 48V Solar Power System With All-In-One Charge Inverter	Pros of ECO 48 volt; 1. Since it can produce up to 16000 WH in 4 hours, it charges the system battery for 6 hours. 2. Investment worthy.	Cons of ECO 48 volt; 1. The company does late deliveries 2. Product delivered in multiple deliveries which is unprofessional
ExpertPower 12V Solar Power Kit	Pros of Expert Power 12V; 1. It has a lithium battery that does not require an BMS board 2. Versatile wave inverter.	Cons of Expert Power 12V; 1.Low production, does not give 100% efficiency
EcoWorthy 800W Solar Wind Power Kit	Pros of ECO 800W; 1. Long battery storage 2. Long lasting quality	Cons of ECO 800W; 1. Under harsher weather, it can experience durability issues.

With all this in place, let's finally take a look at various sizing options that ultimately
relate to your usage...

Chapter 26

Sizing Variations – Can you run it?

Our journey of going solar is finally coming to an end, and I want to begin this chapter by saying that YOU ARE READY to shift to an off-grid solar power system.

We will now take a look at various kW sizes based on energy consumption needs, and which appliances can typically be run. Like in chapter 4 you were introduced to the most important of solar power systems, the panels.

Throughout this research, I asked myself one question in particular: How many solar panels do I need? While I have dealt with this question in great detail, in chapter 4, and throughout the book as well, the answer is– it all depends on your electricity usage and power consumption, honestly.

Solar panels enjoyed a massive rise in popularity in the recent decades, which was due to the inclination of becoming environmentally responsible, and the desire to decrease electricity bills by switching to cleaner and a renewable energy source.

We know that the two important aspects of understanding electricity usage of a household are correlated to the power consumption (kilowatts-hours) and power rating of each appliance.

So, how can you determine the contributing factors, namely power rating, and consumption? It's simple:

Use of power rating

1. You can start by looking for the power rating near the power cord which is listed in either amps or watts.
2. Use the formula amps x volts= watts to determine the power of the appliance.
3. Afterwards, multiply the wattage to the number of hours the appliance operates per day, and then divide it by 1000 to figure out the kilowatt-hours/day.

Power consumption

1. Use a tracking monitor to track an appliance's consumption if you are unable to find the listed power rating.

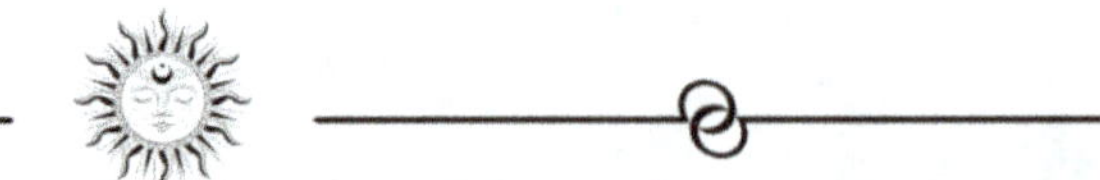

2.   Start by multiplying the energy consumption, which you can attain from the bills as mentioned in the previous chapter, with the expected operating hours.

3.   This would give you an estimated watt-hours/day.

Circling back to your question, in order to estimate the number of solar panels that you need, focus on these three variables:

1.   **Solar panel ratings** which are treated as the power output generated by a specific solar panel when there is access to ideal weather conditions.

2.   **Production ratio** is treated as the ratio between the approximate energy production overtime and the real size of the system.

3.   **Annual Electricity Usage** is the amount of electricity that you use to power your household within a year.

Through these variables you can determine how many panels are required by your residential or commercial premises.

As mentioned in chapter 11, there are different systems for Cabins, RVs and boats. Let's inspect them briefly.

So, the most obvious question would be with regards to cabins; can you power your off-grid cabin with solar energy? You absolutely can! The main requirement here is access to sunlight.

Moreover, how much solar power would you need to power your off-grid cabin? In this regard, you will have to determine how much solar power you require evidently. If your system suffers from inadequate power supply it will not work, which is why you should always keep an estimated account of the minimum power threshold.

So, how can you calculate the power requirement for your cabin?

1.   Calculate the system's energy needs.

2.   Find peak sun hours.

3.   Determine the monthly peak sun hours.

4.   Determine the size of the system and number of panels.

Moreover, an off-grid solar system runs and stores energy by being completely disconnected from the utility grid. So, we know solar panels need around 50-100% sunlight exposure to be effective. However, any percentage less than 50 will not work. There are three level to this:

1.   **Limited use** of appliances is interlinked with the less use of household items, which also limits the occupancy of your cabin.

2.   It is also important that you make use of the **average use** medium that is between the limited and maximum use of the sun's light.

3.   Maximum use contributes to the system when you want all your appliances, that you would use in a fully functioning home, to be connected to the utility grid.

With regards to RVs, there are certain requirements to generate solar energy thus you will need specific components for this which include:

1. Solar panels
2. Charge controller
3. Solar batteries
4. Inverter

Thus, since RVs are nothing like grid-tied systems, a battery bank is the main source of backup. Hence, RV batteries will store the power produced by your panels and ensure that it is available when you need it the most.

What kind of batteries are available?

Gel batteries, Lithium-ion batteries, Absorbed glass mat batteries.

Lastly, the best system for boats is difficult to choose as boats use a lot of energy. In fact, solar panels can aid the production of energy for the boat to carry out main tasks, without using up the boat's battery. Depending on your energy use and boat size, you need more, or less, solar power to provide you with electricity.

Finally, in terms of running a system there are 4 main types of sizes in terms of kW; 1kW, 2kW,5kW and 10kW

1 kW	1. On an average day it can produce 4kWh of electricity. 2. It is capable of generating 5000 watts in a day using the sun 3. It is suitable for you if you want to run 800 watts worth of appliances.
2kW	1. Reliable, as many appliances with low power consumption can be powered by it. 2. You can use 10 panels of 200watts or 20 panels of 100 watts 3. It can also run-on AC 4. This system supplied 8kWh on an average day. 5. It needs a 24,000 watts battery bank to operate
5kW	1. It can produce 20kWh energy everyday 2. It produces 5000 watts during the peak hours.
10kW	1. It can produce 11,000-15,000 kWh per year. 2. However, it can cover the whole household in terms of electricity. 3. This will need 27-35 solar panels to generate good energy.

This marks the end of our informational journey regarding off-grid solar power systems. We dealt with several main issues in great detail.

Conclusion

Beginner

In this 1ˢᵗ book, there is comprehensive information regarding the off-grid solar power system. This book contains five main parts. In each part, there is complete information regarding the off-grid system. Firstly, there are important discussions regarding the advantages of going solar. After this, there is information regarding the difference between off-grid and on-grid solar panels in detail. There are three types of grid systems that include off-grid solar panel system, on-grid solar panel system, and hybrid.

The 6-step process outlined in chapter 10 includes, 1) planning and designing, 2) choosing the best location for panels, 3) ordering the components, 4) building a battery house, 5) installation of panels, 6) wiring up the DIY off-grid solar system to get your system up and running.

The potential with solar power is endless, and with the right mindset of designing an off-grid solar system, you are ready to take on any challenge.

Providing people with the knowledge, skills, and ideas to go independent, especially when it comes to harnessing solar energy, has been the biggest intent behind bringing this book.

Fossil fuels still form a large part of human use, but that can be changed when every individual is able to adopt clean, green, and renewable energy sources.

Your review – and it only takes two minutes to write one – can be the voice of reason to bring this shift globally. As more and more people take to solar energy, along with other renewable resources, we can build a cleaner future that's also easy on the pockets and allows greater independence in living our lives.

Give power to the green revolution with your voice: leave a review on Amazon.com about your experience with this off-grid solar system guide.

Advanced

So, this is it. If you have come this far; I am proud of you for choosing to go solar, and if you have chosen otherwise that's okay too.
Let me summarize the book for you.

Throughout the book I discuss the installation, implementation, sizing, and tips on going solar. Some of the main, and most interesting, aspects that I covered was the 7 pointers that you should consider before going solar.

1. Investigate your home's energy efficiency
2. Assess your solar potential and any limitation
3. Assess your potential for going solar

4. Estimate your solar energy needs
5. Obtain bids and site assessments from contractors
6. Understand available financing expenses
7. Work with your installer and utility to install the system and set up agreements

Furthermore, in this book we discussed the types of solar power panels. They are as follows:

- Crystalline solar panels have the highest efficiency out of all panels.
- Monocrystalline panels are between 15-20% efficient, making them the most efficient of all crystalline panels
- Polycrystalline panels are between 15-17% efficient and can be the most cost-effective option.
- Thin film solar panels are best for unorthodox roof styles and are the most resilient.

Monocrystalline solar panels are the most expensive option due to their manufacturing process. Manufacturers make use of the Czochralski process which is energy-intensive with a resultant wastage of silicon. Since the manufacturers include the cost of the waste silicon the price tags are usually towards the higher end.

Polycrystalline solar panels are usually cheaper compared to their single cell counterparts. This is mainly due to the fact that polycrystalline solar panels are made from two different types of silicon crystals. This is a simpler manufacturing process; therefore, it costs lower for the users and the creators.

Thin-film solar panels have two outcomes. In fact, installing a thin film solar panel is less industrious because they are lighter and maneuverable which reduces labor cost and eventually the overall cost of installation.

Moving on to the mounting of solar panels. There are two types of mounting systems, namely, Ground and Rooftop mounting. The effect that solar energy might have on the warranty on your roof's age and condition. The shingles on your roof have a 25- to 30-year warranty. Ground mounting can be the best option for you if your household consumption is greater than you expected. While rooftop mounting is preferred by many homeowners, if you want to produce more electricity, go for ground mounting.

Moreover, off-grid systems require batteries, whereas grid-tied systems can use them if they so choose. There must be a way to store the power generated by the panels in every solar energy system. You can basically use the utility grid as a huge battery by feeding that energy into grid-tie systems. There are three types of batteries that form the main aspect of the whole system:

Lead Acid: In the solar battery industry, lead acid batteries are the tried-and-true technology. Since the 1800s, deep-cycle batteries have been

utilized as energy storage devices. Additionally, their dependability has enabled them to remain.

Ionized lithium batteries: The newest addition to the field of energy storage is lithium-ion batteries. Manufacturers of electric vehicles discovered lithium ion's potential as an energy storage solution as the popularity of electric vehicles began to rise.

Batteries based on nickel: The use of nickel cadmium (Ni-Cd) batteries is less common than that of lead acid or lithium-ion batteries. Ni-Cd batteries first appeared in the late 1800s, but in the 1980s, they were given a makeover that significantly increased the amount of energy they could store. They are favored by the aviation industry.

Battery Flow: In the field of energy storage, a recently developed technology is flow batteries. They circulate between two distinct battery chambers, or tanks, and contain an electrolyte liquid based on water.

MPPTs convert higher voltage DC output transferred from the solar panel down to a lower voltage needed to charge batteries associated with a PV system. PWM controllers aid the transition between the solar panels and the batteries. It actively controls the current flowing from the solar panel to the batteries, thereby, preventing the batteries from overcharging.

An inverter is an equipment that converts DC power into AC power, changes the voltage and keeps the current the same is called a power adapter. Moreover, since the power output received by the solar panels is not consistent as it is interlinked with the weather. Therefore, on account of these fluctuations, every inverter includes MPPT solar charge controllers that are able to optimize the generation of solar energy.

Subsequently, as explored in the last few chapters of this book, sizing plays a key role in the overall decision of purchasing and installation of solar panels. So, we have established that choosing the right size of wire, connector and charge controller in your PV system plays a crucial role in terms of performance and safety. If the wires you use are undersized, there will be a significant voltage drop due to excessive loss of power. Simultaneously, if the wires are undersized, there is an active risk that they may catch fire. These features alongside components such as breakers, fuses, and arrays, have an impact on the overall performance of your PV system.

As we know, solar power has immense potential, for both personal as well as commercial use, and the sooner you adopt it, the sooner you start to reap the rewards. But it is important that you always remember to calculate and size for your needs – you don't want to be left stranded with underperforming systems after having done so much work. This is why I have created a separate chapter on sizing to ensure that you are aided in every way possible.
And it's always good to ask for opinions or consult experts, if you are ever in doubt.

In the end, all I'd like to say is stay safe, harness that solar potential, live a happy life with a very tiny carbon footprint, and without worrying about bills.

Since my experience is dotted with highs and lows, it also enabled me to learn from my mistakes and improve over what I was implementing, especially in terms of solar power systems.

I wanted to share this experience with you all and help people who intend to migrate into a solar power system, leaving behind the excessive usage of non-renewable energy sources.

This book is an attempt to help you do exactly that – build over your knowledge and gain confidence with various aspects of planning, sizing, and designing your solar power systems which are refined and condensed for your needs, so that you can do what's right without hesitation.

Nevertheless, I'd love to know your experience in expanding existing systems or in creating new ones. Make sure to leave a review on Amazon on how this guide helped you – it also might work as an incentive for others to realize how much they can achieve with solar power and bring a global shift.

Bonus

Solar Power Planner

Record

Home or Business Address: **Date**..

....

....

....

Project Total Cost Summary

$ ....

Installation Company or   **Self-Installed**   ⊟

....

....

....

....

....

Phone# ....

Date ....

System Design:

Off-Grid   **On-Grid**   **Hybrid**

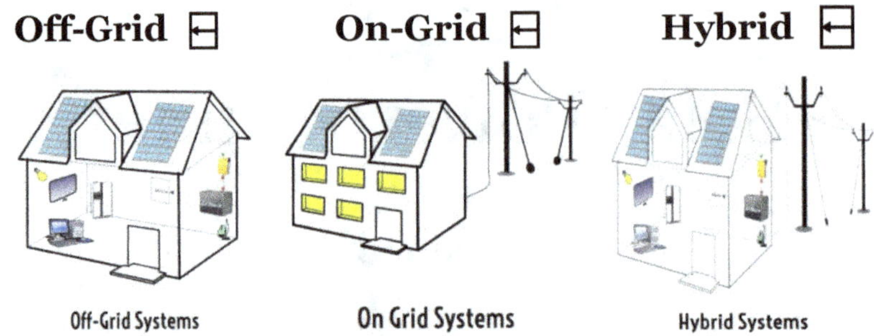

Off-Grid Systems   On Grid Systems   Hybrid Systems

Calculate your power consumption.

Appliance	Watt	Qt	Total Watt	Days/M	Hrs/Day	Watt Hrs	Comments
Cable Box	35	1	35	30	24	840	
Coffee Machine	1000	1	1000	30	4	4,000	
Dishwasher	1500	1	1500	15	1	750	
TV – LCD	150	3	450	30	16	7,200	
Circular Saw 8-1/4"	1400	1	1400	1	10	467	
Satellite Dish	25	1	25	30	24	600	
Freezer – Chest – 15 cu. ft.	1100	1	1100	30	1	1,100	1080 Wh/Day**
Fridge – 20 cu. ft. (AC)	1500	1	1500	30	1	1,500	1500 Wh/day**
Microwave	1000	1	1000	15	0.5	250	
Oven – Electric	1200	1	1200	30	2	2,400	
Toaster	850	1	850	10	0.1	28	
Box Fan	200	1	200	15	24	2,400	
Ceiling Fan	120	3	360	30	24	8,640	
LED Bulb – 60 Watt Equivalent	13	10	130	30	12	1,560	
Space Heater NA	1500	1	1500	15	24	18,000	
Computer	500	1	500	30	24	12,000	
Miner	4000	1	4000	30	24	96,000	
Laptop	100	1	100	30	24	2,400	
Window Air Conditioner 12,000 BTU NA	3250	1	3250	15	24	39,000	
LCD Monitor	100	2	200	30	24	4,800	
Well Pump – 1/3 1HP	750	1	750	30	24	18,000	
Modem	7	1	7	30	24	168	
Clothes Dryer – Gas	1800	1	1800	15	2	1,800	
Router	7	1	7	30	24	168	
Clothes Washer	800	1	800	15	2	800	
Smart Phone – Recharge	6	3	18	30	12	216	
Tablet – Recharge	8	3	24	30	12	288	
					Total Watt Hours per Day	225,375	
					Kw Hours per Day	225	

Reviewing your monthly electrical statement will give you an estimate of use.

- Analyze the yearly report to determine overall power use.
- Taking a daily meter reading will help understand demand.

Purchase a Kw meter and connect to each appliance to calculate your daily load. Or use this sample as a guide.

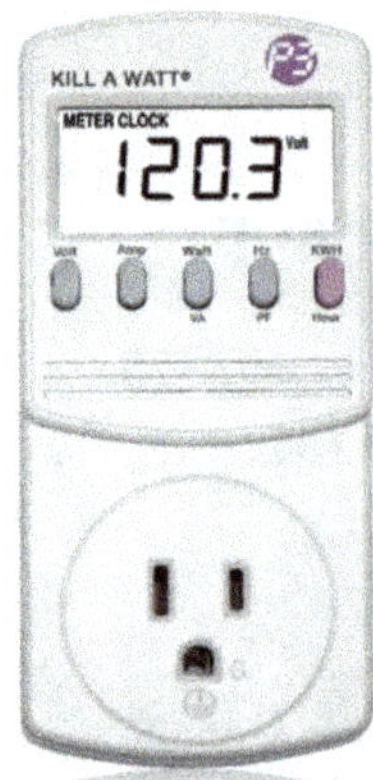

Determine Electric seasonal use   Kw

....

Summer

....

Fall

....

Winter

....

Spring

....

Yearly Total Kw

....

Round Up Total

....

Calculation of Panels = Total Kw divided by .07 = number of panels required.

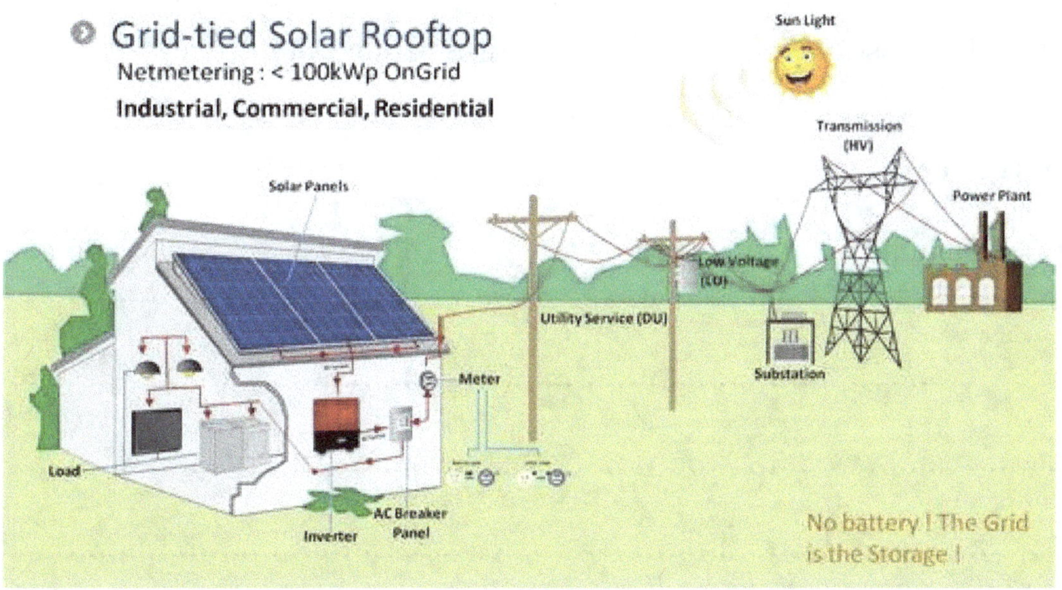

Solar Panels

Qty	Manufacturer	Type	Size	Price	STotal

GTotal...

Date of Purchase   Installation Date

Controller

Qty	Manufacturer	Type	Price	STotal

....

....

....

GTotal..

Date of Purchase   Installation Date

Inverter

Qty	Manufacturer	Type	Price	STotal

....

....

....

....

....

....

....

GTotal..

Date of Purchase   Installation Date

Batteries

Qty	Manufacturer	Type	Price	STotal

....

....

....

....

....

....

GTotal..

Date of Purchase   Installation Date

Monitor

Manufacturer	Type	Price

....

....

....

....

GTotal..

Date of Purchase   Installation Date

Wiring

Manufacturer	Type	Qty	Price

GTotal...

Date of Purchase   Installation Date

Connectors

Qty	Manufacturer	Type	Price

....

....

....

....

....

....

....

....

....

....

....

....

GTotal...

Date of Purchase   Installation Date

Mounts

Qty   Manufacturer   Type   Price

....

....

....

....

....

....

....

....

....

....

....

....

....

GTotal..

Date of Purchase   Installation Date

Miscellaneous Purchases

Qty	Manufacturer	Type	Price

About the author

I'm an adventurous person who has served my country in the Military and have spent most of my life raising 2 sons who now have their own families. My wife succumbed to Acute Leukemia at 38 and her sons were only 1 & 2 years old.

On the creative side, I've been a Cabinet Maker, owner, and operator of a business supplying commercial cabinets to the Movie theater industry and Western jewelry display cases to Montana Silversmiths both of which were shipped nationwide. I fulfilled my childhood dream of building my own aircraft and flying throughout the US. Living in south Florida with my 2 young sons we took many flights including to Disney world and on a flight at sunup to watch a shuttle launch while circling at 9000 ft.. We eventually sold the Lancair ES and moved to Traverse City, Michigan where I had spent most of my young single life. While there for 20 years I owned and operated a Fantastic Sam's hair salon franchise. With my sons on their own, I sold our Cinderella home and I'm now following dreams of traveling and living full-time in my Class A motor home and back in Central Florida near Disney world "The happiest place on earth."

Thank you so much.

Den Collier

Beginners Resources

Figure 1. Global Energy Mix. Source: Brookings

Figure 2: TimberHome goes off-grid - Source: Timberhomes Vermont

Figure 3: Illustration of the sun in space - Source: Shutterstock

Figure 4. Solar Spectrum. Source: globalchange.umich.edu

Figure 5: Solar resource map in the U.S. - Source: NREL

Figure 6: Inside a Photovoltaic Cell – Source: U.S. Energy Information Administration

Figure 7: Formation of an e-h pair - Source: The Physics of Solar Power from Colorado College

Figure 8: Flow from the electron through the load – Source The Physics of Solar Power from Colorado College

Figure 9: Recombination process of the e-h pair - Source: The Physics of Solar Power from Colorado College

Figure 10: Solar water heating system -Source U.S. Department of Energy

Figure 11: Solar PV Global Capacity, by Country and Region, 2010-2020 -Source: REN21

Figure 12: Cost $/W for a PV system - Source: NREL

Figure 13: Overview of a Space Solar Power System -Source: Arya, M. et al

Figure 14: Algal Biofuels - Source: The Biologist

Figure 15: Solar Panel in hand - Source: Shutterstock**Valeur, B. and Berberan, M.**

Figure 16: Portrait of Edmond Becquerel -Source:**Valeur HYPERLINK**

Figure 17: First Solar Panel Installation by Charles Fritts, NewYork, 1884 -Source: Smithsonian Magazine

Figure 18: Series-Parallel Connection for a 30V Half-Cell Solar Panel (Two parallel sets of 30 cells in series, 60 cells in total) - Source: SolarQuotes

Figure 19: Solar panel covered with dust - Source: Security Self-Storage

Figure 20: Layers of a solar panel - Source: CER

Figure 21: Solar panels with 3 and 4 bypass diodes - Source: Panasonic Solar

Figure 22: Popular Connectors for Solar Source: CED Greentech

Figure 23: Structure of an absorber layer - Source: ACS

Figure 24: Solar Cell Conducting Electrons through the Busbars -Source: Electrical Engineering

Figure 25: SunPower's IBC Solar Panel - Source: IBC Sola

Figure 26: PERC SolarPanel -Source: **Adani Solar**

Figure 27: Electrons (Red) Recombining with holes before flowing through the load - Source: Colorado College

Figure 28: Half-Cell Solar Panel - Source: Qcell

Figure 29: Functioning of a Bifacial Solar Panel - Source: NREL

Figure 30: All-Black Solar Panel -Source: Solaria

Figure 31: off grid effect -Source: Canva.com

*Figure 32:*Infographic of Grid-tied and off grid solar system. Source: get-green-now

Figure 33: graphic for off-grid as alternative for rural areas. Source: get-greenow

Figure 34: Avoid power outages from off-grid solar power system infographic. Source: get-green-now

Figure 35: On grid systems. Source: vmechatronics

Figure 36: Off-grid systems.Source: umechatronics

Figure 37: Hybrid solar power system. Source: vmechatronics

Figure 38: Different types of solar panels with names. Source: cleanenergyreviews

Figure 39: Panel sizes. Source Renubblewise

Figure 40: Various types of solar inverters. Source: cleanenergyreviews

Figure 41: Difference between lead-acid and lithium-ion batteries. Source: cleanenergyreviews

Advanced References

Gil Knier. (2008, 6). How do photovoltaics work? Science Mission Directorate | Science. https://science.nasa.gov/science-news/science-at-nasa/2002/solarcells

Kareta, N. (2020, August 7). The photoelectric effect and its role in solar photovoltaics. Power & Beyond. https://www.power-and-beyond.com/the-photoelectric-effect-and-its-role-in-solar-photovoltaics-a-954425/

Pros and cons of solar energy. (2022, January 7). Unbound Solar. https://unboundsolar.com/blog/pros-cons-solar

Fundamental 3: The different types of solar systems. (2022, April 13). SolarQuotes.com.au. https://www.solarquotes.com.au/good-solar-guide/system-types/

Grid-tied vs. off-grid solar: Which is right for you? (2021, December 21). Unbound Solar. https://unboundsolar.com/blog/grid-tied-vs-off-grid-solar

Martin Newkirk. (2016, July 15). How solar power works - on-grid, off-grid, and hybrid systems — Clean energy reviews. CLEAN ENERGY REVIEWS. https://www.cleanenergyreviews.info/blog/2014/5/4/how-solar-works

Pmmilum. (2021, April 6). The 3 types of residential & commercial solar power systems. Ilum Solar. https://ilumsolar.com/the-3-types-of-residential-commercial-solar-power-systems/

Do-it-Yourself home energy assessments. (n.d.). Energy.gov. https://www.energy.gov/energysaver/do-it-yourself-home-energy-assessments

EERE success story—Sun number partnership with Zillow brings solar potential scores to millions of Americans. (n.d.). Energy.gov. https://www.energy.gov/eere/success-stories/articles/eere-success-story-sun-number-partnership-zillow-brings-solar-0

Net metering guide: How the utility credits you for solar power. (2021, November 12). Unbound Solar. https://unboundsolar.com/blog/net-metering-guide

Reducing electricity use and costs. (n.d.). Energy.gov. https://www.energy.gov/energysaver/reducing-electricity-use-and-costs

What is net metering and how does it work? (2022, April 4). Solar Reviews. https://www.solarreviews.com/blog/what-is-net-metering-and-how-does-it-work

Community solar basics. (n.d.). Energy.gov. https://www.energy.gov/eere/solar/community-solar-basics The DIY solar permitting process and other options. (2022, August 3). Baker Electric Home Energy. https://bakerhomeenergy.com/blog/2016-04-08/diy-solar-permitting-process-and-other-options/

Is it better to lease or buy solar panels? What you need to know. (2022, September 1). Solar Reviews. https://www.solarreviews.com/blog/benefits-of-owning-vs-leasing-solar-panels

REenergizeCO. (2022, August 18). Do you plan to sell your house? REenergizeCO Energy Audits and Performance Upgrades | Denver, CO. https://www.reenergizeco.com/blog/solar-panels-increase-home-value/

Solar power purchase agreements. (n.d.). SEIA. https://www.seia.org/research-resources/solar-power-purchase-agreements

What is community solar? (2022, June 3). Solstice Community Solar. https://blog.solstice.us/solstice-blog/what-is-community-solar/

10 best solar companies (2022 guide). (n.d.). This Old House. https://www.thisoldhouse.com/solar-alternative-energy/reviews/best-solar-companies

Homeowner's guide to the federal tax credit for solar photovoltaics. (n.d.). Energy.gov. https://www.energy.gov/eere/solar/homeowners-guide-federal-tax-credit-solar-photovoltaics

Incentives for DIY solar installations. (n.d.). SolarTown Renewable Energy & Rooftop Products, Fast Shipping. https://solartown.com/learning/solar-policy-and-incentives/incentives-for-diy-solar-installations/

The top solar incentive programs in the U.S. in 2022 and how to find solar incentives available in your area? (2022, August 22). Solar Reviews. https://www.solarreviews.com/blog/the-top-solar-incentive-programs-in-the-us

Should you get a monitoring system with your solar panels? (2022, April 13). SolarQuotes.com.au. https://www.solarquotes.com.au/good-solar-guide/monitoring-systems/

Solar monitoring systems: Everything you need to know. (2022, February 27). Treehugger. https://www.treehugger.com/what-is-solar-monitoring-5218338

Solar panel monitoring: How it works & best monitors. (2020, October 24). Unbound Solar. https://unboundsolar.com/blog/best-solar-panel-monitoring

Best off-grid solar systems in 2022. (2022, May 13). SaveOnEnergy® | Electricity Companies in Texas | Call 800-825-1252. https://www.saveonenergy.com/solar-energy/best-off-grid-solar-system/

Gheorghe, S. (2022, March 31). Off grid solar system kits: Renewable energy for your home. Homedit. https://www.homedit.com/off-grid-solar-system-kits/

What are the best off-grid solar systems to buy? (2022, January 4). Solar Reviews. https://www.solarreviews.com/blog/best-off-grid-solar-systems-to-bu

Alex Beale. (2021, 4). 3 ways to test solar panels: Output, voltage & current. Footprint Hero. https://footprinthero.com/how-to-test-solar-panels

Aurorasolardev. (2022, May 20). Comprehensive guide to solar panel types. Aurora Solar. https://aurorasolar.com/blog/solar-panel-types-guide/

Dricus De Rooij. (2015, July 23). Solar panel maintenance: Tips to maximize solar system output. Manage risks and maximize ROI for your PV and energy storage projects. https://sinovoltaics.com/learning-center/system-design/solar-panel-maintenance-tips/

How hot do solar panels get and how does it affect my system? (2022, March 28). Solar Reviews. https://www.solarreviews.com/blog/how-hot-can-solar-panels-get

How many solar panels do you need: Panel size and output factors. (2022, August 3). SunPower - United States. https://us.sunpower.com/solar-resources/how-many-solar-panels-do-you-need-panel-size-and-output-factors

How to size a solar system: Step-by-step. (2021, December 21). Unbound Solar. https://unboundsolar.com/blog/how-to-size-solar-system

Jalo, Y. (2022, August 1). Types of solar panels: What you need to know | EnergySage. EnergySage Blog. https://news.energysage.com/types-of-solar-panels/

Makers, C. (2022, October 14). Best solar panels in 2022: Top products compared | EnergySage. EnergySage Blog. https://news.energysage.com/best-solar-panels-complete-ranking/

Measuring the output power of a solar panel. (2022, 6). Alternative Energy Tutorials. https://www.alternative-energy-tutorials.com/solar-power/measuring-the-power-of-a-solar-panel.html

Neumeister, K. (2022, October 16). 10 best solar panels for homes in 2022 [Updated solar guide]. EcoWatch. https://www.ecowatch.com/solar/best-companies/panels-for-homes

Palmetto. (2021, July 28). How to remove and reinstall solar panels. Home Solar Energy Solutions - Save Money with Palmetto. https://palmetto.com/learning-center/blog/how-to-remove-and-reinstall-solar-panels

See our step-by-step guide on how to clean your solar panels. (2022, April 13). Zen Energy. https://www.zenenergy.com.au/knowledge-base/popular-topic/how-to-clean-solar-panels/

Snodgrass, R. (2022, August 31). Top 10 solar panel companies & manufacturers in 2022 | EnergySage. EnergySage Blog. https://news.energysage.com/best-solar-panel-manufacturers-usa/

Solar panel cleaning. What to do, and NOT to do! (2022, March 21). Shoalhaven Solar. https://www.shoalhavensolar.com.au/knowledge-base/solar-panel-cleaning-what-to-do-and-what-not-to-do

Solar panel maintenance: Everything you need to know. (2022, April 4). Solar Reviews. https://www.solarreviews.com/blog/solar-panel-maintenance-everything-you-need-to-know

Solar panels 101: A guide to solar energy and systems. (2021, September 2). Unbound Solar. https://unboundsolar.com/solar-information/solar-power-101

Types of solar panels: Which one is the best choice? (2021, December 29). Solar Reviews. https://www.solarreviews.com/blog/pros-and-cons-of-monocrystalline-vs-polycrystalline-solar-panels

What is a solar panel? How does a solar panel work? (n.d.). Solar Panels • Solar Panels For Sale For Your Home & Business. https://www.mrsolar.com/what-is-a-solar-panel/

Corey. (2022, September 19). Ground-mounted solar: Top 3 things you should know | EnergySage. EnergySage Blog. https://news.energysage.com/ground-mounted-solar-panels-top-3-things-you-need-to-know/

Ground-mounted solar panels (2022 guide). (2022, October 17). EcoWatch. https://www.ecowatch.com/solar/ground-mounted-solar-panels

Solar ground Mount vs. roof Mount racking: Which is best? (2020, October 24). Unbound Solar. https://unboundsolar.com/blog/ground-mount-vs-roof-mount-racking

Solar panels 101: A guide to solar energy and systems. (2021, September 2). Unbound Solar. https://unboundsolar.com/solar-information/solar-power-101

Wolf, S. (n.d.). How solar panels are attached to your roof. Commercial and Residential Solar Panel Installer | Paradise Energy. https://www.paradisesolarenergy.com/blog/how-solar-panels-are-attached-to-your-roof

Aurorasolardev. (2022, July 28). Solar panel wiring basics: How to string solar panels. Aurora Solar. https://aurorasolar.com/blog/solar-panel-wiring-basics-an-intro-to-how-to-string-solar-panels/

Choosing-right-wire-size - Web. (n.d.). Windy Nation. https://www.windynation.com/jzv/inf/choosing-right-wire-size

Connecting batteries together for more battery storage. (2022, 10). Alternative Energy Tutorials. https://www.alternative-energy-tutorials.com/energy-storage/connecting-batteries-together.html

DC circuit breaker for solar system - Beny. (2021, October 15). BENY Electric. https://www.beny.com/dc-circuit-breaker-for-solar-system/

Electrical panel requirements for solar. (2021, December 21). Unbound Solar. https://unboundsolar.com/blog/electrical-panel-requirements-for-solar

Electrical wiring diagrams from unbound solar. (2022, July 6). Unbound Solar. https://unboundsolar.com/solar-information/electrical-wiring-diagrams

How to wire solar panels in series vs. parallel. (2022, January 12). Solar Reviews. https://www.solarreviews.com/blog/do-you-wire-solar-panels-series-or-parallel

How-properly-fuse-solar-pv-system - Web. (n.d.). Windy Nation. https://www.windynation.com/jzv/inf/how-properly-fuse-solar-pv-system

Life, A. (2021, September 5). Complete solar panel wire size guide (Which wire Gauge you need). AsoboLife. https://www.asobolife.com/solar-panel-wire-size-guide/

Marketing, A. (2021, April 2). Batteries: Series and parallel connections. DIY Solar & Renewable Energy Resources. https://www.altestore.com/diy-solar-resources/batteries-series-and-parallel-connections/

One moment, please... (n.d.). One moment, please... https://www.mpptsolar.com/en/batteries-series-parallel.html

Solar cable Gauge calculator, solar panel calculator. (n.d.). Find your energy freedom, DIY off grid solar system | Renogy. https://www.renogy.com/calculators#tab_solar-cable

Solar cell busbar: 3BB, 5BB or 0BB? (2016, May 13). Manage risks and maximize ROI for your PV and energy storage projects. https://sinovoltaics.com/technology/solar-cell-busbar-3bb-5bb-or-0bb/

Solar Combiner box: A beginner's guide. (2022, May 6). BENY Electric. https://www.beny.com/solar-combiner-box-a-beginners-guide/

Solar panel installation: How to install solar step by step. (2022, August 25). Unbound Solar. https://unboundsolar.com/blog/step-by-step-diy-solar-installation#wiring-and-electrical

Solar panel wiring - Basics - AE solar. (2022, March 10). AE Solar. https://ae-solar.com/solar-panel-wiring-basics/

Types of connectors for solar panels: Most popular type and comparison. (2021, December 16). A1SolarStore. https://a1solarstore.com/blog/solar-connector-types-popularity-and-comparison.html

What are the different types of solar panel connectors? (2021, December 2). Semprius. https://www.semprius.com/solar-panel-connectors/

What size cable for 12V solar panel? » wire size & length. (2022, June 23). Mission New Energy. https://www.missionnewenergy.com/what-size-cable-for-12v-solar-panel/

Should you get a monitoring system with your solar panels? (2022, April 13). SolarQuotes.com.au. https://www.solarquotes.com.au/good-solar-guide/monitoring-systems/

Solar monitoring systems: Everything you need to know. (2022, February 27). Treehugger. https://www.treehugger.com/what-is-solar-monitoring-5218338

Solar panel monitoring: How it works & best monitors. (2020, October 24). Unbound Solar. https://unboundsolar.com/blog/best-solar-panel-monitorin

(2022, March 29). Ayixa. https://www.ayixa.com/2-kw-solar-system-is-it-worth-it-what-appliances-no-of-batteries-and-solar-panels-to-use/

Browning, K. (2022, February 3). A beginner's guide to owning a solar-powered cabin. Climatebiz. https://climatebiz.com/solar-powered-cabin/

Browning, K. (2022, May 24). How many solar panels do I need for my RV? (Expert advice). Climatebiz. https://climatebiz.com/solar-panels-needed-for-rv/

Elliott, J. (2021, August 20). Off grid power systems: Possible with a 10kW solar system? Solar Choice. https://www.solarchoice.net.au/blog/off-grid-with-10kW-solar-and-battery-storage/

Everything you need to know about installing solar panels on boats. (2022, February 11). Solar Reviews. https://www.solarreviews.com/blog/solar-panels-for-boats

Freitas, T. (2021, October 4). How many solar panels do you need to power your house? CNET. https://www.cnet.com/home/energy-and-utilities/find-out-how-many-solar-panels-you-need-to-power-your-house/

Is a 10kW solar system right for your home? (2022, September 1). Solar Reviews. https://www.solarreviews.com/blog/10kw-solar-systems-are-becoming-very-popular-here-is-why

Kerry. (2022, June 24). RV solar panels: What you need to know | EnergySage. EnergySage Blog. https://news.energysage.com/rv-solar-panels/

Palmetto. (2022, January 5). How many solar panels do I need to power my home appliances? Home Solar Energy Solutions - Save Money with Palmetto. https://palmetto.com/learning-center/blog/how-many-solar-panels-are-needed-to-power-home-appliances

Understanding levels of solar power for a log cabin. (2021, December 8). Log Home Products | Log Siding, Log Cabin Siding | Knotty Pine Paneling. https://www.woodworkersshoppe.com/levels-of-solar-power-for-a-log-cabin/

What can I run with a 5kw solar system? (2021). https://solarocean.com.au/what-can-i-run-with-a-5kw-solar-system/

What does 1kW of solar energy look like? I simply solar. (2021, August 27). Simply Solar. https://simplysolar.com/blog/1kw-solar-energy/

Anderson, S. (2021, May 7). String inverters vs. power optimizers vs. Microinverters | EnergySage. EnergySage Blog. https://news.energysage.com/string-inverters-power-optimizers-microinverters-compared/

Checklist before buying a solar PV system. (n.d.). Inverter, Solar Inverter, Home Power Inverter | inverter.com. https://www.inverter.com/checklist-before-buying-a-solar-pv-system

Hardy. (2021, February 19). What is a solar inverter? Types, pros, and cons | EnergySage. EnergySage Blog. https://news.energysage.com/solar-inverters-comparing-inverter-technologies/

Marketing, A. (2021, April 2). The role of an inverter in a solar electric system. DIY Solar & Renewable Energy Resources. https://www.altestore.com/diy-solar-resources/the-role-of-an-inverter-in-a-solar-electric-system/

Mason. (2021, May 26). Comparing Microinverters and power optimizers | EnergySage. EnergySage Blog. https://news.energysage.com/microinverters-power-optimizers-compared/

Metaye, R. (2021, August 28). 3 types of inverters for solar panels. Climatebiz. https://climatebiz.com/inverters-for-solar-panels/

Solar inverters: Types, pros, and cons. (n.d.). Solar.com. https://www.solar.com/learn/solar-inverter/

Solar panels 101: A guide to solar energy and systems. (2021, September 2). Unbound Solar. https://unboundsolar.com/solar-information/solar-power-101

Understanding power optimizers. (2021, 23). Just Solar. https://www.justsolar.com/blog/solar-inverter/power-optimizer

Aurorasolardev. (2022, September 23). How to choose the best solar battery for your needs. Aurora Solar. https://aurorasolar.com/blog/how-to-choose-the-best-solar-battery-for-your-needs-2/

Best solar battery systems 2022 — Clean energy reviews. (2022, September 4). CLEAN ENERGY REVIEWS. https://www.cleanenergyreviews.info/blog/best-solar-battery-systems

Choosing the best solar battery: What to know. (n.d.). Get competing solar quotes online | EnergySage. https://www.energysage.com/energy-storage/how-to-get-storage/choosing-battery/

Erasmus, J. (2021, October 25). How many solar batteries do I need? | EnergySage. EnergySage Blog. https://news.energysage.com/how-many-solar-batteries-needed/

Lead-acid vs. lithium batteries: Which are best for solar? (2021, December 21). Unbound Solar. https://unboundsolar.com/blog/lead-acid-vs-lithium-batteries

Solar battery bank sizing calculator for off-grid. (2021, December 6). Unbound Solar. https://unboundsolar.com/solar-information/battery-bank-sizing

Solar battery care, maintenance, and safety: Don't touch the terminals! (n.d.). SolarTown Renewable Energy & Rooftop Products, Fast Shipping. https://solartown.com/learning/solar-panels/solar-battery-care-maintenance-and-safety-dont-touch-the-terminals/

Solar panels 101: A guide to solar energy and systems. (2021, September 2). Unbound Solar. https://unboundsolar.com/solar-information/solar-power-101

What are the different types of solar batteries? (2021, January 10). Solar Reviews. https://www.solarreviews.com/blog/types-of-solar-batteries

What to look for in a battery enclosure for solar systems. (2017, December 8). SunWize | Power Independence. https://www.sunwize.com/tech-notes/what-to-look-for-in-a-battery-enclosure-for-solar-systems/

Best MPPT solar charge controllers 2022 — Clean energy reviews. (2022, January 8). CLEAN ENERGY REVIEWS. https://www.cleanenergyreviews.info/blog/best-solar-charge-controllers

Buyer guide - do I need a PWM or MPPT solar charge controller? (n.d.). Solar 4 RVs. https://www.solar4rvs.com.au/buying/buyer-guides/choosing-the-right-solar-charge-controller-regulat/

Factors to consider when deciding to purchase a charge controller. (n.d.). Renogy United States. https://www.renogy.com/blog/factors-to-consider-when-deciding-to-purchase-a-charge-controller/

Jim Bruce. (2021, November 3). MPPT vs PWM test | What is the difference between MPPT and PWM? Comparing Solar Companies. https://www.solarempower.com/blog/what-is-the-difference-between-mppt-and-pwm-mppt-vs-pwm-test/

Lin, M. S. (2022, June 9). A buyer's guide to solar charge controllers | EnergySage. EnergySage Blog. https://news.energysage.com/what-are-solar-charge-controllers-do-you-need-one/

Solar charge controller basics. (n.d.). Northern Arizona Wind & Sun. https://www.solar-electric.com/learning-center/solar-charge-controller-basics.html/

Solar charge controller sizing and how to choose one. (n.d.). Renogy United States. https://www.renogy.com/blog/solar-charge-controller-sizing-and-how-to-choose-one-/

What is a PWM charge controller? EcoDirect. (n.d.). Solar, Energy Storage Solutions & Renewable Energy | EcoDirect.com. https://www.ecodirect.com/What-is-a-PWM-Charge-Controller-s/144.htm

What is maximum power point tracking (MPPT). (n.d.). Northern Arizona Wind & Sun. https://www.solar-electric.com/learning-center/mppt-solar-charge-controllers.html/

(2022, March 29). Ayixa. https://www.ayixa.com/2-kw-solar-system-is-it-worth-it-what-appliances-no-of-batteries-and-solar-panels-to-use/

Browning, K. (2022, February 3). A beginner's guide to owning a solar-powered cabin. Climatebiz. https://climatebiz.com/solar-powered-cabin/

Browning, K. (2022, May 24). How many solar panels do I need for my RV? (Expert advice). Climatebiz. https://climatebiz.com/solar-panels-needed-for-rv/

Elliott, J. (2021, August 20). Off grid power systems: Possible with a 10kW solar system? Solar Choice. https://www.solarchoice.net.au/blog/off-grid-with-10kW-solar-and-battery-storage/
Everything you need to know about installing solar panels on boats. (2022, February 11). Solar Reviews. https://www.solarreviews.com/blog/solar-panels-for-boats
Freitas, T. (2021, October 4). How many solar panels do you need to power your house? CNET. https://www.cnet.com/home/energy-and-utilities/find-out-how-many-solar-panels-you-need-to-power-your-house/
Is a 10kW solar system right for your home? (2022, September 1). Solar Reviews. https://www.solarreviews.com/blog/10kw-solar-systems-are-becoming-very-popular-here-is-why
Kerry. (2022, June 24). RV solar panels: What you need to know | EnergySage. EnergySage Blog. https://news.energysage.com/rv-solar-panels/
Palmetto. (2022, January 5). How many solar panels do I need to power my home appliances? Home Solar Energy Solutions - Save Money with Palmetto. https://palmetto.com/learning-center/blog/how-many-solar-panels-are-needed-to-power-home-appliances
Understanding levels of solar power for a log cabin. (2021, December 8). Log Home Products | Log Siding, Log Cabin Siding | Knotty Pine Paneling. https://www.woodworkersshoppe.com/levels-of-solar-power-for-a-log-cabin/
What can I run with a 5kw solar system? (2021). https://solarocean.com.au/what-can-i-run-with-a-5kw-solar-system/
What does 1kW of solar energy look like? I simply solar. (2021, August 27). Simply Solar. https://simplysolar.com/blog/1kw-solar-energy/

www.ingramcontent.com/pod-product-compliance
Lightning Source LLC
Chambersburg PA
CBHW080831160726
47999CB00009B/2850